ro Maker is a must read for pastors and leaders serious about moving
m growing a church to the courageous call to multiply churches. I
ow few people who have been used to catalyze church multiplication
e my friend Dave Ferguson.

—Mark Jobe, lead pastor, New Life Community Church—
Chicago; author; founder, New Life Centers

us spent his life multiplying his leadership, and billions of lives were
anged for eternity. If you do what *Hero Maker* says, you will be able to
the same thing.

—Dr. Ajai Lall, director, Central India Christian Mission

e you tired of small gains through addition? Do you long to see your
e and ministry get to the multiplication stage? Dave Ferguson reached
ese goals by being a hero maker. Read *Hero Maker* and learn from one
the best.

—Dr. James MacDonald, senior pastor, Harvest Bible
Chapel; author, *Act Like Men* and *Vertical Church*

sus made it clear that to take the gospel to the ends of the earth, we
ust make disciples who make disciples who make disciples. If you need
ractical help with disciple-making, read *Hero Maker*.

—Joby Martin, lead pastor, The Church of Eleven22

he most important feature of *Hero Maker* is that Dave and Warren turn
e term hero inside-out and upside-down. In their hands, *hero* becomes
rvant of God, servant of the gospel, servant of others, and servant of the
orld. Read and learn how to make heroes of others.

—Scot McKnight, Julius R. Mantey Professor of
New Testament, Northern Seminary

ead this book! The message of *Hero Maker* will change not just you but
ery leader you raise up.

—James Meeks, senior pastor, Salem
Baptist Church of Chicago

Dave Ferguson and Warren Bird are leaders of leaders. *Hero Make* only impact you; it will impact the leaders you are raising up.

—Mark Batterson, author, *The Circ*
lead pastor, National Communit

Dave Ferguson and Warren Bird are a great leadership combi church praxis and leadership research. *Hero Maker* inspires a le development approach in a fresh yet ancient way.

—Dave Gibbons, CVO, Xealots.org,
author, *Small C*

If my friend Dave Ferguson wrote it, I'm going to marinate in t of every page. And when you add Dr. Warren Bird to the w *Hero Maker* becomes an indispensable resource for pastors planters.

—Derwin L. Gray, founding and
Transformation Chu
The High Defin

If you're looking to raise and empower great leaders, Dave Fe book, *Hero Maker*, is packed with valuable insights. Each of ciples Dave unveils is practical, doable, and helpful to every l

—Craig Groeschel, pastor,
author, *Di*

When I am around Dave, I get the feeling that I can achie anything. Aided by researcher Warren Bird, *Hero Maker* is on decades of the experience of someone who is proving to significant apostolic leaders in our day.

—Alan Hirsch, award-winning a
100 Movements, 5Q Collec

Dave Ferguson and Warren Bird help us unpack five essential practices to grow our leadership and the leaders we are mentoring. *Hero Maker* is for every influencer who knows that the harvest is plentiful, but the workers—and leaders—are few.

—Tony Morgan, founder and lead
strategist, The Unstuck Group

Dave Ferguson and Warren Bird have a heart for the church and a head for knowledge. In *Hero Maker*, they are two great guides for every leader.

—John Ortberg, senior pastor, Menlo Church; author,
I'd Like You More If You Were More Like Me

As long as I've known Dave Ferguson, he has always used a kingdom scoreboard to measure both his life and his ministry. In *Hero Maker*, Dave lays out five simple and powerful practices that will help anyone who applies them become a more effective hero maker and ministry multiplier.

—Larry Osborne, pastor and author,
North Coast Church

At last: the core message of the Exponential conference boiled down to five simple, practical, powerful practices. Start here!

—Andy Stanley, author, communicator, and
founder of North Point Ministries

Dave Ferguson has raised up an amazing number of leaders, church planters, and pastors. He has an unmatched heart and passion for multiplication, and I'm thankful for him. Read *Hero Maker* to find out how he does it.

—Ed Stetzer, Billy Graham Distinguished
Chair, Wheaton College

Hero Maker offers every leader a chance to catch the biblical principles that multiply leadership impact *and* create sustainable momentum for long-term kingdom advance. Get this book. Inhale this message, and let's breathe out heroes!

—Danielle Stickland, speaker, author, advocate

As a leader of a multicultural church in the inner city of Detroit, I find leadership development to be one of the greatest ways to make a real impact in both my church and the community we're called to serve. *Hero Maker* will steer church leaders and laity alike into practices that make our lives greater than what they could ever be in the silos we often unintentionally create.

—Harvey Carey, senior pastor, Citadel of
Faith Covenant Church

In this fantastic book, one of my mentors, Dave Ferguson, not only addresses the heart behind being a hero maker rather than a hero, but he gives us practical steps to implement a plan. Challenge and change your leadership today. Get this book!

—Lèonce B. Crump Jr., founder and pastor,
Renovation Church; author, *Renovate*

I am grateful for books like the one you're holding. It gently presses while it superbly encourages. Dave Ferguson lays out God's plans and calls us to walk in them.

—Matt Chandler, lead pastor, The Village Church

Dave Ferguson makes proven biblical principles accessible to you and your team in five simple practices. If you're looking to multiply your impact, start with *Hero Maker*.

—Carey Nieuwhof, founding pastor, Connexus Church

I have known and respected Dave Ferguson for almost twenty years. In my view, *Hero Maker* is his best book yet.

—Bill Hybels, senior pastor, Willow Creek Church;
founder, Global Leadership Summit

HERO MAKER

Other Books in the Exponential Series

(More titles forthcoming)

HER⚡
MAKER

FIVE ESSENTIAL PRACTICES FOR
LEADERS TO MULTIPLY LEADERS

DAVE FERGUSON
AND WARREN BIRD

ZONDERVAN REFLECTIVE

Hero Maker
Copyright © 2018 by Dave Ferguson and Warren Bird

Requests for information should be addressed to:
Zondervan, *3900 Sparks Dr. SE, Grand Rapids, Michigan 49546*

ISBN 978-0-310-58893-1 (International Trade Paper Edition)

ISBN 978-0-310-53694-9 (ebook)

Library of Congress Cataloging-in-Publication Data

Names: Ferguson, Dave, 1962- author. | Bird, Warren, author.
Title: Hero maker : five essential practices for leaders to multiply leaders / Dave Ferguson
    and Warren Bird.
Other titles: Five essential practices for leaders to multiply leaders
Description: Grand Rapids, MI : Zondervan, [2018] | Includes bibliographical references
    and index.
Identifiers: LCCN 2017048399 | ISBN 9780310536932 (hardcover)
Subjects: LCSH: Mentoring in church work. | Christian leadership.
Classification: LCC BV4408.5 .F47 2018 | DDC 253—dc23 LC record available at https://
    lccn.loc.gov/2017048399

Cover design: Faceout Studio, Tim Green
Cover photo: Shutterstock
Interior design: Denise Froehlich

Printed in the United States of America

22 23 24 25 /LSC/ 15 14 13 12 11 10 9

Contents

Foreword by J. D. Greear

I don't know how many places Jack Welch and John Calvin agree. It can't be that many. But they both are clear on this: one of the most valuable investments a leader can make is identifying and raising up other leaders.

Jack Welch, the CEO who engineered the turnaround at General Electric, says, "The future belongs to passionate, driven leaders . . . who can energize those whom they lead. One of the jobs of a leader is to pump confidence into his or her people. And when you've got somebody who's raring to go, and you can smell it and feel it, give 'em that shot."

And John Calvin, leading Protestant Reformer in the 1500s, agrees: "The more focused a leader is on upbuilding other leaders, the more highly [he or she is] to be regarded."

Surely, if Jack Welch and John Calvin agree on something, it is settled in heaven!

The book you hold in your hands has been written with a passion to see that focus become a reality in the church. My friends Dave Ferguson and Warren Bird, writing from years of experience, demonstrate that those who care the most about the future of the Great Commission will devote themselves to multiplying and sending, not gathering and counting. A focus on multiplying leaders doesn't mean we neglect growing our own ministries; it just means that we add multiplication as an essential element of our "scorecard."

Multiplying will not happen on its own. If we aren't choosing to make it happen, it's probably not happening.

It's time for us to put forward a new vision for the church. Actually, it's not a *new* vision but an old vision recently forgotten. Jesus' vision for completing the Great Commission was never platforming a few hyper-anointed megapastors to pack an auditorium with their electrifying sermons, but empowering ordinary believers to carry the gospel everywhere they went.

In Acts, thirty-nine of the forty miracles the Holy Spirit performs occur outside of the church. We need to expect that kind of ratio today too. If we really want to see the power of God, it's not going to be found primarily in the pulpit. I'm all for the pulpit, but the real power of the gospel is released as ordinary, Spirit-filled people multiply the gospel wherever they go, into every part of their communities.

Dave and Warren take this passion for multiplication and break it into its parts. It's one thing to inspire; it's another to instruct. This book does both. A mentor of mine once told me that when it comes to accomplishing great visions, it's never the dreams you dream but the small decisions you make. *Hero Maker* not only helps you dream the dreams; it helps you start the process. This book will walk you through the steps to catalyze your congregation to become the leadership factory God intended it to be.

In the final section of the book, Warren and Dave identify the obstacles you'll likely encounter. They help us see where difficult decisions will have to be made and delicate tensions will have to be managed. What I most appreciate about this book is that its authors are practitioners, not theorists. Dave has years of experience leading a church, filled with its own needs and concerns, to multiply. Warren has years of observing and coaching church leaders in multiplication. Dave and Warren aren't lobbing platitudes into a world they know nothing about; they are warriors returning with tales from the front lines.

The gospel of Jesus Christ is the most important message in the world. It tells us about a God who loved us so much that he took our sin upon himself so that we could have eternal life with him. Getting that message to others is a matter of life and death. This is no time for small dreams or weak ambitions. It's no time for territorial jealousies or status quo ministries. It's time to dream great things for God, and then attempt great things for God.

The good news is that Jesus promised that his Spirit is willing and able to lead us in this. But if we want his power, we have to do it his way. All of Jesus' promises about the greatness of the church are tied to sending, not gathering.

Hero Maker takes you into the execution of those promises. What will the next generation of church expansion look like if today's leaders take these promises seriously? I get excited just thinking about that.

Jesus once promised his disciples that they would do greater works than he (John 14:12). That promise staggers the imagination, and most of us, frankly, don't really believe it. Do you feel you have thus far done greater works than Jesus? He promised that you would. Of course, he didn't mean we'll preach greater sermons than the Sermon on the Mount, or pray greater prayers than his intercession in John 17, or do greater miracles than raising Lazarus from the dead. Greater refers to the reach and extent of our works as we see the Spirit multiplied through us into the lives of others. Greater happens only as we pursue multiplication.

The days of faithful leaders being satisfied with a single, thriving ministry are long behind us. The new measure of success is multiplication.

Truthfully, that has always been Jesus' standard; we've just become so enamored by the glitz of the megachurch that we've forgotten that. Dave and Warren show us why multiplication is at the heart of the gospel, and how, with God's help, it can become a reality in our ministries.

Introduction

"I have already won the awards, gotten the trophies, and been personally successful. Now I want more!" These words came from Barry,[1] someone whom all his college friends remember as the guy who made the heroic last-second shot to win the championship their senior year.

Today Barry is a middle-aged business executive and follower of Jesus, a gifted "big dog" leader with an impressive resume and a bank account that most would envy. When you walk into a room where Barry is present, people assume he is in charge. He knows how to lead.

But recently there seemed to be a lid on his leadership. He felt like he was missing something.

As a Christ follower, he wanted to make a greater impact with his life.

A mentor challenged him: "You accomplished much in your work life. What are you dreaming about next?" Barry wanted to maximize his leadership but felt even his most heroic efforts weren't paying off.

It was then he started focusing *less* on his own leadership and *more* on the leadership of others. He told me that as he pursued this in his work and life, he began to understand an important distinction. He phrased it like this:

> EVERYONE WANTS TO BE A HERO.
> YET ONLY A FEW UNDERSTAND THE
> POWER IN BEING A HERO MAKER.

Hero or Hero Maker?

I met Barry after he made this discovery, and he finished his thought: "Dave, I've put behind me the days of being the hero. I am making it my mission to dramatically change the trajectory of the lives of ten young leaders." As of this writing, he's found and invested in seven, and his hope is that they will be even more successful than he is.

Barry is becoming what I am calling a hero maker.

The term *hero maker* first came to my attention at the recommendation of Todd Wilson,[2] my friend and coleader of the Exponential conference. Warren Bird and I (this book is written by both of us but will be in my—Dave Ferguson's—voice) took Todd's phrase and gave it this definition:

> HERO MAKER: A LEADER WHO SHIFTS FROM
> BEING THE HERO TO MAKING OTHERS THE
> HERO IN GOD'S UNFOLDING STORY.

Todd also modeled the phrase for me. More than a decade ago, he came to me and said, "I will do all the behind-the-scenes work and run the operations if you will be the president and the onstage presence of the Exponential conference."

"It's a deal," I replied.

Since that time, I have served as president and Todd has served as executive director of the Exponential conference, which has grown to be the largest church-planting conference in the world (that we know of). Many people think that since I'm the president and I stand on the stage and welcome everyone that I must be the genius behind it all. Not true. Todd and his team do most of the work (marketing, organization, registration, logistics), caring only about the mission and not who gets the credit. He creates the platform and then lets me stand on it. Todd Wilson is a hero maker.

Along the way, Todd has also reminded me to quit trying to be the hero and instead to make heroes out of others. I remember a conversation sitting on a plane when he was looking at an article I had written that included a bar graph about one of our Easter services. More than ten thousand people had shown up at Community Christian Church, the church I lead in metro Chicago, and I was excited about that stat. Todd pointed to the article and reminded me of my dream when we planted the church: "I thought your dream was to see a movement of multiplying churches," he said. "This article makes it sound like your dream is to be one church with a really big attendance."

The words stung, but Todd was right. I hadn't *intended* to focus on growing only the church I was leading. Then Todd reminded me that the number of people being reached on that same Easter weekend through NewThing, the church-planting network we started, was more than fifty thousand. Todd pushed me again: "Dave, you should use a graph that tells the stories of what your church plants and church planters are doing, and not just what you and Community Christian Church are doing." He was encouraging me to change from being the hero to being a hero maker.

By the way, so that I don't confuse you with my stories, let me explain that I wear three hats: I'm the lead pastor at Community Christian Church; I'm the visionary of NewThing, a network of multiplying churches; and I'm president of Exponential, best known for its church multiplication conferences.

I tested my idea about whether hero-making leadership is essential to a multiplying movement on my Australian friend, Steve Addison. Steve has studied, written about, and understands better than anyone on the planet what it takes to start a movement of multiplying churches. He told me, "Dave, movements are started by leaders who have died to their own success."

This is not the thinking of the typical leader, pastor, or church planter. Yet that is how a hero maker thinks.

Our challenge for you as a leader is, don't settle for wanting to be a hero but instead discover what it means to be a hero maker. You might be a business leader like Barry or a pastor like me. You might be a volunteer leader of a group or a team like my coauthor, Warren. Whether you are leading ten people or ten thousand, we want you to maximize your leadership, make the greatest impact for Jesus and his kingdom, and join our multiplying movement by becoming a hero maker.

> **Whether you are leading ten people or ten thousand, we want you to maximize your leadership and join our multiplying movement by becoming a hero maker.**

Hero Maker in Sections

To help you clearly understand what it means to be a hero maker, we have divided the book into three parts.

Part 1: A Hero-Making Challenge. My conversation with Todd Wilson and other global leaders brought a turning point in my leadership and now in the leadership of a growing number of other leaders around the world. We stopped asking the same old questions about how to grow a church and began to ask new questions: "What does it take to be a leader who multiplies leaders and disciples to the fourth generation?" and "What does it take to catalyze a movement of multiplying churches?" Since then, we've become even more specific: "How can we see the number of reproducing and multiplying churches in America go from 4% (where we are now) to a tipping point of 10% (where we want to be)?" At Exponential, we call it our four-to-ten mission. Our answers to each of these questions point us to the need for hero makers, because they have discovered the secret that results multiply through others and not through themselves.

In the first section of *Hero Maker*, we refer to multiplying churches as Level 5 churches. If that's new terminology, don't worry. The gist of it is that Level 1 churches are declining in attendance, Level 2 are plateauing, Level 3 are growing, Level 4 are reproducing (adding a new campus or planting a new church), and Level 5 are multiplying (starting multiple outreaches that in turn each start multiple outreaches). If we focus on multiplication, we can achieve God-size impact and results. (If you want to see the five levels visualized, flip ahead to Figure 2.1.)

Hero makers have discovered the secret that results multiply through others and not through themselves.

In this first section, we challenge you to think about the questions you are asking and the leadership practices you are using and to reflect on whether those questions and practices are needed to meet the challenges ahead.

Part 2: Five Essential Practices of Hero Making. This section is the heart of the book, and it introduces the hero maker model. The five practices are sequential, building on each other. To give you a glimpse of what is ahead, I've summarized all five practices by contrasting them with common leadership practices.

1. Multiplication Thinking
   COMMON PRACTICE: *leading until you've reached the limit of your time and energy.*
   HERO-MAKING PRACTICE: *dreaming big and strategically investing yourself in others to multiplying your impact.*
2. Permission Giving
   COMMON PRACTICE: *leading with a tight rein on others.*

HERO-MAKING PRACTICE: *making yes your default response as a leader.*

3. Disciple Multiplying

COMMON PRACTICE: *prioritizing personal growth.*

HERO-MAKING PRACTICE: *investing in the work of helping others multiply apprentices.*

4. Gift Activating

COMMON PRACTICE: *making sure every slot is always filled.*

HERO-MAKING PRACTICE: *releasing leaders to new opportunities as their gifts and skills grow.*

5. Kingdom Building

COMMON PRACTICE: *defining success by what you gather and acquire.*

HERO-MAKING PRACTICE: *defining success by what you release and send out.*

For each of the five practices, I describe the biblical basis for the practice, highlighting it in Jesus' life and ministry. I also offer numerous examples of people putting this practice to work. Plus we give you a simple tool you and your team can use, starting today. So we rotate between motivation and methodology, between theory and practice.

Part 3: Hero Makers Get Results. In part 3, I give you an inspiring vision of what is possible through your leadership. In this third and final section, you'll learn how to create a culture of hero making, and I'll challenge you with a big dream for what we all could do together. I close this section with some motivating words from a friend of mine and a hero maker, Pastor Oscar Muriu in Nairobi, Kenya (whom you'll meet in chapter 4). We've also included a few appendixes to give you even more practical resources, which we summarize in the table of contents.

Jesus the Hero Maker

While hero maker is a term we are introducing to today's leadership genre, it is based on ancient truths that we see consistently lived out in Jesus' life and ministry. You can't study Jesus' ministry practices without seeing him as a hero maker, someone who puts the spotlight on others. First,

Jesus puts the spotlight on God the Father. Then he puts the spotlight on the leaders around him, who in turn do likewise for others. Notice this multiplying-generation sequence of leaders in the gospel of Luke:[3]

- In Luke 8:1–3, Jesus traveled around proclaiming the good news, taking the Twelve and others "with him" (the concept of *diatribo* that I'll describe in chapter 7). That's Jesus impacting a second generation of leadership.
- In Luke 9:1–6, Jesus sent out the Twelve, giving them "power and authority" and the assignment "to proclaim the kingdom of God and to heal the sick." That's the second generation impacting a third generation of leadership.
- In Luke 10:1–2, Jesus sent out seventy-two others on a similar mission, but he told them to pray for even more workers, emphasizing that "the workers are few." That is four or more generations of leadership.

The growth of God's kingdom—all of God's collective work around the world—seems to be in direct proportion to the number of called, trained, empowered "harvest hands," as *The Message* translates Luke 10:2. So Jesus not only involves others in the mission, but he multiplies himself through others. And he tells them each not to pray for just *one* more worker but rather to ask the Lord of the harvest that the workers be many. Jesus was a hero maker, and his example challenges us to be the same.

You Can Be a Hero Maker

This book is about changing the world by changing others. Throughout these pages, I'll remind you of the insight my friend Barry embodied: everyone wants to be a hero, but only a few understand the power in being a hero maker. Barry, like so many of the people you'll encounter in this book, not only became a hero maker, but he had a hero maker who encouraged him to be a hero maker.

I want to help you become a hero maker so you can help others be hero makers too.

That is what I hope to do for you. I want to help you become a hero maker so you can help others be hero makers too. I am convinced that

God wants you to become that type of world-changing leader. He wants to see you multiply your impact and legacy for the sake of seeing the people he loves find their way back to him. Turn the page and we will start with a secret that Jesus knew, passed on to his closest followers, and longs to pass on to you as well.

PART 1

A HERO-
MAKING
CHALLENGE

CHAPTER 1

Jesus' Leadership Secret

Big Idea: Hero makers have discovered that dying to self and living for God's kingdom through others is the secret of multiplied results and greater impact.

Want to know the secret?

I'm not trying to be clever or sly with that question. But over the last twenty-five years, I've learned that there really is a secret to multiplying great leaders. It's a secret for pastors and volunteer leaders alike. And it's what leaders in business and social sectors are looking for. You might lead a megachurch or a small group, but this secret is scalable and will allow anyone to exponentially multiply his or her difference making. Not only is this leadership secret available to all of us, but if you keep reading, you can begin to apply it today.

The Secret

Long before I ever dreamed of starting and leading a church, I dreamed of starting and playing in the National Basketball Association. That's pretty ambitious for a guy who's five foot eleven and has always had the vertical leap of a middle-aged white guy! But like I said, it was a dream.

My sons share my love of the game. They introduced me to *The Book of Basketball*,[4] the definitive, 719-page book on the NBA by Bill Simmons. An award-winning sports writer, Simmons is one of the few people who could write a credible bible of basketball. Chapter 1 of Simmons' book is titled "The Secret." Simmons says there is a secret about basketball that almost no one realizes. He admits that he didn't detect the secret even though he

> You might lead a megachurch or a small group, but this secret is scalable and will allow anyone to exponentially multiply his or her difference making.

was a lifelong fan, veteran sportswriter, and viewer of thousands of professional basketball games. He didn't understand the secret until he had a conversation with Hall of Famer Isiah Thomas, best known for leading the Detroit Pistons to two NBA championships. (And Isiah is only six foot one, which gives me hope for the next NBA draft!)

In an interview, Simmons asked Thomas about the secret to winning an NBA championship. Thomas paused and smiled, hinting that there's definitely a secret to winning championships.

"The secret of basketball," Thomas finally said, "is that it's *not* about basketball."[5]

This clearly wasn't the response Simmons expected. Seeing his confusion, Thomas shared a few stories about the incredible chemistry on his team. And that chemistry was not unique to the Pistons; it was something the Lakers and Celtics teams each had at their peak. Thomas said that he learned the secret when his team made an in-season trade of a star, high-scoring player for an aging, less-stellar performer. That player knew and understood the secret to winning. The Pistons gave up Adrian Dantley, who had a preoccupation with his own statistics, for little-known Mark Aguirre, who was a childhood buddy of Thomas. More important, though, Aguirre saw his role as doing anything he could to make the rest of the team successful. That trade didn't make sense on paper, but it led to amazing results. The Pistons turned their season around and went on to win the championship.

Thomas drove home his point. "Being the best in basketball is really all about *team*," he told Simmons. "Everyone must put the team first." Recalling the championship years, Thomas observed, "Lots of times, on our team, you couldn't tell who the best player in the game was. . . . It's the only way to win."[6]

Most people think winning in basketball is all about having the star players who score the most points, get the most rebounds, have the highest shooting percentage, and have all the right statistics. But Thomas believes that even having all that doesn't guarantee success. In fact, what he suggests runs counter to the prevailing wisdom. Instead of star players who are individually successful, the real secret to success in basketball is having players who are willing to sacrifice personal success for the sake of the team, even forgetting about their own stats at times.

To win, you need people who will forfeit their own success for the greater benefit of their team. That's the secret to winning over the long haul.

"You cannot get seduced by numbers and stats," Simmons concludes.[7] "It's not about statistics and talent as much as making teammates better and putting the greatness of your team ahead of yourself. That's really it."[8]

Jesus Knew the Secret

Jesus had a team. His team was the disciples. Jesus knew the secret and never got seduced by numbers and stats. He was explicit about his desire to equip his followers to do the heroic: "Very truly I tell you, whoever believes in me will do the works I have been doing, and they will do even *greater* things than these, because I am going to the Father" (John 14:12, emphasis added). Jesus told his followers that he was investing his life in them so they would do greater things than he would. He was setting them up so they could reach more people, go more places, and make more disciples than he ever would during his three years of earthly ministry.

> Jesus told his followers that he was investing his life in them so they would do greater things than he would.

Paul Knew the Secret

The apostle Paul begins chapter 12 in his first letter to the Corinthians by, in effect, asking us a question: "Do you want to know the secret?" It's a secret he has learned not about basketball but about the kingdom of God and how each of us has something to contribute to God's work in his kingdom. He writes, "Now about the gifts of the Spirit, brothers and sisters, I do not want you to be *uninformed*" (1 Cor. 12:1, emphasis added).

Paul goes on to reveal and explain the secret in verse 12. He explains that the church has a specific design, a way in which it is intended to work. It's a body. It's a team. And whether we're looking at the church locally or globally, the entire church is created by God to work together as a team, using everyone's Spirit-empowered gifts and all other resources to build up the whole body and to accomplish our God-given mission.

The "secret" is fairly simple, right? Rather than focusing on our individual success or the success of our local church, we need to think about the greater work of God's kingdom—all the places where he is acknowledged as Lord. That whole takes priority over any individual part. You and I are part of a mission that is bigger than what either of us can accomplish by ourselves, no matter how gifted we might be. The kingdom Jesus gave his life for is far bigger than the local church you serve or the denomination or network you're part of. As we each contribute to God's team, it's a win for the kingdom of God as more people are added, regardless of which local congregation they land in.

Thinking this way, as simple as it sounds, radically transforms our approach to leadership. Previously, whenever I'd read any of the hundred-plus *kingdom* references in the New Testament, my first thought would be how that applies to my own context, to

The "secret" is simple: you have to think about the kingdom of God more than about yourself or even your church.

Community Christian Church. Now when I read *kingdom*, I try to imagine our church *and* the churches down the road, my friend's church in downtown New York, the thirty-two-member rural church in Oklahoma, the underground church in China, and all the other global churches within God's kingdom.

This speaks to our priorities. It's what Jesus was getting at when he said, "Seek *first* his kingdom" (Matt. 6:33, emphasis added). Jesus draws our attention to the work of kingdom multiplication through parables about seeds (Mark 4:26–34) and yeast (Matt. 13:33). And there is a reason why he does this. When I begin to seek God's kingdom more than *my* kingdom, his power and purposes are revealed to us and through us.

We cannot advance the kingdom of God or accomplish Jesus' mission if we don't apply this secret to our lives and leadership. Every true movement of the Jesus mission begins with a heart change in the leader, and that happens *as we learn to take the spotlight off ourselves*. When we make this vital shift, we begin to shine the spotlight on others—we put the best of our efforts and energy into equipping other Christ followers and emerging leaders—empowering them to be the heroes, wherever they end up serving. Here is what lies at the heart of Jesus' leadership. This is his secret.

In short, we must shift from *being the hero* to *becoming a hero maker*. Table 1.1 shows the contrast.

Table 1.1: Hero versus Hero Maker

PRACTICE	HERO	HERO MAKER
Multiplication Thinking	I *think* ministry happens through my own leadership.	I *think* ministry happens through multiplied leaders.
Permission Giving	I *see* what God can do through my own leadership.	I *see* what God can do through others, and I let them know what I see in them.
Disciple Multiplying	I *share* what I've learned in ways that add more followers.	I *share* what I've learned in ways that multiply disciples.
Gift Activating	I ask God to *bless* the use of my own gifts.	I ask God to *bless* leaders I'm sending out.
Kingdom Building	I *count* people who show up to my thing.	I *count* leaders who go out and do God's thing.

Warning: Shifting to the hero-making practices detailed in this book means that we die to self in order to live more for Christ and his kingdom. It might mean that we never get the public credit because we've chosen to live in a shadow rather than to seek out a spotlight.

Even though we know these decisions are the right ones because we're advancing God's kingdom, that doesn't make them easy. As one of the leaders at Community Christian Church commented as we discussed being a hero maker,

> You're reminding us that real leaders first die to any vision of personal glory. The dying involves a very real transition, one of grief and loss of ever becoming that culture-defining leader who will shape all others around us. Of ever becoming big. Of ever receiving the recognition on this side of eternity.
>
> It's a difficult death for pastors because we all live for the dream. It goes against the grain that we may never appear on the radar but will instead spread in small units all over our city, country, and globe. We may never find the spotlight, but we will shape a whole new generation. And that's what makes it worthwhile.

In this book, I want to help you learn the secret of affirming, mentoring, and cheering other leaders into greatness and releasing them for work across God's kingdom, and the multiplication effect they create as they in turn mentor and release others. That's our role in advancing the kingdom of God.

Leaders in India Know the Secret . . . and Here Too?

I vividly remember the day I looked at my schedule and saw an appointment with a guy named Sam Stephens. I asked my assistant, Pat, why I had this meeting and who this guy was.

"I thought *you* knew him," she said. "All I know is that he is from India."

I went into the meeting wondering if this would be a waste of my time. I greeted the man, extended my hand, and asked him to tell me his story. Sam started back in the 1950s, with a story about his father. Sam's father had started a mission to plant churches in India, and by 1992 they had experienced some growth. They now had two hundred churches, and all could be traced to that first church started by Sam's dad in the '50s.

Wow, I thought. *Two hundred churches!* Sam had my attention now.

Sam wasn't comfortable talking about his own work; he's very humble. So I had to drag the details out of him. He told me that in 1992, he had taken over the mission, and he made a simple but strategic shift in the way they did things. He began to insist that every church planter not only plant a church but also have an apprentice church planter. This was someone who would come alongside the planter and learn firsthand how to plant a church, so the reproduction would continue year after year.

Now I was really curious. "How is that going?"

Without much expression, Sam replied, "Well, we now have seventy thousand churches."

At that point, I was glad that I was sitting down. I was beginning to realize that this was an incredible story. I asked Sam, "How many people does that represent?" And again his reply took my breath away.

"I think about 3.5 million," he said. Then he added, "But we are praying for one hundred thousand churches and 5 million people!"

At that, I began to wonder: how did this kind of exponential multiplication happen?

In talking further with Sam, I learned that he had discovered the secret. That simple shift he had made back in 1992 had transformed the results of their church-planting efforts. Sam had discovered that there were people and leaders all over India who had gifts, and he found that if he could empower them, encourage them, and make *them* successful, then Jesus' mission would be accomplished at a completely different level of productivity. Sam mentored leaders who in turn mentored other leaders who in turn did the same for many others. In addition to being Spirit-led and missional, what they were doing involved reproducing and multiplying through apprenticeship.

What Isiah Thomas had revealed to Bill Simmons, Sam Stephens had just shared with me.

In my office that day, Sam looked at me and said, "Dave, do you want to know the secret to what Jesus wants for planet Earth? It's not about your personal stat line, Dave. It's not just about growing your church. It's about the kingdom, and by learning how to make heroes of others, look at what God can do through you!"

> It's not about your personal stat line. It's not just about growing your church. It's about the kingdom.
>
> —SAM STEPHENS

Volunteer Leaders Know the Secret Too

Since that day, I've come to see firsthand that you don't have to be a pastor, global missionary, or church leader to be a hero maker and a kingdom multiplier. Michelle Bird, the wife of my coauthor, Warren, plays in neighborhood tennis leagues. Michelle was increasingly burdened to start a small group with her friends in the tennis league to better introduce them to Jesus, so after praying about it, she invited a friend from church to be her apprentice, to help her lead the group.

"I'll help you out, but I'm not a leader," Michelle's friend Hannah replied.

"I hear you, but would you be willing to talk by phone each week to pray, debrief the last meeting, and help me plan the next one?" Michelle countered.

"Sure, as long as you know I don't want to be a leader," Hannah said.

Every week, Michelle had Hannah do something different: greeting people at the door, leading the opening prayer, or asking the first discussion question. Hannah would agree to do it, but she would always remind Michelle, "I'm not going to be a leader."

The women in the group loved their time together, and they asked to keep the group going and do another study. Michelle once again asked Hannah if she would be the apprentice leader. And again Hannah declined, but she said she was willing to help.

Two groups later, Hannah finally agreed to lead, shifting the location to her neighborhood, and to invite some of her friends as well. "I guess I can do this." Hannah recruited her friends and led the group, now with Michelle assisting. And in the next group, Hannah led with an apprentice leader she had recruited. Michelle would join them for planning and prayer, now playing the role of supporter and coach.

Two more groups later, Hannah's apprentice is now leading another group, and Hannah is cheering her on. Across the years as groups have met, several women have found their way back to God and are being discipled. Michelle, seeing that it's not easy for Hannah's apprentice to reproduce herself, is constantly asking, "How's it going with developing your own apprentice?" The net result: the number of trained kingdom workers is being multiplied.

This is what we mean by hero making, and you don't need a pastor or church staff in the mix to make it work.

Share the Secret

Some secrets are meant to be kept quiet. But this secret isn't the kind you keep to yourself.

I remember one Christmas season when my kids were all younger and I took them Christmas shopping to buy gifts for my wife, Sue. After looking in several stores, they each found something for her. Our youngest, Caleb, was three years old at the time, and he had picked out a nice pair of winter gloves for his mom. As we got into the car to drive home, I said to him, "Now, Caleb, these gloves are a secret." I probably should have explained to him what a secret is. When we walked into the house, my wife teasingly asked the kids, "Did you get me any Christmas gifts?" Quite excited, Caleb chimed right in. "Yes, I got you gloves . . . and they are a secret!"

While I generally encourage you to keep your word and not share secrets, in this case I want you to be like Caleb. This is a secret that is meant to be shared! In fact, that's my motive in writing this book: to share in-depth details that reveal Jesus' leadership secrets to you, so you'll share those secrets with others, who share the secrets, and so on.

Those who understand and live out Jesus' secret today—people who get the link between "kingdom" and "team"—are those who play for the team name on the *front* of their basketball jersey and not for their individual name on the *back* of it. Throughout this book, I'll keep coming back to this idea. We want to understand how Jesus worked with a handful of followers to start a kingdom movement.

My hope is that *Hero Maker* will help you redefine your success as a leader, shifting your focus from your personal accomplishments to the accomplishments of those you are raising up and multiplying. We want this book to help church leaders—and leaders in other areas as well—rethink how they measure success. We need to change the scoreboard, the way we tally the points that determine whether we are winning or losing the game. Then we will begin to see our personal success through a kingdom perspective versus seeing the kingdom through the lens of our own efforts. Our priority will shift as well, from making disciples and planting churches to making disciples who make disciples and planting churches that plant churches. *That* is what we mean by hero making!

The key to becoming a leader who multiplies great leaders is having a kingdom mindset. This means helping people identify their unique calling and then releasing them to pour into others. In doing this, you grow as well, both personally and as a leader. You begin to exponentially increase your

> When you invest in helping as many people as possible identify their unique calling and release them to pour into others, you exponentially increase your impact.

impact, even as you focus your efforts and attention on investing in others. You become a hero maker.

The work of hero making can happen at any scale and in any context. Suppose your God-given capacity is to lead a small group of ten. Great! What would happen if your primary goal was not simply to be the best small group leader but to do your best to make sure someone else was an even better leader? What if that person in turn invested their gifts and energy into someone else? When we make heroes of others, the potential for eternal impact grows beyond our limited abilities and efforts.

But let's take it one step farther. Now let's imagine that this is happening in every role in the church, from the lead pastor to every staff member to every volunteer ministry leader. And what if this kingdom mindset of investing in others spilled out beyond the church to every community and business leader? You'd have a multiplication movement in the making. Hero making is the foundation of every movement because it is a *force multiplier*. It takes whatever work we do as individuals and multiplies it over and over again.

I believe that as you read and prayerfully apply the insights and teaching in this book, drawing on the power of the Holy Spirit, and believing that Jesus wants to do "greater things" (John 14:12) through *you*, a new normal will begin to arise in your heart and mind. You'll see how God has called and equipped you to make and multiply disciple makers of Jesus Christ for his purposes and for his kingdom. What could be more important than that?

Hero making is a force multiplier.

If you want to better understand the secret of how Jesus' kingdom was designed to multiply, or to gain more skill and confidence in putting his leadership secret to work, turn the page. Not only will this secret change your own leadership and your church, but it also has the potential to change the world—literally!

Hero Maker Discussion Questions

OPEN

- Tell about a time when you were part of a special team (sports, arts, friends, or work). What made it special?
- What's an "aha!" moment you've had in ministry or leadership, when you discovered the secret to something?

DIG

- Read John 14:12, which is about doing greater things. Prior to reading this chapter, what did you think Jesus meant when he said his followers would do greater things than he himself had done?
- If Jesus is our role model, and he told his followers they would do greater things, how would you apply this to your ministry and leadership?

REFLECT

- Judging by what you've read so far, what do you look forward to in this book? What, if anything, makes you uncomfortable?

CHAPTER 2

The Wrong Questions

Big Idea: Hero makers know that if we focus only on addition, we never get to multiplication.

I've never been shy about asking for advice. In fact, I've put a lot of energy into finding ways to get time with big-dream, high-achievement people who might offer me wisdom. To meet personally with them, I've offered to do everything from hosting their events to treating them to a great restaurant to driving them to and from the airport.

One time I got to pick up Bill Hybels from the airport. He's the founding pastor of Willow Creek Community Church, one of the most influential churches in America. He has been a pioneer in outreach and growth and is a bestselling author of more than twenty books. He's also chaired the board of the Willow Creek Association, a fellowship of more than twelve thousand like-minded churches across roughly fifty countries.

I asked one of our team members to drive the van so I could give full attention to my conversation with Bill. I had a pad of paper with far too many questions for the short time I'd have with him. Throughout our hour together, I rapid-fired questions, and with machine-gun quickness he shot back brilliant answers.

I remember the occasion for several reasons: first, because it was Bill, one of the more impressive leaders I've ever been around; second, because of the insightful answers he gave; and third, because on a later occasion he paid me a compliment, telling me great leaders ask questions, and commended me for bringing a list of them to the airport and wanting to grow as a leader (even though later I discovered that I could have brought much better questions!).

Even more important, his answers have provided helpful guidance as I lead Community Christian Church and NewThing, our church-planting organization, into new territory. In responding to what I asked him, he mentored me well.

Unfortunately, today I look back at that interview with regret. It was a lost opportunity because I asked the wrong questions. I asked questions that focused only on my leadership and my church: "How do I grow a church?" and "How do I develop myself as a leader?" My questions were all about making my current model better or bigger. I didn't realize at the time that my questions would not lead to a new level, a higher perspective that could alter the status quo by changing how I was leading and doing church.

The questions I asked Bill were the same familiar questions that a generation of church leaders have asked over and over again. And for the last fifty years, the answers to those questions have led to practices that focus on simply growing our churches and developing ourselves rather

> **I asked the wrong questions, not hero-making questions but rather questions about how I could be the hero.**

than reproducing churches and multiplying leaders. You might say they are good questions, but not great ones. These are not hero-making questions but rather questions that make us the hero, whether or not we intend that to happen.

We need to think critically about the questions we are asking. Reminds me of a story about two men leaving church after hearing a sermon on prayer. Joe says, "I wonder if it would be all right to smoke while praying." George replies, "Why don't you ask the pastor?" So he does: "Reverend, may I smoke while I pray?" The pastor replies, "No sir, you may not! That's very disrespectful toward our faith." Joe reports the news to his friend. George says, "I'm not surprised. You asked the wrong question. Let me try." So George asks the pastor, "Rev, may I pray while I smoke?" To which the pastor eagerly replies, "By all means, my son. You can always pray whenever you want to." Think about the questions you are asking. The right questions make a difference!

I remember church growth consultant Carl George telling me, "When you are really onto something, it will lead to questions that are more and more profound." When Community Christian first stumbled onto becoming a two-site church, several years ago, we knew we were onto something unique. After becoming a multisite church, we started asking, "How could we multiply to ten locations or more?" And as we approached ten locations, we began to ask a more profound question: "How could God use us to multiply networks of reproducing churches around the world?"

When you understand Jesus' leadership secret (chapter 1), you become discontent with questions of bigger and better. You find yourself asking more-profound questions about reproducing, multiplying, and movement making. I want to encourage and challenge you to reexamine the questions you ask. The answers to your questions lead to the practices you implement in your leadership.

In the introduction to this book, I outlined five levels of church development. In short, Level 1 churches are declining, Level 2 are plateauing, Level 3 are growing, Level 4 are reproducing (churches that are planting new churches and launching sites where planting is planned and programmed versus automatic and spontaneous), and Level 5 are multiplying (starting multiple outreaches that in turn each start multiple outreaches).[9] See Figure 2.1 for a visualization. In the rest of this chapter, we're going to examine different levels of questions and the resulting leadership practices. Here is my challenge for you: Take your questions up a level! In the questions you raise, don't settle until you reach Level 5.

FIGURE 2.1

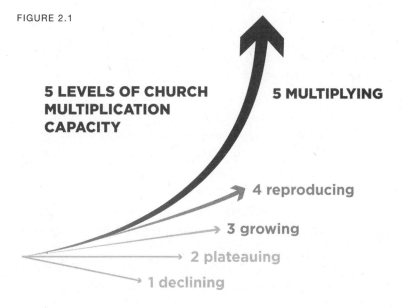

5 LEVELS OF CHURCH MULTIPLICATION CAPACITY

5 MULTIPLYING

4 reproducing

3 growing

2 plateauing

1 declining

Level 1, 2, and 3 Questions Lead to Level 1, 2, and 3 Practices

Level 1 churches are among the most common out there (as are Level 1 ministries within churches, which could be a Sunday school, a youth group, a prison ministry, or anything else). Attendance can be in decline for any number of reasons. You may be in or leading a church that has experienced this or is currently working through it. Sometimes the church no longer has clarity of vision and purpose. Maybe the church has become too internally focused. Maybe the church's neighborhood has changed over the years and the church hasn't changed with it. We've all seen this happen. I've also seen churches lose relevance. The way the church has reached out in the past is no longer engaging the community. Maybe there has been unaddressed division within the church, or unhealed scandal. Maybe the church is even struggling to survive.

I've seen how it's tempting for leaders of Level 1 churches to voice questions like those listed in Figure 2.2.

These are all important questions, but none of them will take the

FIGURE 2.2

LEVEL 1

Questions That Lead to Declining

· How do I keep leading this ministry when no one volunteers to help?

· How do I keep from being discouraged when we're just not getting the same results we used to?

· How can we best honor the legacies of those who are dying or moving away?

· How could we simplify or consolidate various ministries, since we don't have enough volunteers to support them?

· How can we trim costs in order to pay the bills, enabling us to remain financially viable?

church out of its pattern of decline. I've observed how questions like these lead to practices that are more reactive than proactive, more about managing the decline than reversing it.

By the way, nothing requires you to keep asking Level 1 questions. One way to stop asking them is to make statements that reflect the dream of a different future for your church or ministry. How could the following build faith and hope that the pattern of decline can be broken?

- If God's Word says there is an abundant harvest within reach of our church, then what if this coming Christmas (or Easter or Mother's Day) we were to . . .
- If God says all things are possible through him, then why couldn't we develop a plan to . . .
- I believe there are people out there who need our help to find their way back to God, so could we pray and then brainstorm ways that our church could reach out to them and . . .

And as you will soon discover, it's Level 4 and 5 questions that allow you to dream big.

Like leaders of Level 1 churches, leaders of churches at Level 2—those that are plateauing—ask questions relevant to their situation. These churches are gaining ground each year, but their losses during that same time neutralize their gains. Often their identity is wrapped around being whatever size they are; they feel they're in their sweet spot if they can simply maintain their current size, from programming to finances.

If this describes your church, you're not alone—far from it. Churches at Levels 1 and 2 together represent roughly 80% of all U.S. churches.

Some examples of common Level 2 questions are shown in Figure 2.3.

FIGURE 2.3

LEVEL 2

Questions That Lead to Plateauing

- How can I train someone to take my place, so that this ministry will keep going after I step down?

- How can we maintain past participation levels in the church's workdays when we spruce up the property?

- How do we make this the best church possible for the people God has brought to us?

- How do we get enough volunteers to keep all our ministries staffed?

- How can we use church funds better to maintain our facilities and better support our paid staff?

These too are important questions, but none of them will lead to practices that take the church out of its pattern of holding even.

Nothing prevents you from addressing Level 2 questions necessary for survival while at the same time asking better questions. I think of Mike Slaughter, who, fresh from seminary, received an assignment from his United Methodist denomination to pastor a hundred-plus-year-old church in a central Ohio hamlet of fewer than twenty homes, named Ginghamsburg. Since its founding, Ginghamsburg Church had hovered at around fifty people. Mike set out to meet their needs but also to ask better questions, all centered on, "How can I lead this congregation to discover new heights in what it means to be a follower of Jesus?" He started a discipleship group among these saints, and as the months went by, they not only grew personally in their faith but also started inviting friends to join their journey. As Mike reflects, "I jokingly called the process 'sanctified Amway' because of how devoted people became to our product—a life-changing relationship with Jesus Christ. I foresaw the leaders who emerged from our small-group community becoming the Joshuas and Deborahs of tomorrow's church."[10]

And they did! Mike stayed at that church for more than thirty years, and so did a large portion of that original group. During this time, not only did attendance grow tenfold, but Ginghamsburg sent out several teams to birth five more Methodist churches in their area. And two of those births have helped birth other Methodist churches. Likewise, they've started ministries from urban Dayton to poverty-stricken Sudan in Africa. The Sudan effort, by the way, began with a congregation-wide question one year: "What does Jesus want from us for this coming Christmas?"

Level 3 churches are experiencing growth, anywhere from slow to rapid. Sometimes the growth is misleading. Perhaps it's just a reshuffling of the saints because the church across town had a split and your church has a better children's ministry. I've also seen growth as merely an extension of class or race, as when middle-class minorities are moving into an area, many of them already followers of Christ, and one particular church is an affinity match for them.

Other times, however, the growth comes mostly from conversions as the church helps people find their way back to God. Maybe the church has an outstanding student ministry, high-visibility young adult gathering, vibrant missional communities, and/or an effective program of Christ-centered recovery groups. Typically, the teaching ministry is also relevant in content and regularly invites people to take next steps in becoming a follower of Jesus Christ. More often than not, the church is reaching out in tangible ways to show the community the love of Jesus, especially by serving the disadvantaged.

Level 3 churches make up approximately 16% of all Protestant churches in the United States. Figure 2.4 shows the kinds of questions that leaders of Level 3 churches ask.

FIGURE 2.4

LEVEL 3 — Questions That Lead to Growing

- Should my leadership style change now that we've grown so much?

- How can we help all the recent newcomers get to know us and each other so they feel better connected?

- How can we close the back door so that more of our newcomers engage in our discipleship process?

- How can we decide between a building expansion or adding another worship service to keep us from bottlenecking the growth?

- How can we keep growing the mission in light of so many new people who don't yet tithe?

These are also good questions, but none of them will lead to practices that move the church from its pattern of growth by addition to one of reproduction or multiplication.

Level 4 questions will lead to reproduction, and Level 5 questions to multiplication. We'll go into those in the next chapter. For now, I want you to see and understand that Levels 1, 2, and 3 are about the shift from subtraction to addition. It is good to grow (Level 3), but why settle for good when what God wants for his church is something better (Level 4) or even the best (Level 5)?

Does Something Tell You There Has to Be More?

Asking the wrong questions gives us status quo answers and status quo results. Worse, it leaves too many of us thinking, *There has to be more than this.* We're stuck and don't know what to change. The day-to-day, week-to-week patterns we've settled into aren't consistent with the dreams we had when we entered ministry. When we start to ask the hard questions and honestly assess where we are, we realize we've gotten sidetracked, spending all our time and energy running the church instead of focusing on multiplying disciples and accomplishing the mission of Jesus—the mission we gave ourselves to in the beginning.

I remember a meeting early in Community Christian Church's history. We were trying to clarify our vision and mission, and our young team was struggling with how to articulate where we were going. Troy Jackson, an intern with us, finally spoke up, saying, "I got it, I got it. I know our vision!" Then with a deadpan delivery he said, "We . . . want . . . to . . . be . . . a . . . really . . . really . . . really . . . BIG . . . church!" We all started laughing, and not just because of his delivery. We knew that what he said was true! But we also knew that we had to do more. Even then, we realized that if we and other churches continued to follow our current pattern of growth by addition, we would not win the world to Christ and make disciples in all the nations. Essentially, we would be disobeying Jesus' clear and passionate call to *all* of his disciples (then and now) in his Great Commission (Matt. 28:19–20).

> Asking the wrong questions leaves too many of us thinking, *There has to be more than this.* We're stuck and don't know what to change.

Let me put it as bluntly as I can. Too many church leaders are stuck asking the same old question: "How do I grow my church?" Let's ask questions that are more profound! Let me give you four reasons why that's the wrong question and why we need to take our questions up a level.

1. "How do *I* grow my church?" We were not meant to do this alone or versus others. That "I" should be replaced with a "we." Hero makers know that the mission is accomplished only through the multiplying of other leaders.

2. "How do I *grow* my church?" This is only partially right. Yes, the

church was meant to grow. And yes, healthy things grow. But growth is not the endgame. Hero makers understand that growth is not about creating more *seating* capacity; it's about creating more *sending* capacity and expanding God's kingdom. Also, the phrase "grow my church" should be changed to "multiply my church."

3. "How do I grow *my* church?" It's not yours or mine; we are only stewards. We've each taught this stewardship lesson hundreds of times to our people regarding their finances and every area of their life, but we need to look at ourselves and the churches we are responsible for and apply it to our own ministries and giftedness. Hero makers know it's all God's, so they say "grow *God's* church" rather than "grow *my* church."

4. "How do I grow my *church*?" It's not just about the church (or whatever ministry you lead within a church); it's about the kingdom of God. This question of how to grow the church is almost always asked with the lowercase *c* church in mind. That's shortsighted. Hero makers are far more concerned about the growth of God's kingdom. They see their church through a kingdom lens versus seeing the kingdom through the lens of their local church. Hero makers substitute "grow God's *kingdom*" for "grow my *church*."

A far better question than "How do I grow my church?" is the Level 5 question, "How can we multiply God's kingdom?"

One-Question Assessment

Let me suggest a simple leadership exercise: replace the question, "How do I grow my church (or ministry)?" with the weightier question, "Am I trying to be the hero, or am I trying to make heroes out of others?"

Ask that question every day, and I guarantee you will multiply the impact of your leadership. How does it work? Like this:

- If you are leading a small group, ask, "Am I trying to be the hero in this group, or am I mentoring other leaders to make heroes out of them?"
- In your teaching, ask, "Am I trying to be the hero in my teaching, or am I developing other teachers who will be the heroes?"

- In leading your staff or team, ask, "Am I trying to be the hero of this team, or am I developing and investing in others so they will be the heroes?"

Making it a daily practice to ask one question is simple but challenging. However, keeping this question in the front of your thoughts and prayers may be the single greatest adjustment you ever make in your leadership.

You Are More Ready Than You Realize to Be a Hero Maker

As a young leader, I thought I had a very big vision for my church (notice I was saying "my church." Ugh!). I wanted to lead a church that would reach one thousand people. Then I heard a paradigm-shifting challenge from author Neil Cole that caused me to start asking different questions. He said, "Take your current dream for your church and multiply it by one million." I quickly did the math. One thousand times one million equals one billion! I started thinking about trying to reach a billion people, and it immediately challenged my current practices. I knew that I couldn't turn my dream into reality with one leader or one church. I knew that I would have to multiply my efforts through hundreds, maybe thousands or tens of thousands, of leaders. It took my questions to a whole new level!

Don't stay where you are. Don't stay stuck asking the same old questions. If you do, you will get the same old answers and same old results. You were made for more. Ask yourself every day, "Am I trying to be the hero, or am I trying to make heroes of others?"

What is the dream for your leadership? Multiply it by one million. Now, how could God accomplish that? If you want to know, let's move on to the next chapter, where we start asking the really big questions.

Hero Maker Discussion Questions

OPEN

- Tell a story about a time when asking the wrong question got you into trouble. Extra points if it's a humorous situation.

DIG

- Read Acts 1:6, where the disciples asked the wrong question. John Calvin said that there are as many errors in that question as there are words in it! What are some of the ways their assumptions behind that question had to change in order for them to understand the response Jesus gave them in Acts 1:7 and Acts 1:8?

REFLECT

- What disillusionment about church, ministry, or leadership, if any, has caused you to think, *There has to be more than this*?
- What in this chapter has given you hope?

CHAPTER 3

The Right Questions

Big Idea: Hero makers understand that if we focus on multiplication, we can see God-size results.

Asking the right question can change everything.

In an article in *Forbes* magazine, David Sturt and Todd Nordstrom describe how half a century ago, someone asked a profound question that fundamentally changed how we communicate with each other every day. He asked the question in an era when every phone was tethered to a wall in our homes by a short, squiggly cord. In some rural communities, people still used a "party line," where everyone would listen for the pattern of rings when the telephone sounded to determine if the call was for them or for the next farm down the road.

As Sturt and Nordstrom tell the story, it was then that Marty Cooper, a young engineer at Motorola, asked a very insightful question: "Why is it that when we want to call and talk to a person, we have to call a *place*?" That contrary question led to a new era of communication and the invention of DynaTAC 8000X, the very first cell phone.

The Tanner Institute interviewed Marty and more than 250 other great innovators like him and found that the genesis of almost every brilliant innovation was asking the right question. The just-right question can be a disruptive agent, cutting through years of complacency to redirect a leader's or team's focus toward extraordinary new insights.[11] Makes you wonder what question Steve Jobs asked that led to the Mac computer, what Elon Musk asked that brought the electric car to market, and so much more!

As we learned in the previous chapter, if we start with the wrong questions, the result will be a certain set of answers and practices that lead to status quo results. Instead if we dare to start with the right questions

(Levels 4 and 5), our pathway will lead to a different set of answers, better practices, and multiplied results.

FIGURE 3.1

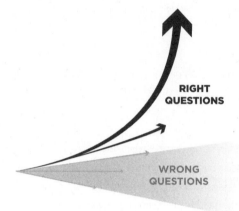

RIGHT QUESTIONS

WRONG QUESTIONS

If I could give you only one leadership question to ask yourself every day to maximize and multiply your influence, it would be, "Am I trying to be the hero, or am I trying to make heroes out of others?" As you ask that question, know that God has given you a unique vision for your life, and for that reason, I want you to gain clarity in how to ask all the right questions to lead a multiplying movement.

> If I could give you only one leadership question to ask yourself every day to maximize and multiply your influence, it would be, "Am I trying to be the hero, or am I trying to make heroes out of others?"

This chapter has stories, Scripture, and statistics all pulled together to encourage you to ask the right questions so you can get multiplied results. My hope is that you never settle for parroting the familiar questions of leaders before you.

I challenge you to ask the questions that God wants you to ask, questions that will lead you to the practices he wants you to implement. Your choice of questions is critical. To enhance their quality, I want you to do the following:

- *Pray for guidance.* When we pause to pray, it opens us up to the deeper, richer thoughts of heaven that are often chased away by our hectic rush through our daily schedule. In the early stages of our difference-making quest, the simple act of paying attention to the prompting of God's Spirit can provide the kinds of subtle adjustments that bring about the greatest innovation. Pause to ask God to bring to mind the right questions for you and your leadership vision.

- *Pray for people.* Tell God about the people you want to help. Ask God to bring to mind faces of individuals and groups that he wants you to reach. Don't be surprised if the faces are not always familiar or the groups are not always local. As God brings people to mind, ask him to use you to reach them.

- *Pray big!* What would you love to see happen through your leadership? Not just *like* to see happen. Not just feel good about. What would you *love* to see result from your time and energy? What is the big dream? Now give that dream a number. Once you have that dream and number, multiply it by 100x. Such as a hundred times more conversions or volunteers or small groups or new churches. If you have the faith to ask for 1,000x or even 1,000,000x, ask God for that.

Did you pause and pray? Please do it right now.

Einstein had this to say about asking the right questions: "If I had an hour to solve a problem and my life depended on it, I would use the first 55 minutes determining the proper question to ask, for once I know the proper question, I could solve the problem in less than five minutes."[12] If you are an Einstein, just spend your time thinking about it. If you are not (like me), spend that time in prayer with God!

Gathering for Asking Questions

I and eleven other senior leaders from some of the most highly visible and fastest-growing churches across the United States agreed to gather in Chicago to explore new questions. Each of us had spent the last ten years or more asking the Level 3 question, "How can I grow my church?" I remember laughing a lot and learning a lot, but I also remember that every one of us felt like there had to be more than what we were experiencing. We formed a two-year cohort we called Future Travelers, which I wrote about with my friend Alan Hirsch (Alan is a recognized expert on multiplication movements) in *On the Verge*.[13] Over the next twenty-four months, we asked new questions about multiplication and movement making and pursued answers together.

Steve Andrews was typical of the leaders gathered. He had planted Kensington Church in the Detroit suburb of Troy, Michigan, and in less than twenty years, the church was exceeding ten thousand people in weekly worship across several campuses. Yet, as Steve said, "I found myself pretty empty. I was feeling like I had in a big way missed some of God's purposes in my life. We had thousands and thousands of people coming to church, but without the New Testament results that I knew God longs for."

Steve realized that the problem was that his current leadership practices wouldn't allow his church to do all God wanted to do. "There's not enough years in my life to keep growing this thing bigger," he said. Steve got so busy staffing his church's programs that there seemed no escape from Level 3 growth by addition, even though it was rocket-speed growth. "How could I champion releasing people as missionaries when I can't even staff my own programs?" he shared.

"All these good things hold me back from Level 4 reproduction and Level 5 multiplication," Steve explained. "I am more interested than ever in changing our conversation from finding the next person to add to our numbers, shifting instead to how to release 150 leaders to start new churches and ventures and impact our city through multiplication."

> I found myself pretty empty. We had thousands and thousands of people coming to church, but without the New Testament results that I knew God longs for.
>
> —STEVE ANDREWS

Steve and the rest of us were done asking only, "How do I grow my church?" An angst of regret lingered in the room as the group realized that for years (even decades), we had been asking the wrong questions and implementing the wrong practices.

Sometimes Better Questions Start with a Personal Calling

It's not just pastors who learn to ask better questions. Joanne Russell is passionate about seeing women come to know Christ. When she and her husband relocated to Southern California, they found a church and began building relationships in their new community. After two years of meeting people through the PTA, a book club, and other community activities, she began a women's Bible study in her home.

What began with nine women in her living room became the next year twenty-four women, and as of this writing six years later, there are 350 women in thirty-four groups. The ministry is now based at one of the campuses of her church, North Coast Church. She has become a staff pastor there and is known as the founder and leader of a ministry that brings women together in small groups to build relationships with each other and to study the Bible together.

One trigger for this amazing ministry growth is Joanne's dissatisfaction with the lack of confidence that many women live with, which in turn limits their ability to boldly share the love of Christ with others. "I long to help women see their lives as God sees them," she explains. "One of my life verses is 1 Thessalonians 2:8, which says, 'Because we loved you so much, we were delighted to share with you not only the gospel of God but our lives as well.'" So her focus has been on creating an environment where women can do just that: share their lives as well as the gospel. In doing so, she helps them believe that they can facilitate a group. She invests in them, encourages them, and in turn helps them invest in and mentor other women.

If Joanne had fixated on "how can I share my life and faith with others?" she certainly would have had an eternal impact on many. But she asked a far better question: "How can I help other women share life and faith with others, who will in turn do likewise with still others?" That shift of question has translated into a much greater impact.

Addition or Exponential Multiplication?

To understand the dramatic difference between addition and multiplication, imagine two people on the first day of a month each receiving a dollar. The first person gets more dollars each day by addition, and the second person benefits from a multiplier effect. The first receives money this way: two dollars more on day 2, three dollars more on day 3, four dollars more on day 4, and so on. But for the second person, the running tally

Table 3.1: Addition versus Exponential Multiplication

DAY	ADDITION	MULTIPLICATION
Day 1	$1	$1
Day 2	$3	$2
Day 3	$6	$6
Day 4	$10	$24
Day 5	$15	$120
Day 6	$21	$720
Day 7	$28	$5,040
Day 8	$36	$40,320
Day 9	$45	$362,880
Day 10	$55	$3,628,800
Day 11	$66	$39,916,800
Day 12	$78	$479,001,600
Day 13	$91	$6,227,020,800
Day 14	$105	$87,178,291,200
Day 15	$120	$1,307,674,368,000
Day 16	$136	$20,922,789,888,000
Day 17	$153	$355,687,428,096,000
Day 18	$171	$6,402,373,705,728,000
Day 19	$190	$121,645,100,408,832,000
Day 20	$210	$2,432,902,008,176,640,000
Day 21	$231	$51,090,942,171,709,400,000
Day 22	$253	$1,124,000,727,777,610,000,000
Day 23	$276	$25,852,016,738,885,000,000,000
Day 24	$300	$620,448,401,733,239,000,000,000
Day 25	$325	$15,511,210,043,331,000,000,000,000
Day 26	$351	$403,291,461,126,606,000,000,000,000
Day 27	$378	$10,888,869,450,418,400,000,000,000,000
Day 28	$406	$304,888,344,611,714,000,000,000,000,000
Day 29	$435	$8,841,761,993,739,700,000,000,000,000,000
Day 30	$465	$265,252,859,812,191,000,000,000,000,000,000

doubles on day 2, triples on day 3, quadruples on day 4, and so forth. The payout would look like Table 3.1.

On day 30, the first person has a total of $465, while the second person has an astounding $265,252,859,812,191,000,000,000,000,000,000 (that's thirty-three figures). If you're curious, this number reads as two hundred sixty-five nonillion, two hundred fifty-two octillion, eight hundred fifty-nine septillion, eight hundred twelve sextillion, one hundred ninety-one quintillion.[14]

This second person has gathered all of the planet's wealth by day 17 alone! The second person's tally is exponentially larger because of where multiplication can lead.

When leaders and churches change from additive models to multiplicative models, they suddenly have the potential in a short time to reach every person on earth.

Steve's problem—the glass ceiling caused by his church's growth by addition—does have a solution, and one with infinite impact. It comes through asking questions about multiplication. And the answers to those questions will lead to practices that maximize the church's influence.

> When leaders and churches change from additive models to multiplicative models, they suddenly have the potential in a short time to reach every person on earth.

My friend Eddie Yoon, author of *Superconsumers: A Simple, Speedy, and Sustainable Path to Superior Growth* and someone who has helped his clients achieve more than $1 billion in growth in annual profits over the past two decades, told me the following over a conversation about hero making:

> A lot of my work with growing companies has led me to believe that the vast majority of businesses try to grow by pie-splitting vs. pie-growing. All my data and experience says that pie-growing companies grow faster, are more profitable and are far more valuable to Wall Street.
>
> I bet the same is true for churches. If they focus on church shoppers (pie-splitting) I suspect they'll experience far less growth potential than if their focus is, "Am I actually multiplying God's kingdom?"

He also made one more observation:

My guess is that too many leaders think "glory" is a zero-sum game:
If I help someone else get glory, then there's less for me. The truth
of hero making may be that you're choosing to defer glory until
your rewards in heaven. But it may be that there's actually so much
more glory on this side of heaven if we help more people make more
disciples. ("This is to my Father's glory, that you bear much fruit,
showing yourselves to be my disciples," John 15:8).[15]

Level 4 and 5 Questions Lead to
Level 4 and 5 Practices

Here's the reality: 96% of all U.S. churches have never reproduced themselves.[16] They may be young or old, little or big, denominational or
nondenominational, urban, suburban, or rural, but the overwhelming
majority of churches that you and I know about have never birthed a new
church or launched a new site or sent out a leader to start one, whether
ten, one hundred, or one thousand miles away. They might have led many
people to Christ, and that's terrific. They might have discipled many new
believers—children, youth, and adults—and that's huge. They might have
been involved behind the scenes, praying for and helping fund missionaries at home or abroad, and that's really important.

Yet something is missing in the 96%: they've never gotten on the front
lines and trained and released a person or team to give life to a new church
that will "go and make disciples of all nations." They've never experienced
Level 5 practices.

How does that reality translate into Level 5 church thinking? It
means that 96% of all U.S. churches are either declining (Level 1), plateauing (Level 2), or growing (Level 3). Only 4% are at Level 4 (reproducing)
or Level 5 (multiplying). And that 4% is lopsided on the Level 4 side, with
extremely few truly multiplying.

Imagine what would happen if the needle on the gauge moved from
4% of churches in America reproducing or multiplying to greater than 10%
doing so. After an Exponential conference, I had a late-night conversation with Pastor Tim Keller, who is a student of movement making, and
he is convinced that 10% represents the tipping point. This same tipping

point is confirmed by Levitt and Dubner, the authors of *Freakonomics*.[17] Bottom line: people who study movements say if 10% of all churches were reproducing or multiplying, it could dramatically influence the spiritual landscape of America. Every 1% increase represents tens of millions of lives changed for eternity.

Clearly, that would be a move of the Holy Spirit. But have you ever considered this: what if this kind of kingdom-advancing, Great Commission multiplication is what God already wants to do, and we're holding it back by asking the same old Level 3 questions? Could it be that the vision of becoming a multiplying church is consistent with the original vision Jesus had for his church in Acts 1:8—that the church would start and multiply other churches who would move from Jerusalem to Judea to Samaria and to the ends of the earth? Jesus knew that through the fulfillment of this vision, his mission would be accomplished.

Michael Marquardt has spent more than twenty-five years training leaders. In his book *Leading with Questions*, he wrote, "Good

> **What if this kind of kingdom-advancing, Great Commission multiplication is what God already wants to do, and we're holding it back by asking the same old Level 3 questions?**

leaders ask many questions. Great leaders ask the great questions. And great questions can help you become a great leader."[18] My translation? The better question gets a better answer, and here are the best questions of all for a leader and for a church:

- Leader: "Am I trying to be the hero, or am I trying to make heroes out of others?"
- Church: "How do we multiply God's kingdom?"

You've Likely Found Partial Answers Already

Many church leaders have found partially right answers to questions on how to move from addition to reproduction or multiplication.

- The *missional movement* asked questions about how to get Christians out of their holy huddles and back into the neighborhoods and into relationships with the people they live, work, and play with each day.

- The *multisite movement* asked questions about how to reproduce one location's effective ministry in another community or city.
- The recent *church-planting movement* has asked questions about releasing leaders and resources to start new churches in order to reach new people.

Overall, many leaders, churches, and denominations are searching for more-profound questions that can help us make more disciples.

Many are discovering that reproduction is even more strategic than growth (addition). Reproduction happens when a church plants a new church or starts a new site or location. When we start a new group or team, reproduction equally happens at all other levels of ministry. For example, a grief support group can grow in size, which is great. But it can also birth a new group (and then *both* groups can grow). I call that Level 4 reproduction.

Some examples of questions Level 4 churches ask are shown in Figure 3.2.

FIGURE 3.2

Questions That Lead to Reproducing

LEVEL 4

- How can we be more active in planting a new church?
- Should our church go multisite by launching an additional campus?
- How can we strengthen our culture of apprenticeship so that more ministries will replicate themselves?
- How could we take on an intern or leadership resident as a way of helping train future church leaders?
- How can I strengthen our bench by creating a leadership path and putting a greater emphasis on leadership development?

At Exponential, we have worked to create simple, sticky language such as "leadership resident," which is a church planter in training, or "level 4 church" or "level 5 church" to describe churches that are reproducing or multiplying. I'm encouraged to see a growing number of leaders and churches adopting this new vocabulary, which Exponential has also been promoting through our excellent ebooks, such as *Becoming a Level 5 Multiplying Church* and *Spark: Igniting a Culture of Multiplication.*[19]

"Level 5" describes a multiplying church. This is a church—or ministry within that church—that not only reproduces (Level 4) but also builds into that reproduction the DNA of continual reproduction. It's the question, "How many apples are in this seed?" versus "How many seeds are in this apple?"

The thirty thousand leaders who have attended an Exponential conference in the past couple years (plus tens of thousands more who have participated online) are growing more interested in the issue, "How do I begin to ask Level 5 questions?"

A few of the questions that Level 5 churches will ask are shown in Figure 3.3.

FIGURE 3.3

Questions That Lead to Multiplying

LEVEL 5

- What are the practices of a hero maker that I could apply at the church I serve?*

- How do I carve out the time to disciple six or so people that will go on to disciple others?

- If church planting is the best way to reach people for Christ, then how can we get more involved in churches that will in turn plant other churches?

- How can we measure and cheer for what happens outside the walls of our church and the boundaries of our city?

- How do we follow the old Home Depot slogan in moving from "We can do it; you can help" to "*You* can do it; and we can help"?

*By the way, that's what the entire middle section of this book is about.

Is There a Level 5 Church or Ministry Inside You?

If you're feeling a bit scared right now, a bit anxious about the seriousness of playing a leadership role in developing a Level 5 church or ministry within the church, I've got great news. You're only in chapter 3. The next chapter paints a picture of how to lead as a hero maker, of what kind of person God will use (hint: if you love Jesus, it's probably you!).

Then the section to follow shows you step-by-step how to embrace the five practices of a hero maker. If that's not enough, the final section of the book walks you through challenges and questions that often arise as people embrace the kind of hero making that results in a Level 5 multiplying ministry.

Say a prayer, and then jump into the next chapter.

Hero Maker Discussion Questions

OPEN

- Would you rather ask questions or answer questions? Why?
- What is your reaction to Albert Einstein's statement, "If I had an hour to solve a problem and my life depended on it, I would use the first 55 minutes determining the proper question to ask, for once I know the proper question, I could solve the problem in less than five minutes"?[20] Agree or disagree?
- Ever had an experience, or observed one, in which a lot of work was put into asking the right questions?

DIG

- Read Matthew 21:23–25 and Mark 11:27–29, and notice that Jesus responded to some questions with a question. Why do you suppose Jesus did this?
- What would it sound like for you to ask Level 4 or Level 5 questions? Give an example.

REFLECT

- What is your biggest deterrent from consistently asking Level 4 and Level 5 questions?
- Take time to pray, asking God to remove whatever it is that keeps you from asking Level 4 and Level 5 questions.

CHAPTER 4

Leading as a Hero Maker

Big Idea: Hero makers shift from being the hero to making others the hero in God's unfolding story.

"Five . . . four . . . Ferguson picks up his dribble . . . three . . . two . . . one . . . Ferguson shoots and scores! They win! They did it! Ferguson's last-second shot has won the championship!" With my hands raised in victory, I shouted those words in the driveway of my house as a kid. In fact, I created a heroic drama like this hundreds of times every summer.

I bet you did too.

If it wasn't a game-winning last-second shot, how did you imagine yourself as the hero somewhere? My wife, Sue, who became a teacher, saw herself being like Anne Sullivan: teaching the next Helen Keller and helping her students discover how to learn.

Maybe you dreamed of taking a spaceship into outer space as the whole world watched to see whether you would land safely.

Perhaps you envisioned yourself in front of ten thousand screaming fans, nailing a face-melting solo on your electric guitar.

Or maybe you imagined dancing so beautifully that when the music stopped, the crowd erupted with a standing ovation.

I believe God put that dream to be a hero within each of us as our way to make a difference and to leave our mark on planet Earth.

Jesus' death on the cross was heroic. Jesus told his Father, "Not my will, but yours be done" (Luke 22:42), and then he stretched out his arms and gave his life for us.

But Jesus didn't stop with being a hero. He made heroes out of his closest followers. We know that Jesus was a hero maker by how he allocated his time and energy as a leader.

When you think of Jesus' ministry, do you picture him speaking to the crowds—preaching the Sermon on the Mount, feeding the five thousand—or spending time to train the Twelve? One researcher says that the Gospels put three-fourths of their emphasis on the training of the Twelve. He calculates that from the time Jesus told the Twelve that he'd teach them to multiply ("I will send you out to fish for people," Matt. 4:19) until his death, Jesus spent 73% of his time with the Twelve. That's forty-six events with the few, compared with seventeen events with the masses.[21] The ratio of time Jesus spent with the few versus time he spent with the many was almost three to one.

The point: Jesus' ministry emphasis, in terms of where he put the biggest amount of time, was with his twelve leadership residents! He was mentoring them so they would do greater things. This included multiplying themselves through others.

Jesus' ministry emphasis, in terms of where he put the biggest amount of time, was with his twelve leadership residents!

In the years that followed, not only do we see the amazing works of the Holy Spirit through these twelve in and after the book of Acts, but according to history Jesus' earliest followers fulfilled his prophecy that they would do greater things, by making other disciple makers around the world.

What Greater Things Looks Like for Us

Here in Chicagoland, we thought the greater things would be accomplished through one church that grew larger in size and even spilled over into multiple locations. We give God all the glory for the thousands who have found their way back to him through Jesus at Community Christian Church and are being mentored in the ways of Christ. But we have made an important change in the question we are asking. We are no longer asking only, "How can we grow Community Christian Church?" We are asking, "How can Community Christian Church work with other leaders and churches to multiply God's kingdom?"

Because of this, we're discovering that greater things are happening on a far larger scale through our international church-planting initiative, called NewThing. At present, more than twelve hundred churches are part of this network of reproducing churches, some of which we directly started, some of which are daughter churches of those we started, and some of which are churches that affiliated with our network because of their desire to multiply other churches. We estimate that these twelve hundred churches represent more than two hundred and fifty thousand followers of Jesus. And since each of these churches has made a commitment to be reproducing and multiplying, the potential becomes exponential and far exceeds that of our one big multisite megachurch.

And that's only a sliver of the greater things that multiplied from Jesus' early apprentices. Today 2.2 billion people—one-third of the world's population—claim the name of Jesus!

That kind of movement-making multiplication is what we're talking about when we say we want to see the church multiplied. This is the multiplication of disciples that Jesus talks about when he calls for a multiplication of his witnesses in "all nations, beginning at Jerusalem" (Luke 24:47).

Who Are Today's Hero Makers?

The single biggest obstacle to movement-making impact like this is a leader who is stuck always needing to be the hero. For most, it's tough to give up that status.

I have never met a kid who is playing basketball in the driveway and imagines: "Five . . . four . . . Ferguson picks up his dribble . . . three . . . two . . . one . . . Ferguson passes the ball to an open teammate, and his teammate scores! They win the championship!" It almost never happens. But as Isiah Thomas told us in chapter 1, the secret is all about team. For church leaders, the secret is the kingdom of God. We cannot let the story become about me, my leadership, or even my church. It's always about the kingdom and making heroes of others.

Too often even our best difference-making efforts are oriented around positioning ourselves as the hero. You could easily hear the following from any well-meaning Christian leader or maybe yourself:

- "When I heard about it, I went to the hospital, and I led Juanita in a prayer to receive Christ."
- "So I texted the benevolent ministries team, and I got a check and hand-delivered it myself."
- "It seemed that ministry was going nowhere, until God gave me an idea that has taken it to a whole new level."

None of these responses are evil or even wrong. In fact, many of them remind me of myself. Way too many times in ministry, I've jumped in with "I've got it!" or even "This is my sweet spot," and it never occurred to me— until too late—that I was blocking other people from the privilege and joy of using *their* faith or serving in *their* sweet spot. I was the hero, not the hero maker.

One of the more frequent conversations I have with my wife, Sue, ends with her saying, "Um, that wasn't *your* idea!" Oftentimes it was her idea or someone else's idea, and I'm trying to claim it as my own. I don't think I'm doing it with an evil intent, but there is something deep within me (and perhaps in you too) that loves being the hero. And when I'm trying to be the hero, I am not being a hero maker.

If responses of "me the hero" represent your pattern, you will have a limited impact that never involves greater things. These responses suggest a disciple of Jesus who hasn't matured from being a hero to being a hero maker.

What if the opposite happened?

- "When I heard about it, I called Maria, because Juanita lives in her neighborhood. Maria went to the hospital and wound up leading her in a prayer to follow Jesus. When Maria told the story at church, the congregation applauded, no doubt giving many others the idea and permission to 'go and do likewise.'"
- "So I texted the benevolence team and asked if they'd write and deliver a check. You wouldn't believe the joy that Charlie and Joe reported after they hand-delivered that gift."
- "It seemed like that ministry was going nowhere, but I challenged the leadership team to seek God together. They came up with an idea that has taken the ministry to a whole new level. But even better, they're gearing up for another leadership retreat, believing that God has even more for them."

Hero makers shift from being the hero in their church's unfolding story to expecting others to be the hero. Hero making is something anyone can do, and when accompanied by a leadership gift, it becomes explosive as it is replicated in the lives of many.

Meet a Hero-Making Leader from Kenya

While I was dreaming of hitting last-second game-winning shots on a driveway in suburban Chicago, Pastor Oscar Muriu was a kid dreaming of being the hero of the Kenyan national football team and finally bringing them to international prominence. In the same way that I never made it to the NBA (not yet!), Oscar never scored a goal for the Kenyan national football team (not yet!). But Oscar is a personal hero because he is one of the best examples of a hero maker I've ever met, and that's why he also gets the closing words of this book.

Oscar was in his twenties, newly out of seminary, exploring the "What's next?" question for him and his new wife, Bea, when he said yes to pastoring a needy church in Nairobi that had declined to only a dozen people. Yet Nairobi Chapel proved to be a perfect match for Oscar's gifts and vision. The little congregation responded to the risks Oscar asked them to take, such as shifting from serving expatriate Brits to serving Kenyan college students and the people of Nairobi, leaving well-paying jobs to go into ministry, and more. Within the first few years, the number of people attending grew so much that even with multiple services, the sanctuary could not hold everyone. In just ten years, the church had grown tremendously.

While leading this fast-growing church of several thousand, Oscar had a crucial decision to make, one that would determine the legacy of his leadership. He began to ask himself, "Am I going to be the hero, or am I going to make heroes out of others?"

Oscar led the congregation in a gutsy, hero-making decision. In one Sunday, Nairobi Chapel went from being one very large church to being one church in five locations, as Oscar turned over many of the people and resources to four other young pastors. He said, "I can reach more people for the kingdom and have a more lasting impact if I multiply myself through other leaders. From this point forward, I'll be just one of five." Oscar poured himself into mentoring the other pastors who led those new churches.

What prompted such an unconventional, risky decision?

Oscar explains, "When I was a young, rookie, inexperienced pastor, I was reading Psalm 71:18 one day, and I was deeply struck that David's prayer was to declare God's might to the next generation." Oscar quickly reasoned, "If I'm going to be true to the heart of David, then I need to invest myself in the next generation, because they will continue to lead after I'm gone. It was then I made the decision to always have younger people that I'm pouring my life into for the sake of the mission."

Oscar is convinced that the decision to make heroes of others who in turn will multiply still others has resulted in many more people becoming followers of Christ. Today there are twenty-two campuses in Kenya known as Nairobi Chapel, plus eight other Nairobi Chapels in other countries! They have already planted more than one hundred churches in pursuit of their goal to establish three hundred church plants, lead one million people to Christ, and actively disciple one hundred thousand people.

> I made a decision at that point to always have younger people that I'm pouring my life into for the sake of the mission.
>
> —OSCAR MURIU

Oscar explains the church's strategic plan: "We must multiply ourselves at every level. At the individual level, we will be intentional about multiplying leaders, staff, and disciples. At the ministry level, we will seek to reproduce all of our groups and teams on a regular basis. At the church level, we want to begin a church-planting movement locally, nationally, and internationally."

For several years now, Nairobi Chapel has had one hundred leaders annually who move through their three-track leadership resident program and then go out and plant a wide variety of new churches. Some are large, looking and feeling much like Nairobi Chapel. Some are planted overseas, the first one in London. Some are in the economically depressed slums of Nairobi.

Oscar has the leadership gifts and ability to become a solo leader with a tremendous personal following and the spotlight clearly focused on him. Instead he chose to make heroes of others and invest the time to mentor and coach, and the payoff has been experiencing the greater things Jesus promised, things far greater than even Oscar's unique talents could have achieved alone.

Moms, MOPS, and Hero Making

You can do any type of ministry and be a hero maker. Pat Runyon is a mom and a hero maker. At her home in Wheat Ridge, Colorado, Pat and seven other older women with a big heart for the families in their community had a meeting in which they prayed and began to dream about what they might do to help the next generation of young mothers. Those petitions and holy aspirations gave birth to a movement of more than four thousand groups in thirty countries, known as MOPS (Mothers of Preschoolers) International.

Pat recalls, "We honestly didn't know what we were doing." The ladies loved meeting together and began by inviting young moms with their babies into their homes for coffee, support, prayer, and Bible study. "It was the Holy Spirit that led us to partner with churches."

As the groups continued to multiply, the eight founding women kept records of all of them on notepads stored in a shoebox in Pat's garage. After ten years of remarkable growth, the founders knew MOPS had outgrown them, so they recruited and hired Elisa Morgan as their CEO. They released power and authority to her, doing everything possible to make her a success. Why? That is what hero makers do.

"Elisa is a very strong leader," says Sherry Surratt, who eventually succeeded Elisa. "She hired a staff, cast vision that women have tremendous leadership potential, and built an absolutely brilliant leadership development system that grew to involve more than twenty-five thousand female volunteers. It's a system of easy entrance, easy training, and where so many young women first step into leadership." From MOPS's beginning until today, Elisa and the whole MOPS culture have embodied the joy of making someone else the hero.

Five Hero-Making Practices

Hero makers create a platform and then invite other people to stand on it. Great idea, but how do you do it?

The five chapters of the next section are dedicated to making sure you clearly understand how to become a hero maker and to giving you simple tools to help you do it immediately. I have no interest in writing a book that gets read but doesn't get applied in real life. (I also created a website, *HeroMakerBook.com*, to help you with practical application.) So I have gone to great effort to make sure that the five hero-making practices in the next section are well explained, reproducible, and very usable.

FIGURE 4.1

5 ESSENTIAL PRACTICES OF A HERO MAKER

HERO-MAKING PRACTICES	MULTIPLICATION THINKING	PERMISSION GIVING	DISCIPLE MULTIPLYING	GIFT ACTIVATING	KINGDOM BUILDING
JESUS AND HERO MAKING	ACTS 1:8	MATT. 4:19	JOHN 3:22	MATT. 28:19	MATT. 6:33
HERO-MAKING TOOLS	DREAM NAPKIN	I-C-N-U CONVERSATION	FIVE STEPS OF APPRENTICESHIP	COMMISSIONING	SIMPLE SCOREBOARD

As you look at Figure 4.1, note that while hero makers are continually implementing all five of these practices in their leadership, the practices are used sequentially in the development of an individual apprentice. If you are new to hero making and are mentoring someone for the first time, you will want to start with multiplication thinking, then go to permission giving, and then disciple multiplying, gift activating, and kingdom building.

There is a logic in the way these practices are ordered that will allow you to do the work of hero making. Let's consider each one separately.

1. Multiplication thinking. This is a shift in *thinking*, and if you want a quick slogan for this practice, it's "Think it!" You move from thinking that the best way to maximize ministry is through your own efforts to understanding that it is through developing the leadership of others. We see this in the life of Jesus in Acts 1:8. When Jesus casts a vision for taking the gospel to the ends of the earth, he tells his followers, "You will be my witnesses" to explain that he is going to do it through them. Jesus didn't think the mission was going to happen just though him during his time on this earth; he thought it would happen through others who would equip others who would equip still others. Jesus practiced multiplication thinking. To help you easily implement this practice, I will give you a simple tool called a "dream napkin" and challenge you to multiply your impact by 100x. This simple exercise will push you and those you are mentoring into multiplication thinking and into realizing that the only way you can maximize ministry is through developing others.

2. Permission giving. This is a shift in *seeing*, and if you want a quick slogan for this practice, it's "See it!" You will take the focus off your leadership and begin to see the leadership potential in the people all around you. Since you see the people around you as leaders in development, you will begin to lead with a yes and give them permission to fully engage in the mission. We see this in the life of Jesus when he says to a group of ragtag working-class fellows, "Come, follow me" (Matt. 4:19) They never expected a rabbi to see them worth teaching and leading. But Jesus saw in them a group that could change the world. To help you easily implement this practice, I will give you a simple tool called an "ICNU conversation." This simple tool will show you how you can help others see potential in themselves they never saw before, and in so doing, you will give them permission to reach their full God-given potential.

3. Disciple multiplying. This is a shift in *sharing*, and if you want a quick slogan for this practice, it's "Share it!" You will begin to not only share what you know to help others follow Jesus but also share your life and invest in the development of leaders who do the same for other leaders. We see this in the life of Jesus as he spent three years primarily with twelve people (John 3:22). To help you easily implement this practice, I will give you a simple tool called the "five steps of apprenticeship." This tool has the power to multiply movements of disciple makers. The only reason it does not is because people have not fully used it.

4. Gift activating. This is a shift in *blessing*, and if you want a quick slogan for this practice, it's "Bless it!" You will not just ask God to bless the gifts he has given you but ask him to bless the leaders you have developed as you send them out at the end of their apprenticeship. The most obvious example of this is in Matthew 28:16–20; Jesus is turning over the leadership of the movement to his closest followers, and he tells them, in effect, "I have all authority and will use it through you as you go!" To help you pass along the blessing, I will give you a simple tool called "commissioning" (explained in chapter 8). This ancient practice of laying your hands on someone and asking God to bless them as you send them out is a powerful way to activate a leadership gift.

5. Kingdom building. This is a shift in *counting*, and if you want a quick slogan for this practice, it's "Count it!" You are no longer only concerned with who is showing up at your thing; you count who is doing God's thing! Jesus told his followers in simple terms, "Seek first the kingdom of God" (Matt. 6:33 ESV). They heeded this admonition, and all that mattered was what God was keeping track of as the Jesus mission was being advanced around the world. So that you can make this shift in counting, I will give you a simple tool I call a "hero maker's scoreboard." Lots of statistics are important and beneficial, but this simple scoreboard will have churches track only a few vital metrics and ask leaders to track only two key measurements. This scoreboard is designed to help you count what builds the kingdom.

With these five practices, God will use you to change the world. Each practice depends on your willingness to continually ask, "Am I trying to be the hero, or am I trying to make heroes of others?"

Don't Confuse Hero with Hero Maker

By this point, do you see the huge difference between a hero and a hero *maker?*

Please hear what I am about to say, and let it sink deep into your mind and linger in your heart. It's time to quit trying to be the hero. You can do better. Much better. Instead you can be a hero maker.

When my coauthor, Warren Bird, became a Christ follower, he bought the same big, thick Bible his pastor was using. Through daily reading and listening to great teaching, he marked it up for his first ten years of discipleship, before switching to another Bible. By that ten-year mark, practically every page had Warren's own notes, plus the publisher's printed column jammed with cross-references. Warren recently looked in that Bible on the page containing 2 Timothy 2:2 (Paul's instruction to train others, who train others, who train others, who train others). Warren had inked lots of notes on that page, but none referring to this verse. Nor did the publisher's highly praised "chain link" of marginal references mention multiplication. Warren flipped over to other leader-multiplication verses that I've highlighted in this book, with roughly the same finding: no mention of multiple generations of apprenticeship.

You might be like Warren. You're reading this book and aspiring to be a hero maker, but you simply haven't been in a leadership or church setting where this is normative. You want to learn. You've listened to teaching and have even taken great notes. You've put into practice what you have learned, but you were simply never taught hero-making practices.

Then let me say it again: you can be a hero *maker*. It doesn't matter who you are, what your background is, or what your title or role may be. You can multiply the kingdom's influence by investing in the lives of those around you. Want to know how? It starts by learning to think multiplication (which I guarantee you can do, even if your math skills aren't the greatest). That's the first of five practices I will show you in the next section, and as with each practice, I'll give you a simple tool so you can begin to implement it immediately.

Are you ready to quit trying to be the hero? Are you ready to start hero making? Then you're ready for the next section of this book. I think of it as an apprenticeship with Jesus, focusing on how movement-making leadership works. In chapters 5 through 9, you'll discover the five essential practices for being a leader who multiplies leaders. I believe these practices are critical for maximizing your impact, because:

- These are the practices Jesus applied.
- They are what we find in movement-making churches, both historical and contemporary.
- They are affirmed by Leadership Network research.
- They are the consensus of a think tank of leaders from Level 4 and 5 churches, convened by Exponential.

Turn the page and let's get started!

Hero Maker Discussion Questions

OPEN

- Who has been a hero maker to you? (Not a hero but a hero maker.) Think of someone who has unselfishly invested in you to help you become better. Tell the story.

DIG

- Read Mark 4:26–34 (the parables of the seeds) and Matthew 13:33 (the parable of the yeast). How do each of these parables illustrate that multiplication is a part of kingdom growth?
- Maybe it was eye-opening that Jesus focused three-quarters of his leadership and ministry on the Twelve, not on the crowds. How will this understanding impact your own leadership?

REFLECT

- The Gospels tell us that Jesus spent more ministry time with the few than with the many, by a ratio of three to one. What is your ratio?
- If hero makers create a platform and then invite other people to stand on it, what can you do today to create such a platform and invite others to stand on it?

PART 2

FIVE ESSENTIAL PRACTICES OF

HERO⚡

MAKING

CHAPTER 5

Multiplication Thinking

Big Idea: The practice of multiplication thinking is a shift from thinking that ministry happens through my own leadership to thinking that ministry happens through multiplied leaders. Multiplication thinking requires that we dream big and use simple tools, like a dream napkin.

Luke Skywalker needed Obi-Wan Kenobi.
Rocky Balboa needed Mickey Goldmill.
Harry Potter needed Dumbledore.
Katniss Everdeen needed Haymitch Abernathy.
Frodo Baggins needed Gandalf.
Heroes are made and not born. For every hero, there is a hero maker.

The Hero's Journey

Think of some of your all-time favorite books, or remember the movies you love to watch again and again. Many of these great stories are remarkably familiar: an unlikely hero embarks on a journey that has been thrust upon him or her. The hero is ill-equipped for all that lies ahead but meets a mentor or helper who offers wisdom, tools, or the courage to journey on. The hero makes allies and enemies, and maybe even falls in love.

> Heroes are made and not born. For every hero, there is a hero maker.

Then comes the ordeal, in which the emerging hero makes the ultimate choice to sacrifice for the greater good. In the end, it all pays off and, having accomplished the heroic, the hero returns back to where he or she started.

In literary circles, this is known as the hero's journey. In his book *The Hero with a Thousand Faces*, American mythologist Joseph Campbell

FIGURE 5.1

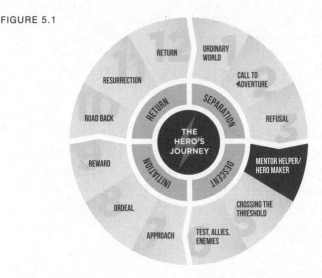

popularized the common journey of every hero and summarized it in twelve stages (see Figure 5.1). Campbell said it is at stage 4, early in the journey, that the hero meets a mentor. The mentor gives the hero the guidance and tools to leave the ordinary and move into the extraordinary. The mentor is a hero maker.

The guidance provided by the hero maker includes giving the emerging hero a vision of a greater cause, a more important battle, or a bigger dream.

- Obi-Wan Kenobi didn't just train Luke Skywalker how to use the Force; he trained him how to lead the rebellion and overthrow the Empire.
- Mickey didn't just train Rocky how to box; he trained him how to inspire his city and eventually his country.
- Dumbledore didn't just teach Harry Potter magic; he taught him how to build an army of students to fight Voldemort.
- Haymitch Abernathy didn't just train Katniss Everdeen how to survive the Hunger Games; he trained her how to lead a revolution against the oppression of the Capital for all the districts.
- Gandalf didn't just recruit Frodo Baggins for a journey; he inspired him to lead a diverse fellowship committed to overthrowing evil.

We see this pattern of hero making across Scripture as well. Who can forget the hero-making role that Moses played with Joshua, or that Naomi played with Ruth, or that Mordecai played with Esther, or that Elijah played with Elisha? Each of these hero makers are investing in their apprentices, and not only training them but also giving them a vision of God's greater story.

Hero Makers Live and Teach Multiplication Thinking

This first hero-making practice has two applications: first, you must live it out; second, you must also pass it on to your apprentices. I call this practice multiplication thinking. It's truly a paradigm shift in how you understand your part in the mission of Jesus.

Multiplication thinking is most often catalyzed by the vision of a greater cause, a more important battle, or a bigger dream.

FIGURE 5.2

I was meeting with Millard Fuller, the founder of Habitat for Humanity, in his office in Americus, Georgia, when he looked me in the eye and asked, "Don't you think everyone deserves a simple, decent place to live?" There was no disputing the truth of his vision for making sure everyone had a roof over their head. Immediately I could feel the adrenaline rushing through my body. I had no idea how to do it, but I knew it had to be done! It was the compelling cause and big dream of Millard Fuller that catalyzed his multiplication thinking: he couldn't do it on his own; he couldn't launch one construction company that could do this; the best and only way to accomplish this vision was to mobilize multiplying numbers of volunteers. His big dream coupled with multiplication thinking is what allowed Habitat for Humanity to become the biggest homebuilder in the world.

In chapter 2, I told you about the paradigm-shifting challenge I received to dream bigger: "Take your current dream for your church and multiply it by one million." Doing the math, I took my dream of reaching one thousand people, multiplied it by one million, and got one billion people! I knew I couldn't do that myself or through my church. It pushed me to multiplication thinking and to wondering, "How can I multiply my efforts not just through one person but through hundreds, maybe thousands or tens of thousands, of leaders? And how can I help start hundreds and thousands of churches?" That big dream pushed me into a new kind of multiplication thinking.

This is the first of our five practices, and in this chapter we'll also explain how Jesus used it in his leadership and then give you a simple tool to do it with too.

FIGURE 5.3

A HERO-MAKING JOURNEY: MULTIPLICATION THINKING

HERO-MAKING PRACTICES	MULTIPLICATION THINKING	PERMISSION GIVING	DISCIPLE MULTIPLYING	GIFT ACTIVATING	KINGDOM BUILDING
JESUS AND HERO MAKING	ACTS 1:8	MATT. 4:19	JOHN 3:22	MATT. 28:19	MATT. 6:33
HERO-MAKING TOOLS	DREAM NAPKIN	I-C-N-U CONVERSATION	FIVE STEPS OF APPRENTICESHIP	COMMISSIONING	SIMPLE SCOREBOARD

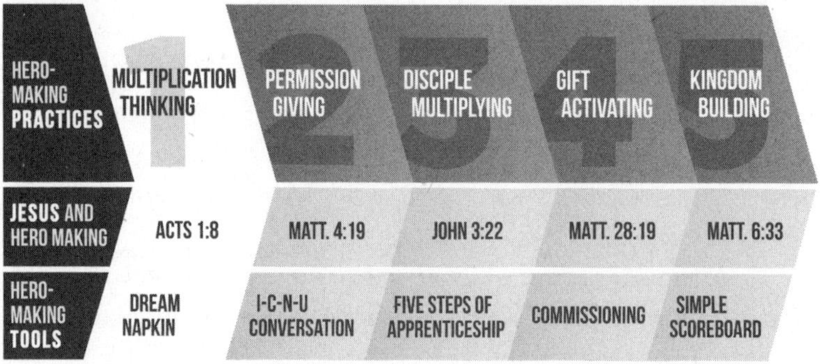

Jesus Taught a Multiplication Mindset

Our world desperately needs a multiplied number of heroes! We need heroic difference makers who aren't afraid to step out and make an impact in the lives of people—kids, students, the poor, those struggling with addictions, the marginalized, those afflicted with wealth, business leaders, and more. One multifaceted hero will never be enough to speak to that much diversity. I love how Tim Keller, in launching a New York City-based church-planting center through Redeemer Presbyterian Church, has repeatedly said that no single church can reach everyone. So they announced to every denominational and nondenominational church planter: if you love Jesus, the Scriptures, the gospel, and the city, we'll train you to plant a church. Redeemer is still doing that today and seeing multiple generations of reproduction.

But even more than we need heroes, we need hero *makers* who think big, who see the scale of God's dream and realize, "There is far more that God wants me to do than I can do all by myself."

Even as Jesus called his first apprentices, he started talking about multiplication. When he said, "Come, follow me," the rest of his sentence was "and I will send you out to fish for people" (Mark 1:17).

Even more than we need heroes, we need hero *makers* who think big!

What did that mean? The next four chapters will offer many examples of what Jesus did to mentor them "to fish for people," but here let me comment on what that meant in terms of scale. When he first called these apprentices, he performed a miracle, helping them to catch "such a large number of fish that their nets began to break" (Luke 5:6).

Later Jesus told them they would likewise reach a huge number of men, women, and children. In Acts 1:8 he said, in effect, "I don't want you to think in terms just of Jerusalem. Don't even limit yourselves to this region, nor to people with your economic or religious background. Actually, by the power of the Holy Spirit that I'll be sending you, I want you to be my witnesses to the ends of the earth. Yes, a handful of people will connect with millions, and later with billions."

Think about it. That promise was the last thing Jesus said before he left planet Earth, before they would go out and share the good news without him in this world as their coach. He cast this big dream: "My Spirit is going to be inside you, and it will give you the courage to do what you would never be able to do on your own. You will be willing to die for this cause. With my Spirit inside you, we are going to take this good news movement from here in Jerusalem to Judea to Samaria to the very ends of the earth."

Can you imagine their mouths gaping wide? "Where?" "How?" The angel shows up, and I can imagine him saying, "C'mon, to the ends of the earth, boys! Go get 'em!" They are walking away, still musing. "How? How? How can we do that?" Then somewhere it hits them: "What if we multiplied through others what Jesus did with us?" A multiplication mindset. And as long as the church has kept that big dream in the forefront and understood the practice of multiplication thinking, the movement has advanced, goodness has prevailed, truth has triumphed, and people have found their way back to God. May that ever be the case!

When you study Jesus' training of the Twelve, you see that he modeled in many ways what he later taught them in Acts 1:8. They did literally take the gospel all over the country: they spoke to Jews and Gentiles, Greeks, Romans, and foreigners, men and women, rich and poor, slave and free. His commission here just affirmed that they should keep doing what they had been doing, even if now on a global scale!

Dream Big!

Let me share something I have discovered. The very act of dreaming big will change how you think, how others around you think, and ultimately how you behave. But the struggle is that we are busy with our lives, our leadership, our ministry, and our church. We get stuck doing the work of ministry, and we forget about the bigness of our God. Futurist Alvin Toffler said something that pulls me out of the muck and mire of trying to be the hero and helps me focus on hero making: "When you are taking care of the little things, think about the big things so the little things go in the right direction." Go ahead and read that again and let it sink in. When we are in the grind of doing ministry, starting a new church,

We get stuck doing the work of ministry, and we forget about the bigness of our God.

or leading a church, it is easy to not think about the big picture and instead to focus on just what's in front of us. However, by focusing on only what's in front of us, we will dwindle our leadership potential and oftentimes concern ourselves with only survival and growth (Levels 1–3) instead of the big picture of multiplication (Levels 4–5). We need to step back and see the bigger dream.

One of the guys who pushed me constantly to dream bigger was Lyle Schaller. If you don't know the name Lyle Schaller, do me a favor and google him. Lyle wrote fifty-five books, edited forty-four others (that stat is from Warren Bird, who wrote a book about Schaller),[22] was called by *Christianity Today* "the dean of church consultants," and was once voted "the most influential Protestant leader in America."[23] Lyle also happened to live in the same town I did and came to Community Christian's very first service. We shared a love for the church and became friends. I loved that old guy!

One of the reasons I loved him was because over and over he would prod me by looking me in the eye and saying, "Dave, your biggest problem is that I have a bigger vision for your church than you do!" And every time he said that, the dream for my church would get bigger. And that bigger dream would force me into multiplication thinking and asking myself how I could multiply more leaders in more places.

I thought I was the only one Lyle picked on. Not true. I was listening to Craig Groeschel of Life Church, currently the largest church in the United States, give a talk titled "Expanding Your Leadership Capacity." He told a story about an old church consultant: "Over and over this consultant would give me grief by looking me right in the eye and saying, 'Craig, your biggest problem is that I have a bigger vision for your church than you do!' And every time he said that, my vision would get bigger!"

I now wonder if a big part of Lyle Schaller's consulting was finding lots of senior leaders and saying, "Your biggest problem is that I have a bigger vision for your church than you do!" knowing that a big dream would catalyze multiplication thinking.

I want to be that faith-stretching voice for you! I want to look you in the eye and say, "C'mon, don't let me or anyone else have a bigger vision for your church or your life than you do!" And more important, what is *God's* vision for your leadership, life, and church? At the end of this chapter, I'm going to ask you to find a napkin and write out your big dream. Not your current dream but a bigger dream for your leadership. I'm going to ask you to take what you are currently dreaming and multiply it by one hundred. And then ask, "How can I do that?" My hope is to push you toward multiplication thinking. Let me explain why multiplication thinking is such an important practice.

MULTIPLICATION THINKING CHANGES THE QUESTIONS

Once you accept the challenge of a big dream, you are forced into questions of how, and multiplication thinking naturally follows. As my dream grew, so did my multiplication mindset. When the dream of Community Christian was to be one church with two sites, I started asking, "How can I reproduce myself?" Now our dream is to be a church that has multiplied two hundred sites and churches in Chicagoland, and

I'm asking, "How can I create a system that is continually reproducing all our leadership?"

A decade ago, our dream was to start a network of new churches, so I had to ask, "How can I attract, train, and deploy church planters?" Now our dream is to see a movement of reproducing churches, so I have to ask, "How can I create systems that reproduce networks and attract, train, and deploy apostolic leaders?"

Do you see how a big dream pushes you into multiplication thinking? And the bigger the dream, the more you are thinking multiplication. If you step into the vision of being a hero maker or accept the challenge of leading a Level 4 or 5 church, multiplication thinking is sure to follow. And that multiplication mindset will cause you to ask questions that get multiplied results.

It was a big dream that led us to build our first Community Christian facility that we call the Yellow Box. We saw it not just as a place to "warehouse believers" but also as a meeting place to train and multiply leaders. That multiplication thinking led us to ask our leaders, "If you could do anything in this new space to reach people, what would you do?" That question sparked the imagination of my wife, Sue, who began to think about new ways to reach women. This led to the birth of a ministry called Connections, which has multiplied more than sixty women's groups, expanded to multiple locations in Chicagoland, and is dramatically changing women's lives.

One of those women who experienced life change is Lori Cooke. She first came to Connections with very little knowledge of the Bible, but with a hunger for God. In the closeknit community of these women, she found her way back to God and was baptized. Her small group leader saw leadership potential in her and asked her to apprentice to become a small group leader.

Then came a day just before Christmas a few years ago. Lori received the devastating news that her twenty-year-old son had collapsed on the basketball court and could not be revived. After seeing Lori and her family through the funeral and the holidays, several people began to question whether Lori would be able to lead her women's group. Sue, Lori's coach at the time, felt that Lori should decide for herself, but she let Lori know that everyone would understand if she did not feel up to it. When asked whether she would like to take time off, Lori responded, "No, I need to be here, and I need to lead." Lori explained that the giving and receiving in her group helped get her through the hard times.

Since then Lori has allowed God to use her painful past and her leadership gifts to apprentice three other women leaders, whom she now coaches. In addition to leading, "Lori is our number one recruiter," says Sue. Lori is always inviting women to join Connections—teachers at her children's school, fellow parents at a dance class for kids, other parents at sports events, a former nanny, and anyone new she meets at church. Lori tells everyone, "Connections changed my life!"

Lori's life was indeed changed. Hundreds of women's lives were changed. All of that change because of a question, multiplication thinking, and a big dream.

MULTIPLICATION THINKING CHANGES OTHERS

Multiplication thinking is contagious. It is infectious. A multiplication mindset not only changes your questions but slowly begins to change the people God has put around you!

I was speaking at the Ambition Conference, hosted by InterVarsity, with about one thousand college students and leaders in Tampa. The purpose of the gathering was very clear: to inspire and equip these college leaders to double the number of college campuses that would have an InterVarsity presence. It was essentially a church-planting conference. It was awesome!

I was privileged to be in on some of the early planning meetings with senior level staff of InterVarsity and hear them dream of seeing InterVarsity go from being on about five hundred campuses to being on one thousand. They had prayed and thought through this vision and had unleashed it on their leaders. The rapid response to this kind of vision was multiplication thinking. Leaders said things like, "For us to double, that means I need to reproduce myself" or "We are going to need a multiplication strategy for developing at least five hundred more leaders." It was working. The InterVarsity staff had found a way to get their leaders to do what Toffler encouraged: "When you are taking care of the little things, think about the big things so the little things go in the right direction."

Before I spoke to these young leaders, I made sure every attender had a napkin. I told my own story about writing out on the back of a napkin in a little Mexican restaurant the dream of becoming a multiplying church. I told them how it was such a big dream that I kept it tucked away for several years, afraid to share it. Then, at the insistence of a friend, I showed it to him, and he said the most powerful words: "Dave, you can do that!" Once I took that dream public, it moved our team and me farther into a multiplication mindset. I ended my talk by asking every one of the leaders to write out their big dream on the back of that napkin I gave them and never hide it!

My favorite moment at the conference was at the end, when organizers asked every person to hold up their dream napkin so we could pray over them and ask God to do what only God can do. It was so awesome! And since that time, I have had college leaders from all over the country text me pictures of, or tweet me an update on, their dream napkin and then share with me their multiplied results.

MULTIPLICATION THINKING CHANGES YOU

Thanks to the encouragement of people like Lyle Schaller and my friend who said, "Dave, you can do that," I have spent most of my leadership life pursuing big dreams with a multiplication mindset. The dream of Community Christian Church being a multiplying church, the vision of NewThing being a catalyst for movements of multiplying churches, and the big dream of Exponential moving the needle from 4% to 10% of churches in the United States being reproducing or multiplying churches—that has changed me forever!

Because of multiplication thinking,

- I continually ask questions that lead to multiplied results.
- I find myself surrounded by people, leaders, and high-capacity influencers who are passionate about big dreams.
- I am more dependent on God than ever! I live with more anticipation than ever!

Multiplication thinking will change you too!

Unlikely Hero Maker Who Gets Multiplication

Multiplication happens as apprentices make other apprentices who in turn make still other apprentices. One of my very favorite hero makers who gets that is my friend Ralph Moore, pastor of a church named Hope Chapel. Their experience is nothing short of *viral* in how one church has birthed at least twenty-three hundred other churches. What was the trigger God used? Ralph says, "Once we made multiplication our focus, the number of churches expanded rapidly as new churches made disciples and multiplied new churches."

If you're imagining Ralph as the kind of leader who takes charge of a room just by his presence, think again. Ralph is so unassuming and understated that you almost have to drag his amazing story out of him. Even after you pull it out of him, he will downplay his role in it.

I was so impressed with the number and quality of leaders Ralph has developed that I lined him up to speak from the main stage at our Exponential East and West conferences. Exponential East came first. Ralph was so humble and chill that he neglected to mention during his time onstage that he is the catalyst behind starting more than twenty-three hundred new churches. Also (don't tell Ralph I said this), his unassuming nature and reluctance to elevate himself didn't exactly grab the audience's attention. Sometimes that happens with hero makers. They're not necessarily used to being in the spotlight. They're not always comfortable being the hero.

> Ralph was so humble and chill that he neglected to mention during his time onstage that he is the catalyst behind starting more than twenty-three hundred new churches.

Since I had him speaking again at Exponential West, he and I had a phone call to discuss it. Ralph confided in me (and has since written publicly) about his struggles with anxiety and depression.[24] He told me about one time when he had a panic attack that was so bad, he couldn't sleep at all for three days and nights. For seventy-two hours, he couldn't focus on anything for more than ninety seconds. "It was the most difficult period of my entire life," Ralph said. Since then, he has regularly taken medications twice a day.

I knew Ralph has one of the best hero-making track records in our country, so I suggested that for Exponential West, we use him in interview format. My thought was that I could ask the question, "So, Ralph, tell us: how many churches have you planted?" And then he would have to tell his story. But then on the day of our interview, in front of thousands of people, Ralph called me out: "You thought I was boring last time, so now you're interviewing me, huh?" At first I was stunned. Then he smiled, and the audience got in on the joke.

In fact, many of the hero makers you'll meet across these pages will be quick to let you know the ways in which they're broken. They're all quick to affirm that any good influence they've had in making heroes of others is only because of a God who delights to work through their limitations, whose "power is made perfect in weakness" (2 Cor. 12:9).

When I think of Ralph, I'm reminded that if God can use a laid-back guy who struggles with poor self-esteem and deals every day with anxiety and depression to start twenty-three hundred (and counting) new churches, then God can definitely use you! Ralph is another example that God can use anyone who is surrendered to make a hero of others.

God can use anyone who is surrendered to make a hero of others.

Following, Ralph shares his story in his own words. Notice his humility in the opening paragraph. I know you'll learn a lot from him.

One word of explanation: For each hero-making profile throughout this book, I've asked the person to speak in his or her own words. I also asked them to come alongside you and include helpful advice for leaders in churches or ministries who are experiencing the first three levels on the multiplication spectrum: Level 1 (declining), Level 2 (plateauing), or Level 3 (growing but not multiplying). I asked them to offer advice that would coach someone toward multiplication—moving their church toward not only Level 4 (reproducing) but also Level 5 (multiplying).

Ralph Moore

HOPE CHAPEL
KANEOHE, HAWAII

*More than twenty-three hundred churches
came from one church's multiplication
movement in less than twenty-five years.*

I got thrust into multiplying leaders by accident, at least from my perspective.

I was leading Hope Chapel church in Hermosa Beach, California, which was using a 1950s approach to ministry—the idea being that growing Christians would come to a church building on Sunday morning, Sunday evening, and Wednesday evening.

That model of church didn't work for a bunch of younger families who lived several miles away. One of the men asked permission to start a Sunday night meeting in his house. It went really well, and a few months later the group asked permission to become a church. Initially I said no, but then someone else tried to recruit the guy to start a ministry and I didn't want to lose him, so I quickly changed my mind and said, "Yes. Great idea!" That turned out to be a good move, because not only did their church go well, but in the next couple of years, he and his wife started several other churches. He showed himself to be a reproducing leader, and I saw in him the potential to lead a Level 5 multiplying church.

Because we had both grown up being trained in multiplication thinking through a group called Navigators, what happened was not a total surprise to me. He and I would meet every Monday morning at 6:30 a.m. to walk around a nearby golf course, pray, talk about Scripture, and do discipleship by hanging out together and dreaming.

I was genuinely trying to make him the hero, because I knew he would then do the same with others. In that relationship, I was more of a teacher and encourager than anything else.

Then I moved from California to pastor a church in Hawaii, where at the time only 1% of the population attended church regularly. I took with me my experience of multiplying leaders and churches. At that point, I believe God told me to start enough churches within the next decade that would help reach a greater percentage of the population for Christ. I knew that to do what God said, we *had* to multiply leaders and churches. I needed to become a hero maker.

I knew that to do what God said, we had to multiply churches. I needed to become a hero maker.

The process we used for discipleship and leadership development was very simple.

For discipling people, we kept the discussion in our small groups based on that week's sermon. After starting with food and fellowship, the leader would simply ask three questions:

1. What did you hear from the Holy Spirit?
2. What will you do because of it?
3. How can we pray for you?

Then they'd pray. It was that simple.

If we were discipling leaders, we would all read the same book. We would gather around food for fellowship and ask three similar questions:

1. What did you hear from the Holy Spirit?
2. How will that impact your ministry?
3. How can we pray for you?

Then we'd pray. Again, a very simple, reproducible approach to developing leaders.

If someone had started three groups, and those groups were moving toward reproducing, we would explore bringing that person on staff or sending him or her out as a church planter. We weren't really that precise or rigid, but it was a very simple, highly relational system that we used month after month, year after year, with amazing results.

The culture of Hope Chapel placed a high value on multiplication, and my job was simply to develop, cheer, and make heroes of people who multiply at any level.

We were a part of the Foursquare denomination, and when they saw our multiplication efforts, they decided to make me a district overseer. I served over one geographic area, alongside Wayne Cordeiro, lead pastor of New Hope Honolulu, who oversaw another jurisdiction. Typically, denominations only allow you to plant within your geographic territory, but in our case, after a while they wisely told both of us we could plant churches anywhere we wanted. And we did!

Our teamwork, along with others like Hawaiian Islands Ministries, led to the transformation of Hawaii's spiritual landscape. According to Barna Research,[25] while once only 1% of our state attended church, now 37% of the population of Hawaii attends church regularly, and 62% of the state call themselves Christians. Hawaii was the only state of the fifty that saw a net increase in church attendance.

Hope Chapel has now seen more than twenty-three hundred churches birthed in Hawaii and around the world, all from that first little church in Hermosa Beach. Who but God could have imagined the fruit that started from twelve people in 1971 and multiplied as disciples made disciples who made disciples!

Ralph's hero maker tip: Here's my advice to someone leading a Level 1, 2, or 3 church or ministry: Give just five hours a week to doing the work of discipling others and/or reproducing leaders. Make it one of your hobbies. Start by selecting three young leaders to mentor, and impart what you know. You never know, one might eventually lead a Level 5 church. If that happens, the time you spend making heroes could help trigger the start of thousands of new churches in our lifetime and truly saturating our communities with the gospel. Really! These churches could literally change the whole world.

Why Do So Few Practice Multiplication Thinking?

To me, Ralph is one of the very few solid examples in North America of a leader who has practiced multiplication thinking and leads a Level 5 church. Some of his backstory is that early in his leadership, someone was a hero maker to him (I'll tell you about that in chapter 6, and it might surprise you who!). But our takeaway from Ralph here is that when leaders disciple and release leaders who then in turn make disciples who plant churches that plant churches—that is how movement making happens! This inherently requires multiplication thinking.

Why are Ralph and others so few in number? It's what motivated me to build this whole book around the term hero maker. Deep inside most Westerners is an aspiration to be a hero. The predominant model of a successful church is Level 3, with the pastor being the hero. At that level, you get invited to speak at conferences, you sponsor a popular podcast, and you've been courted to write a book.

That's what we aspire to, so we adopt that paradigm. As in the movie *The Truman Show*, we don't realize that there's a whole other world out there. But just as Truman Burbank (played by Jim Carrey) punches a hole in the boundaries of his world and is never the same after stepping through it, so more and more church leaders are punching a hole in their Level 3 thinking and are never the same. And just as Truman was urged by the cast and producers to return to the show, church leaders may sense a pull to return to the old paradigm.

I remember being invited to a nationally prominent church, one that had modeled Level 3 growth for many years, to talk about how to reproduce by going multisite and planting churches. Their response showed the backward tug. After my talk, one of their senior staff said to me, "How can we do what you say, when we haven't got this one right yet?" Yet this was one of the most "right" churches in the world!

Simple Tool for Multiplication Thinking

THE DREAM NAPKIN

In *Exponential: How You and Your Friends Can Start a Missional Church Movement*, my brother Jon and I tell the story of the dream God gave us and a handful of others that became Community Christian Church. I mentioned earlier in this chapter how I wrote it out on a napkin in a restaurant. I now have it in my journal, and I carry it every- where I go, praying often as I notice it in there. I call it my dream nap- kin, and I've encouraged thousands of people to use the same simple tool. (See Figure 5.4.) When I speak at conferences, I'll often put a napkin on every seat, and I walk people through the process. At Community Christian Church, we even have a napkin dis- penser on a wall!

FIGURE 5.4

Let me walk you through what to do.

1. *Napkin.* Get a paper napkin. It can be any napkin. Of course, there is nothing special about the napkin. What is special is what's about to happen between you and God. And if you lose the napkin, you can write out your dream again on a different napkin. (I lost my original napkin. People always express sympathy when I tell them, but I just write out a new one!)

2. *Pray and write.* Take a look at your dream. Now honestly ask yourself, "Can I accomplish this dream through my own leadership?" If your answer is yes, you need to get a bigger dream. If you don't have a dream that makes you dependent on God, you need to get a bigger dream. I challenge you to take your dream and multiply it by 100x. This 100x vision is the kingdom-size dream only God can do through you working through others as a hero maker.

3. *Expand by 100x.* Next, multiply your dream by one hundred—or more. You may need to get a second napkin and start all over. What makes this a dream napkin is that this is not what you, your ministry, or your church can do on your own. This 100x vision is the kingdom-size dream only God can do through you working through others as a hero maker.

4. *Pray and believe.* Using all the faith you have to visualize the dream on that napkin becoming reality, ask God, "How can you use me to do this?" Share your desire with God in prayer.

Over the coming months and years, God will take you down new paths and create new opportunities. So you will need to do this over and over again. Dreaming big is a catalyst for multiplication thinking.

Who Is Waiting on You?

Without Obi-Wan Kenobi, Luke Skywalker might never have become a Jedi Knight and led the rebellion against the evil Empire.

If Mickey hadn't challenged Rocky, perhaps he never would have kept fighting, inspiring millions.

Take away Dumbledore's friendship with Harry Potter, and Voldemort might never have been defeated.

If Haymitch had not mentored Katniss in all facets of the Hunger Games, she may not have uncovered and ultimately overthrown the corruption of President Snow.

Who knows if Frodo ever would have made it to Mordor with the ring, leading the fight of good versus evil, if not for his apprenticeship with Gandalf.

There are leaders waiting to be developed and heroes waiting to be made. They might just be waiting on *you*. Becoming a hero maker starts with multiplication thinking but continues with four more practices, which we will explain in the following chapters. Are you in?

To realize this big dream, you will need to be a permission giver. Are you ready to explore that in the next chapter? If you nodded your head, then you just passed the first challenge in that chapter: learning to make yes your first instinct! Turn the page to find out more.

Hero Maker Discussion Questions

OPEN

- What was your big dream as a kid? (Astronaut? Ballerina? Pro athlete?) Who do you know who dreams big? Would you say they also practice multiplication thinking?
- Describe a time when you realized that there was way more God wanted you to do than you could do yourself, stretching you into multiplication thinking. What happened as a result?

DIG

- Read Acts 4:1–22, noting the various responses to the church's growth to five thousand people. To what extent is multiplication thinking implied in how the apostles responded?

FIGURE 5.5

- What biblical parallels come to mind for the dream napkin tool described in this chapter?

REFLECT

- Create and share your own dream napkin (Figure 5.5).
- Who are you mentoring whom you could lead in a dream napkin exercise?

CHAPTER 6

Permission Giving

> **Big Idea:** The practice of permission giving is a shift from *seeing* what God can do through my own leadership to seeing what God can do through other leaders. Permission giving requires that we learn to lead with a yes and use simple tools like ICNU conversations.

"Growing up on the west side of San Antonio, I believed in god—the god of football," says Derwin Gray, the founding pastor of Transformation Church, just outside Charlotte, North Carolina. "The game was my ticket out of an early life saturated with violence, addiction, abuse, and chaos."[26] But it took two hero makers—a high school football coach and a teammate with the locker room nickname "Naked Preacher"—to give him the permission he needed to access that ticket.

His head coach was D. W. Rutledge, who is legendary in Texas high school football. One reason Rutledge was a Hall of Fame coach was because he was able to help young men believe in themselves and to give them permission to succeed when they saw very little of that in other areas of their life. Derwin told me, "Coach saw in me what I didn't see in myself; that's what the best leaders do. They look into the soul of a person and say, 'I see what you could be, and my role is to bring that out of you.'"

> The best leaders look into the soul of a person and say, "I see what you could be, and my role is to bring that out of you."
> —DERWIN GRAY

It was Coach Rutledge who not only turned Derwin into a standout football player but also helped him see his way out of a bad neighborhood and a challenging family setting. Derwin credits Coach Rutledge with helping him envision a better future. "I was one of the only men in my family who had not been to jail, who did not have a substance abuse problem, who did not have a child out of marriage, and who didn't flunk out of high school," Derwin says.

Derwin performed so well in high school that he went to college on a football scholarship and was drafted by the Indiana Colts to play strong safety. "I had made it out and was very successful, and pro football became my god," he says.

Then he met Steve Grant. Grant, a Colts linebacker, would take a shower, wrap a towel around his waist, pick up his Bible, and ask those in the locker room, "Do you know Jesus?" Like most in the locker room, Derwin laughed him off. But over the next several years, he saw this linebacker not only preach his faith but also live it out. It was that "Naked Preacher" who led Derwin to faith.

A few years later, injuries pressed Derwin to retire from the NFL as his body gave out from playing a brutal game. At that point, he says, "I was stripped of everything I thought gave me meaning. I was left with nothing, even though I seemingly had everything." It was remembering the encouragement of his high school coach and the faith given to him by a naked preacher that gave Derwin a new dream for his life. All this led him and his wife to start Transformation Church, a remarkable multiethnic congregation.

Derwin is not just the lead pastor; he's also the lead permission giver. Just as others gave him permission and encouragement to go beyond his wildest dreams, he inspires and encourages people in his church to exceed theirs. If you were to visit Transformation Church,[27] you'd be wowed at how many of their members have taken major volunteer leadership roles in the church or in the community or have gone on to plant other churches.

The people in our own groups, ministries, and churches are full of Derwin Grays, all at different stages, from those struggling to find hope in life to those at the top of their game. Ask yourself, "How can I affirm them and give them permission to go far beyond their wildest dreams?" Then let me share with you some powerful stories of what permission giving can do, plus a very practical tool that you can use to become a stronger permission giver. Figure 6.1 shows how permission giving fits into the sequence of the five core practices for a hero maker.

FIGURE 6.1

A HERO-MAKING JOURNEY: PERMISSION GIVING

HERO-MAKING PRACTICES	MULTIPLICATION THINKING	PERMISSION GIVING	DISCIPLE MULTIPLYING	GIFT ACTIVATING	KINGDOM BUILDING
JESUS AND HERO MAKING	ACTS 1:8	MATT. 4:19	JOHN 3:22	MATT. 28:19	MATT. 6:33
HERO-MAKING TOOLS	DREAM NAPKIN	I-C-N-U CONVERSATION	FIVE STEPS OF APPRENTICESHIP	COMMISSIONING	SIMPLE SCOREBOARD

Jesus Gave His Authority to . . . You!

When Jesus said to some unschooled, off-the-map fishermen, "Come, follow me . . . and I will send you out to fish for people" (Matt. 4:19), he made an amazing statement of permission giving. He didn't say, "Follow me, and watch what God can do through my own leadership," although they certainly did so. He said, in effect, "Follow me, because God's going to work through some leaders other than me: each of you!" And for a respected rabbi to look this group of working-class grinders in the eye and say, "I see something special in you" was mind blowing and life changing.

This was not just a day-one recruitment message. No! Jesus started his ministry with it, practiced it throughout his ministry, and ended his earthly ministry with it.

How? Can you imagine a senior pastor assembling everyone on staff and saying, "You know I'm the boss. I have the authority. Now I'm giving it all to you. Go out there and get the mission accomplished!"

That seems to be exactly what Jesus did. He said, "As the Father has sent me, I am sending you" (John 20:21). In addition, in one of the most familiar passages in the Bible, the Great Commission, Jesus says, "All authority in heaven and on earth has been given to me. Therefore go and make disciples of all nations, baptizing them in the name of the Father and of the Son and of the Holy Spirit, and teaching them to obey everything I have commanded you. And surely I am with you always, to the very end of the age" (Matt. 28:18–20).

In essence, Jesus looks at his apprentices and says, "Hey, guys, I've got all the authority, and now I'm giving you access to it. So go spread the good news everywhere!"

Talk about permission giving! Could anyone hope for a more permission-giving leader? From day one until his final day, Jesus practiced what he taught. How many times across his ministry does Jesus model permission giving? Just three examples:

- You feed them! (Mark 6:30–44)
- You try casting out the demons! (Matt. 17:14–21)
- You go out and share the gospel! (Luke 10:1–3)

"No Thanks, Dude, We're All Set"

Such high-trust permission giving doesn't routinely happen, but should it? *Growing Young*, a recent landmark study about millennials and church, subtitled *Six Essential Strategies to Help Young People Discover and Love Your Church*,[28] says that the more you give millennials permission—handing them the keys of everything from the church facility to the soda machine by the youth room—the more they'll thrive.

By contrast, Sean Sears, at the time in his late teens—just the kind of person *Growing Young* was talking about—had a permission-withholding challenge that's so extreme as to be comical. Yet I fear there's a grain of truth in his experience.

Sean went to a Bible college, passionate about student ministry. There was a popular church near his college, and he tried to get involved in the student ministry there. He found the youth pastor and asked, "How can I plug in? Maybe you need some counselors?"

"No, we have all the counselors we need," the youth pastor replied.

"I'm a freshman, hoping to be part of the church for four years," Sean said. "Maybe there's another way I could help?"

"Nope, we are all set."

Sean really wanted to get his foot in the door, so he offered to give kids rides to youth group.

"No thanks."

He offered to go to some of the students' ball games, just to be an encouragement.

"No thanks."

How about if he showed up the day before youth group to set up the meeting room?

"No."

Sean took one final stab. "What if whenever you hold a youth event, I came afterward and cleaned up the pizza boxes and other debris?"

"No, dude, we're all set."

You already know how Sean felt. Totally discouraged!

His girlfriend (and future wife) had been going to a church that was farther away and considered less spectacular; it was smaller, older, and had fewer bells and whistles. Sean decided to attend, mostly out of interest in her.

After Sean had come a few times, the pastor asked, "Is there any way you'd like to get involved?" Sean felt a surge of energy and explained that he'd like to be a youth pastor someday.

The pastor shot back, "Why someday? Why not now?"

Immediately Sean began to think of all the reasons why the youth pastor at the other church didn't want him. "I was starting to believe I wasn't needed," Sean reflects. "But then this pastor gave me permission to do whatever I needed to reach youth who were far from God."

Sean took the challenge and started a youth group with the church's three middle schoolers. A year and a half later, the group had grown to thirty-five. So the church went from roughly 100 people to 135, with now a fourth of the congregation being what Sean called "preadolescent street punks."

"The old gray hairs were the most loving and patient people I could have hoped for," says Sean. "The kids were loud and rowdy, but the congregation was so excited that kids from the neighborhood were finding Jesus."

The impact on Sean transformed his future. "That experience put inside me a passion to make sure I was never a barrier or roadblock to others serving God," he says. He was determined to be a permission giver, not a permission withholder.

Fast-forward to today, and Sean Sears is a hero maker. Sean planted Grace Church in greater Boston, Massachusetts, and in its first twelve years of life, it planted four other churches. A nineteen-year-old student who helped Sean start Grace became the pastor of their first daughter church. They have an extensive emphasis on developing and giving permission to men and women who are high-capacity but underutilized for kingdom purposes. "Every church I've known, including Grace, is full of leaders," Sean says. "We just haven't done a good job of identifying them, giving them permission, and releasing them."

I believe *Growing Young*'s research is spot-on, but permission giving is not just for integrating and mobilizing the next generation. Jesus wants permission giving to be in the DNA of *every* generation that follows him.

Fears That Keep Us from Permission Giving

Two of the most permission-giving people I know are Larry and Deb Walkemeyer, who have served for more than twenty-five years at Light and Life Christian Fellowship, in greater Los Angeles. Starting with a handful of committed white folks in an established congregation in an aging facility with very limited parking, the church has grown into a multiethnic, outward-focused urban church with one thousand in attendance that has planted forty-four churches and counting.

Larry says there are two kinds of churches: lake churches and river churches. He explains that lake churches are like bodies of water that don't go anywhere, so everything stays in one place. "A lake church keeps everything within its banks, and unless something stirs it up once in a while, it will get stagnant. River churches are different, because the water is flowing to somewhere; nothing stays the same, and the current is always moving." Larry says, "Our focus now is to reach, teach, mend, and *send*. We want to release a river of multiplication in our church, city, and world." Of the fifty-six churches Light and Life has started, twenty are local and domestic church plants, and thirty-six are international, in the Philippines, Ethiopia, and Indonesia.

Every time a new opportunity to send someone arises, there is a temptation to hold and preserve what you have. "It's not easy being a river church, but we feel called to keep sending people out," Larry says. "We have sent many staff, leaders, givers, and money to start new churches. Some of these groups have been small; several times we have given away 10% of our congregation, and on two occasions we sent 25% of our whole church."

In his ebook *Flow: Unleashing a River of Multiplication in Your Church, City and World*,[29] Larry says, "The more I studied the book of Acts, the more I was overwhelmed by the bold fearlessness that marked the early church. Risk was the daily special on the church's menu." He goes on to highlight very real fears that commonly keep pastors from giving permission to plant new churches. Even if you are not a pastor, I think you can identify with each of these fears. Here are the five fears he identifies that keep us from giving permission.

1. *Fear of failure.* Permission giving means giving away not only authority but also people, leaders, and money while knowing that the new project might fail. It means you have fears like, "We are winning at addition; why risk losing at multiplication?" or "What if church planting damages our mother church? Will we recover?" You face those fears and you give permission anyway.

2. *Fear of rejection.* Multiplication means giving permission to transfer allegiance from the sending pastor to the planting pastor. This kind of emotional exchange calls for a deep personal security to overcome inner fears of rejection. Pastors must ask, "Am I secure enough in God and in my own identity to face what will feel like a form of abandonment?"

3. *Fear of loss of control.* Leading with a yes means you are empowering others and divesting of the direct management of leaders and people. It is a lot like a parent who launches a child and must endure the possibility of being hurt by that child's poor choices. Pastors must ask, "Do I trust God enough to hand over large groups of people to novice shepherds?"

4. *Fear of conflict.* Permission giving always changes the status quo and creates the possibility of significant pushback. Everyone loves addition but many fear multiplication; consequently, it's difficult to cast and pursue this vision without generating sparks. Can you and the leaders deal with the fallout from developing this potentially controversial new priority in a church?

5. *Fear of financial hardship.* When you give large groups of people permission to take their giving and leave to join a church plant, you have no idea of the impact on your church's monthly income. You wonder, "Will God still provide all that we need?" Again, you face the fear and then you give permission anyway.

Six Levels of Giving Permission

The Walkemeyers have discovered the secret that kingdom multiplication happens when we become hero makers and give those around us permission to advance Jesus' cause.

But the fears they cite are real, often triggered by painful experiences. Have you ever heard (or thought) something like this: "Oh no. When I said, 'Please run with it,' I wanted you to keep me in the loop. But it looks like you went and already did everything..."

How often have you wanted to give someone permission, but things went south and you ended up taking authority back? Maybe in the process, you inadvertently damaged a relationship or quashed someone's eagerness to serve.

Here are six levels for saying yes and giving permission. They are a perfect response to the five fears we've been discussing. They will help you and the people you're developing avoid misunderstandings. They also offer you a series of steps for giving people more and more authority, as appropriate, as you move them from one level to the next.

Level 1: Watch what I do, and then let's talk about it.

Level 2: Let's together figure out a plan for what you should do.

Level 3: Propose a plan for what I should do, and let's talk about it.

Level 4: Let me know your plan for what you should do, but wait for my feedback.

Level 5: You should handle it completely, and then let me know what you did.

Level 6: You should handle it completely, and there is no need to report back to me.

These six levels work best when you give someone an assignment, and then you ask them to repeat it back to you, by saying, "Please tell me what assignment you just heard from me and what level of permission you received to go and do it." This approach helps you to frame ministry around the word yes. If you are going to be a permission giver, you need to develop a yes reflex.

If someone comes to you and says, "I've got this idea about reaching kids through sports," what do you say? Yes.

If someone says, "I want to care for HIV patients," what do you say? Yes. If someone says, "I want to help provide support for single moms," what do you say? Yes.

A yes reflex stages a coup d'état against hero-only ministry and starts a revolution of difference making, led by hero makers. A yes reflex is a verbal manifesto that says, "I see in you a much-needed role to play in the mission of Jesus."

Realize That Your Default Is Probably No

From day one at our first real job, our bosses, coworkers, and mentors tell us,

"You have to prioritize!"
"You can't do every idea you have!"
"You have to learn to say no!"

So it's not surprising that saying no becomes our default as a form of self-preservation, resisting the stream of asks for time, guidance, and resources. It is easy for us to automatically switch to no mode. It can become our "natural" first response.

Problem! The one thing every hero maker possesses that everyone around him or her needs is *permission*, which needs to come in the form of a yes. If you want to multiply leaders who in turn multiply leaders, you must lead with a yes. If the people around you cannot get a yes, they will never discover the dream God has for their life or reach their redemptive potential. If your followers can't get permission from you with a yes, they will never be engaged in the mission.

> If the people around you cannot get a yes, they will never discover the dream God has for their life or reach their redemptive potential.

The great temptation is to respond with how instead of yes. But questions of how need to wait. If we reply, "How could you do that?" we sow the seeds of doubt by responding to their aspirations with a question about strategy. If we go right to, "How much would that cost?" we are responding to their dream with a question of tactics. The questions of how will come later, but the reflex of a hero maker is to be a permission giver and say yes.

Simple Tool for Permission Giving

AN ICNU CONVERSATION

Let me invite you to adopt a simple tool we have used at Community Christian Church for years, with remarkable results. It unfolds as simply as this conversation between church staff member John Ciesniewski and volunteer leader Greg Sink. Greg, a man in his sixties with a successful career, heard these words from John: "I see in you someone who could be a great campus pastor." This conversation led Greg on a path to retire early and do a leadership residency so he could become a campus pastor at a new location of our church, in an active adult (age fifty-five plus) community.

What happened here is that one person called out greatness in another person. It's a simple formula that helps create a yes environment. All you do is say, "I see [blank] in you." You fill in the blank with the appropriate affirmation.

We use the initials ICNU as in-house shorthand for these conversations. We call ICNU the four most important letters of the alphabet. We encourage everyone—you don't have to serve in any official capacity—to regularly tell others, "I see this ability in you," "I see this gift in you," and "I see God at work in you when you..."

I can't stress enough what a difference it can make when someone you respect takes the time to see something in you and to call that out in you. Most people did not grow up in a family in which they experienced this, nor do they work in an environment where this happens. Our ICNU culture helps those who are affirmed have the confidence to step forward and ask for permission, wanting to hear, "Yes, you can do it."

Yes to Murder Town USA

It was hearing a yes from a spiritual father that sent Derrick Parks to plant a church in Wilmington, Delaware, a place *Newsweek* called Murder Town USA.[30] It was that same yes, accompanied by a "you can do it" from his hero-making mentors, that kept Derrick there when a neighbor was shot and killed just a few doors down from where he lived.

Derrick Parks grew up with all the challenges of being an African American male in poverty-ridden South Camden, New Jersey. He worked his way through them and became a successful school administrator in suburban Philadelphia. So what would cause him to become a church planter in a place like downtown Wilmington? It was Pastor Eric Mason who, as a hero maker, had an ICNU conversation with Derrick, and their relationship has lasted to this day. "He is my father in the ministry," says Derrick. "I phone him all the time."

Eric Mason had completed a pastoral residency program and then planted Epiphany Fellowship in downtown Philadelphia. Derrick, working in a Philadelphia school during Epiphany Fellowship's early years, had gotten involved in the church. He was drawn to the vision, including the dream to plant other churches in needy areas, from Brooklyn to South Central Los Angeles. As Eric describes his hero-making vision, "We want to send out many church planters, going humbly into places that are difficult and unreached."

Along the way, Eric saw Derrick's potential and played a huge permission-giver role in Derrick's life. "God has only just begun with his great work in you," Eric told Derrick, giving Derrick both license and language to advance the mission of Jesus.

When Epiphany Fellowship of Philadelphia planted a new church in Derrick's hometown of Camden, Derrick became an elder there. The pastor there likewise had ICNU moments with Derrick. "Dr. Eric Mason and Pastor Doug Logan were certainly permission givers in my life," Derrick affirms. As Derrick sensed a further calling of God to bring the gospel to "other Camdens," he did a sixteen-month church-planting residency through Epiphany. Then he too got sent out.

So Epiphany Philadelphia planted Epiphany Camden, which planted Epiphany Wilmington. Each was spurred on by permission givers. Likewise, from the first days in Wilmington, Derrick is saying yes wherever possible so God can continue that chain. Derrick says, "I am modeling the same by dreaming for the fatherless young men in my church. There are six young men that I meet with regularly to walk them through biblical manhood principles. Some of them have muted aspirations for ministry, and I encourage them to follow the Lord's calling faithfully."

For all these Epiphany Fellowship churches to be birthed, leadership had to let go of control and release their resources and people to take the good news elsewhere. Without these many permission givers, the story would be very different. Had pastors tried to control and keep the people God put under their leadership, you wouldn't have a Derrick Parks risking it all in Wilmington.

Who Gave Ralph Permission?

You met Ralph Moore in chapter 5. I believe he's one of this country's best examples of a hero maker. For the past five decades, he has practiced permission giving with the leaders God has brought around him, and that has resulted in twenty-three hundred new churches and counting!

Ralph's story is not about a big church but about a big dream. He has pastored only three churches in his life, and all of them were small when he arrived or started them. But Ralph repeatedly demonstrates two values: multiplication thinking and permission giving. When the church he currently pastors was about two hundred in attendance, he announced, "Even if we never grow past two hundred people, I believe that in the next twenty years, we have the potential to plant thirty churches that each will plant other churches. And if we grow beyond two hundred people, then I believe we should increase that twenty-year goal."

One of Ralph's strategies for starting those new churches is to encourage bivocational ministry, sometimes called tentmaking (from the apostle Paul's practice[31]) or marketplace pastors. "My assumption is that these everyday missionaries are heroes in the making who need affirmation more than anyone else," Ralph says. "Every Christ follower is a missionary, and pastors need to give more permission than they do and make heroes of them."

In fact, says Ralph, "From my experience, the greatest potential for growing God's kingdom lies with the people who will remain in their career while establishing a church. I know a doctor, an architect, a private school administrator, a U.S. Marine gunnery sergeant, a furniture store owner, a copy machine salesman, a BMW distributor, a bio-geneticist, and several others who have successfully started new churches. And I'm only naming the ones that I've worked with recently!" Many of those are modern-day tentmakers, part of a rising trend in bivocational pastors.[32]

Who gave Ralph permission to release all these people into various levels of ministry? "Though no one ever discipled me," he says, "I did have significant mentors who were hero makers to me." One mentor was Robert Schuller, founder of what became the Crystal Cathedral (not too far from the location of Ralph's first church), who took Ralph and his wife Ruby under wing. "Ruby and I had been the youngest and newest church planters to attend his annual pastors' conference. He encouraged us and met with us personally on several occasions. He assigned one of his staff to meet with us monthly, in restaurants where we couldn't afford to eat on our own. Eventually, he invited me to speak at his pastors' conference on an annual basis, which gave us further interaction with him and his wife, Arvella. Toward the end of his ministry at Crystal Cathedral, I got invited back to speak at the conference. After we moved to Hawaii, one of his daughters joined one of our daughter churches in Maui. Different as we were in theology and style, he is still one who gave me permission to do much of what I've done."

Ralph knows firsthand what happens when someone you look up to believes in you and says you can do it. That's what he experienced, and that's what he's done with others. Ralph describes how he has implemented the ICNU conversations: "I've made it a point to make disciples, whom I constantly encourage to achieve more than they believed was possible." Ralph explains the power in these personal conversations: "I think the spiritual gift of encouragement is at work in these encounters." He has tried to emulate what Schuller did for him. "An hour spent on the phone with someone I met at a seminar can help a younger leader feel that someone they see as significant believes in them. I do this at every opportunity."

"I Am for You, Even If You Are Not in Our Denomination"

One of my favorite examples of a permission giver is a United Methodist pastor named Jerry Sweat, who had many ICNU conversations with a very gifted staff member named Joby Martin. "I want to help you plant a church, even if it's not United Methodist," Jerry told him. Here's what happened, in Joby's words:

Jerry Sweat and Joby Martin

THE CHURCH OF ELEVEN22
JACKSONVILLE, FLORIDA

*In only four years, a new Jacksonville church
became a permission-giving center for
more than six thousand weekly worshipers
while planting seventy new churches.*

Just three short years after launching the Church of Eleven22, we celebrated salvation number three thousand. That's three thousand lives eternally changed!

I (Joby) trace a lot of those spiritual victories back to an ongoing series of conversations with my former senior pastor, Jerry Sweat, at Beach Church, a United Methodist congregation in Jacksonville, Florida. His passion, to use his words, was "to raise up people and help them live out their calling."

I had the incredible opportunity to serve under him as his youth pastor and executive pastor. At one point, he encouraged me to start a weekly worship gathering to reach people ages eighteen to thirty-five, the lost generation—the unchurched, the dechurched. We held the new service Sundays at 11:22 a.m. (the reference to the time stuck, so Eleven22 became the name of the church).

Three years later, we had grown so much that Jerry proposed another idea: he would support sending me and the majority of people who called Beach Church home to start a brand-new church. Most senior pastors would be intimidated by this idea. Not true of Jerry Sweat. He embraced the growth. In fact, he initiated the decision to expand the reach of Beach United Methodist, and rather than split, to launch it into two brand-new churches. That meant Beach Church would cease to exist as it had been known.

When he told me that idea, he says, he felt peace—and I felt nausea!

The fact that I wasn't raised United Methodist and wanted to align with the more Reformed Acts 29 church-planting network didn't bother him. He even championed that to his superiors. That's right: a United Methodist church birthed a brand-new church with a large number of tithers who will not be United Methodists. And it happened with the full blessing of the district superintendent and bishop!

When the church launched, Jerry's message to me was powerful: "What you're about to do isn't new; it's just your turn." I am forever changed because of all his permission-giving, ICNU words like these. Jerry was my hero maker, he has been my greatest cheerleader, and he also spearheaded a three-year campaign to raise six million dollars between our two churches.

At one of those events, he said, "God has done amazing things. In three years, more people have been saved between the two churches than were attending the one church when we were all together! If we can just get ourselves out of the way, God can do even more amazing things."

Joby's hero maker tip: If you want to move toward Level 5 multiplication, then put priority on *talking* about multiplication. I started talking about multiplying at our very first staff meeting, the morning after we formally launched as a church. We didn't know how, so we partnered with people who were already doing it. We surround ourselves with people who know how to shift those gears. But those conversations have already led us to help plant more than seventy churches so far. Who knows what will come from multiplication conversations that you begin!

ICNU Leads to More Disciple Multiplication

Let me be clear: Leading with a yes does not mean that you will fund their idea. In fact, in most cases you absolutely should *not* fund their ideas. Yes does not mean that you will assign a staff person to oversee it. Sometimes that makes sense; often it will not. Yes does not mean that it gets announced at a weekend celebration service. Yes does not mean that it gets space on the website. Yes simply means that you are giving others permission and blessing to be used in the Jesus mission.

Remember my summary of Jesus' Great Commission: "Here's the mission. I'm giving you my authority to do it. Use it to make disciple makers. I'm with you all the way." If you do that with others, you will soon see an increase in the number of people being discipled and multiplying themselves through others. As you use ICNU to become a more joyful, affirming, creative leader, you're ready to learn the next step in becoming a hero maker. That's what the next chapter is about.

Hero Maker Discussion Questions

OPEN

- Tell about a life-transforming ICNU affirmation that you've received. Tell how you felt and what has come from that experience.
- Describe an ICNU conversation that you've initiated with someone else. How did *you* feel as it happened? What happened in that person's life or ministry?

DIG

- Read John 1:44–51, which describes Jesus' call to Nathanael. In what ways is that an ICNU conversation?
- What impact do you think it had on Nathanael?
- What do you think Jesus meant when he told Nathanael, "You will see greater things"?

REFLECT

- Prayerfully select someone you can approach with an ICNU affirmation. Ideally, pick someone you haven't ever (or recently) affirmed at this level. Who is it? What will you say?

CHAPTER 7

Disciple Multiplying

Big Idea: The practice of disciple multiplying is a shift from *sharing* what I've learned to add followers to sharing what I've learned in ways that multiply disciples. Disciple multiplying requires that we do life with other leaders with the goal of four generations of multiplication and use simple tools like the five steps of apprenticeship.

When I was four years old and my brother Jon was two, my parents moved our family from rural Missouri to Chicago to start a new church, which they led for the next thirty-seven years. Growing up, I saw lots of people find their way back to God; I saw our church start a new site and plant new churches. God has blessed me with great parents and a great upbringing in my home church.

Somehow along the way, though, I came to believe the half-truth that the more committed I became as a disciple of Jesus, the more I would focus on me. My discipleship focused on questions like these:

- Am I having a consistent devotional life of Bible reading and prayer?
- Am I learning more about my faith from the youth group, Sunday sermons, and even the music I listen to?
- Am I looking for opportunities to tell others what Jesus has done for me?
- Am I inviting God to enter every area of my life to make me more like Jesus?

If you're looking to find a problem in those questions, you won't. They represent vital practices taught in the New Testament.

The problem is what's missing. I misunderstood that being a disciple or apprentice of Jesus was primarily about me in the sense of *my* relationship with God and *my* relationship with others. I knew it also included my building up the body of Christ, my loving other people, and my telling the world—including my friends—about Jesus. But note the direct connection to *me* in each case.

One day I realized that something on the fringes of my faith needed to be at the core of my Christian growth. This is the third practice for becoming a hero maker. One test of whether we're a hero maker is whether we're reproducing and multiplying *other* Christ followers, who in turn do likewise.

One of the most mentioned commands of Jesus is the Great Commission: "Go and make disciples of all nations, baptizing them in the name of the Father and of the Son and of the Holy Spirit."

It's firmly planted in our heads but not in our lives.

> **One test of whether we're a hero maker is whether we're reproducing and multiplying *other* Christ followers, who in turn do likewise.**

I now understand that Jesus' command challenges that I haven't really made a disciple if the person hasn't begun in turn making other disciples. I need to be mentoring disciple multipliers into multiple generations. After all, isn't making serial disciple makers the only way to "make disciples of all nations"?

Maybe you're ahead of me, and you've already applied that verse personally. If so, you are definitely ready for the big idea of this chapter: you become a hero maker through the practice of sharing what you've learned by discipling leaders, and not being satisfied till you've seen it multiplied to the fourth generation.

Maybe, however, you haven't figured out how to consistently implement this practice in your leadership or build this practice into the culture you're leading. In this chapter, I want to not only challenge you with the imperative of being a disciple multiplier but also show you how to do it (see Figure 7.1). Every leader who wants to multiply leaders needs to understand how to become a disciple multiplier and equip those around them to be disciple multipliers. You may lead a small group, a prayer ministry, a location of a multisite church, a megachurch, or even a network

FIGURE 7.1

A HERO-MAKING JOURNEY: DISCIPLE MULTIPLYING

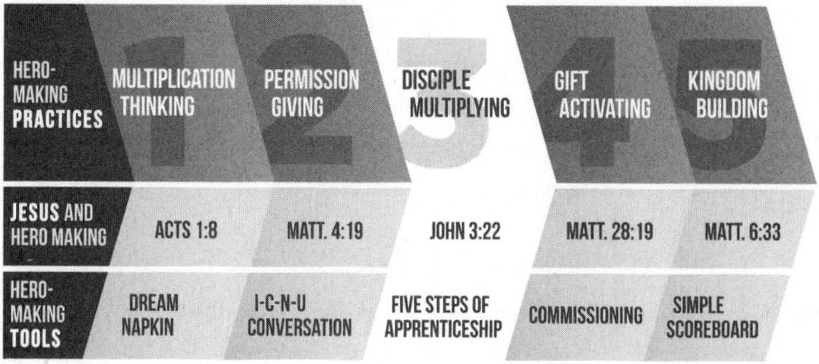

HERO-MAKING PRACTICES	MULTIPLICATION THINKING	PERMISSION GIVING	DISCIPLE MULTIPLYING	GIFT ACTIVATING	KINGDOM BUILDING
JESUS AND HERO MAKING	ACTS 1:8	MATT. 4:19	JOHN 3:22	MATT. 28:19	MATT. 6:33
HERO-MAKING TOOLS	DREAM NAPKIN	I-C-N-U CONVERSATION	FIVE STEPS OF APPRENTICESHIP	COMMISSIONING	SIMPLE SCOREBOARD

of churches, but to become a hero maker, you need to prioritize disciple multiplying. This practice represents a way of sharing what you learn by mentoring other leaders.

Jesus-Style Apprenticeship Is Something Anyone Can Do

In John 3:22, the Bible makes an easily overlooked, seemingly mundane statement: "Jesus and his disciples went out into the Judean countryside, where he spent some time with them."

What Jesus did is really quite simple. He selected just a few people—he focused on twelve—and they hung out with him and did ministry alongside him. Yet when Jesus spent some time with these twelve apprentices, something big happened. The word for "spend time" in Greek is pronounced "dia-*tree*-bo" (and transliterated *diatribo*). *Dia* means "against," and *tribo* means "to rub." So *diatribo* literally means "to rub against" or "to rub off." It literally means "to spend time together rubbing off on each other."

You and I can do that today. When we spend enough time with others, we begin to rub off on them, and they rub off on us. You start talking like each other. You pick up similar interests. You care about the same stuff. Maybe you know some couples who have been married like fifty years, and they have even started to *look* like each other! They've rubbed off on each other.

What Jesus did was not just about hours and minutes. It was *diatribo:* some of him was rubbing off on them. One of the main ways Jesus transformed his followers into people who would impact the world was through apprenticeship, by simply spending time with them. It was through *diatribo*, the Bible says, that Jesus' followers "turned the world upside down" (Acts 17:6 ESV). Even the Son of God, God in the flesh, didn't try to change the world on his own. Jesus *diatribo*'ed others.

Apprenticeship and Disciple Multiplying

To truly have exponential impact, all of us need to be mentoring, developing, and multiplying leaders. Another place where we see Jesus *diatribo*'ing, or rubbing off on, his twelve leadership residents is in the gospel of Mark: "Jesus went up on a mountainside and called to him those he wanted, and they came to him. He appointed twelve that they might be with him and that he might send them out to preach and to have authority to drive out demons" (Mark 3:13–15). There is so much for us to learn from these verses, but let's pull out four practical insights from how Jesus mentored the Twelve to form these future hero makers.

1. Disciple multipliers start with the few, not the many (Mark 3:13–14). In the verses that immediately precede this section of Scripture, we see that the crowds swelled to large numbers. They all wanted a piece of Jesus. They wanted to hear him talk; they wanted to get close to him. But these verses say Jesus "called to him those he wanted." I like to think that he picked twelve people "he wanted" to hang out with and with whom "he wanted" to be friends. Jesus was establishing an apprenticeship based on relationship. Equally important to note is that he didn't give in to the attention and the clamoring of the crowd; instead he started with and focused on the few. Jesus was a hero maker to the few and in so doing changed the world.

> *Hero maker next step:* Select a few people, maybe just two or three, or maybe as many as twelve, whom you will focus on. Invest in them and do everything you can to be their hero maker.

2. Disciple multipliers prioritize relationships, not curriculum (Mark 3:14). A phrase in verse 14 reveals the first reason why Jesus selected the

Twelve; it was so that "they might be with him." It is clear that Jesus was prioritizing the relationship with the Twelve. This was truly an apprenticeship that prioritized spending time together, in which the Twelve could observe, learn, and do what Jesus was doing. Apprenticeship is true to the intent and expression of how Jesus did discipleship. Much of our discipleship efforts today focus on content and curriculum, but our hero maker, Jesus, prioritized the relationship.

> *Hero maker next step:* Now that you have selected a few people to whom you will be a hero maker, determine your relational rhythms. How often will you meet, and what will the format be? Will you meet weekly or monthly? Will you meet face-to-face over coffee or through cell phones or the internet? To "be with" someone, you need to schedule your relational rhythms.

3. Disciple multipliers focus on sending capacity over seating capacity (Mark 3:14–15). The goal of this apprenticeship with Jesus was not for the Twelve to go through a set of curriculum, and then double that number to twenty-four who would go through the class, and then eventually have forty-eight, and then ninety-six, and keep growing the crowd who sat at Jesus' feet. No!

The goal of the apprenticeship was that "he might send them out" and they would do with others what he had done with them. Jesus wanted his apprentices to get to the place where they could do what he was doing. Once they could "preach and . . . have authority to drive out demons," the apprenticeship was complete. Our hero-making approach should involve the same kind of apprenticeship.

> *Hero maker next step:* Once you have selected your few people and established a set of relational rhythms, it's important to be clear about your expectations. You don't want the people you are mentoring to continue to serve as an assistant or even as a coleader. You want them to grow to their full capacity. If you are developing them to lead a group or lead a band or start a church, vocalize that expectation. Make it very clear, and get their agreement.

When is the apprenticeship complete? That's simple: when both you and your apprentice think they are ready to bring on their own apprentices. At that point, commission them and send them out with your blessing.

4. *Disciple multipliers hand off authority rather than hold on to it (Mark 3:15).* Not only did Jesus send out his apprentices; he also gave them authority, often substantial enough to "drive out demons." Don't overlook or underestimate spelling out the authority you're giving people. With authority, they'll feel fully empowered, commissioned to minister, and blessed to go even farther than you did.

> *Hero maker next step:* Ask those you're mentoring to state back to you the authority you've given them: "Please tell me what you think I've authorized you to do." You will then know how they interpreted your words of empowerment and commissioning. You'll know whether they're still acting as merely your assistant or ready to lead.

Apprenticeship Made All the Difference for Our Core Group

We started Community Christian Church with just a handful of friends from college. We had no people, no buildings, no money—and many said no sense! But we did have a passion to help people find their way back to God through Christ.

We lived in Chicago, a city of eight million people. We knew that 80% to 90% of those people, depending on what neighborhood they lived in, would not be in church on any given weekend, and we suspected that most of those were far from God. How do fewer than ten people reach all of them?

We all went out and started small groups. We each began to *diatribo* with anywhere from six to sixteen people. That was great. We saw God do amazing things. But that left 7.99999 million other people.

To continue to reach others, we each selected at least one apprentice leader. That apprentice leader would come alongside us and learn from us how to lead a group and *diatribo* with another six to sixteen people. In time, usually six to eighteen months, those apprentice leaders were ready, and they went on and led the existing group or started a brand-new small group.

Now, more than twenty-five years later, there are thousands of kids, students, and adults at multiple locations who call Community Christian their church home. Every year across Chicagoland, hundreds and hundreds of people are baptized, finding their way back to God.

But I've witnessed firsthand that when you're committed to being a disciple multiplier, the impact reaches beyond your church and your city. One of my early apprentice leaders was a guy who worked at General Mills, named Troy McMahon. He did a great job as an apprentice in my small group, and soon I made him the leader of the group, while I went on to start another group. In time, Troy became a coach for small group leaders. Then he joined our staff, and eventually he became our first campus pastor. All along the way, I was mentoring him, and he was mentoring others, who were mentoring down the line for literally *hundreds* of others.

Eleven years ago, we sent Troy off with our blessing plus about twenty-five people he had recruited at Community Christian to plant a new church in Kansas City with NewThing, our international network of reproducing churches. Now not only does Troy lead that church with one thousand people at three locations, but that church has helped plant forty-one churches. On top of that, he is leading a network of churches in Kansas City that is focused on planting one hundred *more* churches in that city! This is the kind of multiplication that advances the four-to-ten mission I talked about in chapter 1.

> I've witnessed firsthand that when you're committed to being a disciple multiplier, the impact reaches beyond your church and your city.

When we see disciple multipliers birthing new communities of faith, we will begin to move the needle from 4% of churches in America reproducing and multiplying to 10% and beyond!

We could have started just one church with one site and had an impact, but through apprenticeship and a commitment to being disciple multipliers, we have been able to reach exponentially more people.

Volunteers Can Be Disciple Multipliers

Is successful apprenticeship the opportunity or responsibility only of church staff? Absolutely not! In fact, the growth and impact of God's kingdom is in direct proportion to the number of people who multiply disciple makers *outside* of being hired at church. For every Troy McMahon, there should probably be fifty to one hundred hero makers like my friends Mary and Dr. Bill. Their stories inspire me.

Mary has always been very successful, both in business and as a volunteer at Community Christian Church. Despite her success, she didn't always see in herself what others and God saw in her. Mary has remarkable leadership gifts and the ability to influence hundreds and thousands of people. It was at a retreat called Ultimate Journey that she began to see the truth about herself and about God. She was so excited about the healing and the changes that were taking place, she immediately invited four other women to go through a small group to study the same content she had studied. Over the next few years, other women began to have the same Ultimate Journey experience she had, and they talked about it with great enthusiasm. Mary could see the difference she was making and set a goal to mentor other leaders and see ten new small groups.

Within a few years, she had met that goal and surpassed it. At this writing, Mary has trained fourteen leaders, and small groups are now being led in three churches. One new group leader is preparing to use Ultimate Journey in a church plant in Johannesburg, South Africa!

Mary is a disciple multiplier. When I asked Mary about her dream for these groups, she said, "I want to mentor enough leaders that we can have Ultimate Journey at every Community Christian location, that it can expand into more churches, and that we'd also see it begin to be used by men too!"

My friend Dr. Bill shares the same multiplying vision. He was leading a medical mission trip to the Philippines. He was the only medical doctor on the team, supported by a handful of nurses and volunteers. So he was charged with overseeing the medical clinics they would run during this fourteen-day trip. Because Bill has been around a church that values reproducing everything, he started the trip by giving the team this pep talk: "Everything we do needs to be reproducible. Just like we reproduce churches, I want all of

The growth and impact of God's kingdom is in direct proportion to the number of people who multiply disciple makers *outside* of being hired at church.

you to be able to take what you learn here and be able to reproduce a clinic to help others in other countries. So what I am about to teach you can be easily reproduced anywhere you go."

He is vision casting for multiple generations of medical apprentices. I love it!

Multiplying Apprentices in the Arts

I like to give grief to my coauthor, Warren Bird, by telling him that he needs a recovery group for people addicted to visiting growing churches. His boss at Leadership Network tells me that Warren has done more large-church study visits than anyone on the planet. Whenever Warren finds a church with a strong apprentice culture, a particular interest of his, he starts digging around the various departments to find out what's working.

What does he find? Inevitably, the hardest and last area of a church to reproduce and multiply is the worship arts. Why? Warren hears a lot of stereotyping:

- "Artists want the platform for themselves and don't want to share it with others."
- "Artists by nature aren't good people developers."
- "Artists are kind of quirky, and you don't *want* them to reproduce."
- "Artistic quality demands that you keep the bar high and work only with the proven few."
- "Artists on church staff are paid too much to spend time training others."

Ouch! If you're an artist, you perhaps aren't happy that I voiced these painful stereotypes. But stay with me. I want to show that they're often wrong, and maybe they could be proved wrong at your church as well.

Tug-of-War or Riding a Bike?

Let me start with Community Christian Church. From our early years, we challenged every person at every level to reproduce themselves. I mentioned in the previous chapter that our church started with just a handful of people, all leading small groups and developing other small group leaders. To this day, I still lead a small group and develop an apprentice leader.

We didn't stop with small groups. We did likewise with children's ministry, student ministry, first impressions ministry, and yes, the arts as well. The book *The Big Idea*[33] is a three-way authorship by me, my brother Jon, and Eric Bramlett, the creative arts director at Community Christian Church. In it we tell how I asked Eric, when we first hired him, to place his desk right next to mine. I wanted to *diatribo* (rub off on) him and reproduce in him and the arts the multiplication that was happening in the rest of the church. Eric and I became fast friends, and to this day he continues to serve as the leader of our creative catalyst for our artists at Community Christian Church.

Today Eric laughs when someone tells him that artists can't reproduce themselves at every level. Eric's team has done it year after year, and they've taught many other churches to do likewise. But it's never easy, because most artists feel they are stuck in a tug-of-war between excellence and multiplication.

If you focus on excellence, you trust only a few very talented artists, and you never multiply or develop anyone else. If you focus on multiplication, you develop lots of new artists, and in the process excellence suffers. This mental paradigm seems always to produce a no-win situation. If you have to choose between excellence and multiplication, you will lose, the congregation will lose, young emerging artists will lose, and the mission of Jesus will lose.

Artists need to hear, "You have been forced into a false dichotomy! You do not have to choose between excellence and multiplication."

A better analogy than a tug-of-war is how Eric and our artists think of it at Community Christian: it is more like riding a bicycle.

A bicycle has two pedals, and in this case one pedal is excellence and the other is multiplication. To create forward motion, you need to push them both, one at a time. (See Figure 7.2.)

Focusing on either excellence or multiplication is like trying to ride a bike by pushing only one pedal. It's hard to get any momentum. We need to push the pedals of both excellence *and* multiplication. The pedal of excellence will attract artists, while the pedal of multiplication will develop more and better artists. If we are to see a movement through starting new churches, we must think about the next generation, and we

FIGURE 7.2

must learn how to push the pedal of artistic excellence and then the pedal of artistic multiplication.

Here is what will happen: As we gain speed, we will alternate pedals so quickly that it will seem as though we are pushing both pedals at once. And pushing both pedals will create momentum. And that momentum will lead to movement!

Eric has the artistic gifts to be a solo performer on any stage. But he understands the secret of teamwork to grow God's kingdom, so instead he and our other artists work at eagerly mentoring new generations of Erics, who in turn are raising up others. Together they coordinate Christ-centered creativity and worship across all the locations of Community Christian Church, which represents over thirty weekly services.

Mentoring Artists Is the New Normal at Other Churches Too

Bayside Church in Granite Bay, California, has likewise rejected the tug-of-war mindset and is riding the bicycle of excellence and multiplication. They are so committed to artist development that they have created a school for it.[34] The church, which was started in 1996, today hosts about eighteen thousand people every weekend in twenty services across five campuses and has also started seven new churches.

You may not have heard of Bayside Church, but I bet you've sung a song by one of its worship leaders, Lincoln Brewster—songs like "All I Really Want," "All to You," "Everlasting God," and "The Power of Your Name." The church is led by a team of four senior pastors: Ray Johnston (who founded it), Andrew McCourt (who led the largest church in Belfast, Ireland), Curt Harlow (twenty-year veteran of college campus ministry), and Lincoln Brewster (recording artist and songwriter). Notice that Lincoln is only one of the worship leaders, and he's one of the senior pastors as well.

Lincoln came on Bayside's staff when the church first started and was meeting in a school. He was already a well-known worship leader and recording artist; he landed his first mainstream recording contract by the time he was nineteen years old and had played with rocker Steve Perry (formerly of the band Journey).

But even as Lincoln, who predictably became a stellar worship leader for Bayside Church, continued to rise as a solo recording artist, he sensed something was missing on that trajectory. "I can have only so much effect doing concerts by myself," he reflected. "I could do more if I'm teaching *others* how to lead worship, especially if they catch the vision that they too can teach others." This challenge became very practical as Bayside began exploring the idea of starting new churches and campuses. Early on, Bayside had started a worship-leading conference called Thrive, and out of that they created Thrive School of Worship, a yearlong training opportunity that lets artists study during the week what they do onstage. (They later started Thrive School of Leadership.)

To Lincoln, the logic was clear: to multiply the kingdom, the platform had to be shared. He knew that he could have only a one-to-one ratio—him to one congregation. But if he developed fifty leaders who then created fifty leaders of their own, it would have a much bigger effect. An exponential effect!

Lincoln is arguably one of the most gifted guitar players in the world, but he knows that to maximize his impact, he cannot go it alone. So he *diatribo*'s; he puts time and heart into mentoring others who lead worship. Lincoln Brewster is creating the platform and then letting other worship leaders stand on it and lead others in worship in campuses and churches all across the country. That's hero making through disciple multiplication.

Could You Do This Too?

If getting aspiring artists to mentor or apprentice others is one of the more challenging areas to being a disciple multiplier, by contrast one of the easiest is through the development of interns. I hope you read the following story and conclude, "Our church could do that too; we could get a bunch of interns, pay them next to nothing, and see fruits of multiplication beyond our wildest dreams." (By the way, see appendix 5 on the legal appropriateness of paying your interns "next to nothing"!)

That's almost how it happened for Chris Hodges, who was on staff at Bethany World Prayer Center. He moved to Birmingham, Alabama, to start Church of the Highlands, which launched in 2001. He had a vision to develop young leaders and place them in ministry. Within months, his only staff member and youth pastor, Layne Schranz, recruited seventeen students to be a part of their ministry school. The church was meeting in a high school on Sundays and had no office space, so for most of the first year, the interns met in the basement at Layne's house.

"Even before we launched, Chris's vision was to use, train, and reproduce leaders at every level of the church," says Layne. That's how they started: Chris's family, Layne's family, the interns, and a mass mailing that drew four hundred people to the first service.

That was more than sixteen years ago. Today the church is one of the five largest in the continent, drawing more than forty thousand people weekly. The ministry school has grown as well; every year, more than nine hundred students attend what is now known as Highlands College.[35] (More to come on this topic: we later devote much of chapter 11 to using residencies as a way to accelerate the development of your church's hero making culture.)

Yet I believe the church's biggest impact is beyond their walls. Here's the backstory: Just before Church of the Highlands started, Greg Surratt, senior pastor of Seacoast Church in Charleston, South Carolina, was convinced that God had given him a vision to help start two thousand new churches. But he knew it couldn't happen through his leadership alone. So he gathered several prospective church planters in whom he could see great potential, including Chris Hodges, and they formed a church-planting organization named the Association of Related Churches (ARC).[36]

Through ARC, Greg offered Chris twenty-five thousand dollars to fund the new church, plus any monthly support needed to meet budget for Highlands' first year. Greg asked Chris, once Highlands was up and running, to pay it forward and invest that same amount into other church planters. I've known Greg Surratt for several years, and this is just one example of how he is a hero maker.

Now back to those interns. What Chris and Layne discovered is that churches who reproduce micro will also reproduce macro. The interns eventually got out of Layne Schranz's basement and caught a vision for being not just ministers but minister makers. Today some of the interns finish their course and come on staff at Highlands Church. Many go to other churches. But the largest number go on staff at churches who planted through ARC. Highlands has become the growth engine behind ARC, even housing its offices. At the time of this writing, ARC has launched 673 new churches and is raising more than four million dollars annually to support the starting of new churches.

In Many Ways, Our Continent Is Trailing Others

Next, I want to introduce you to my friend Mario Vega and have him tell you his story of remarkable apprentice multiplication. It's important for you to hear from him, because while most of my illustrations come from North America, he is outside that context; and frankly, beyond the American borders is where we keep finding our best examples of the hero maker practice of disciple multiplication. (And maybe the best way to change the American, individualistic, Lone Ranger mindset is for all of us to befriend a pastor or leader in a Level 5 church that gets hero making better than we do!)

As you hear from Mario, be sure to notice two features of how he does ministry. First, they have a six-month training track for mentoring and developing leaders for their small groups (which they call "cell groups"). They also have a weekly meeting to plan the small group meeting, and a separate coaching huddle each week.

Second, the small group leader is asked to name people in his or her group who will be asked to take on various roles. This is the core of how they do apprentice multiplication.

Mario Vega

ELIM CHRISTIAN MISSION
SAN SALVADOR, EL SALVADOR[37]

*Apprentice multiplication is in the cell group
DNA at one of the world's largest churches.*

Without a doubt, our cell ministry has been the most important multiplication factor at Elim Christian Mission. In fact, we have planted churches across Central America, North America, Europe, and Australia, in part because of the evangelism and leadership development built into our cell group system.

Cell ministry is so important that we track the metrics of group life and multiplication more than worship attendance. In our mother church in San Salvador, we now have 110,000 people in our 9,000 weekly Saturday cell groups. Cells are groups of three to fifteen adults who meet weekly outside the church building for the purpose of evangelism, community, and spiritual growth, with the goal of multiplication. Cells are organized geographically, so that each group multiplies within its own geographical area.

We view our cell groups as an army that is penetrating the city for Jesus. We view our planning meeting like an army preparing, planning, and strategizing for battle. Cell leaders meet on Wednesday to pray, plan, and prepare to evangelize those who don't know Jesus. We want to fulfill Christ's marching orders to make disciples of all nations until he comes again.

Our cell ministry is rooted in New Testament teachings about the priesthood of all believers. Our cell groups take us back to the basics of Scripture.

People are not asked to be cell group leaders, but we have created a culture in which they are expected to do so. Leadership is seen as something natural for every believer. The pastor's role is to equip them to do the work of the ministry. When they move to other cities, they continue doing what they learned in El Salvador: open the doors to their home and introduce their neighbors to Jesus.

That makes every believer a potential minister of the gospel. For that purpose, a training course for new cell leaders has been designed by Elim that is offered to each convert starting the week after conversion. This course lasts for six months and consists of twenty-six lessons imparted weekly.

Leaders at Elim have four meeting commitments each week: Sunday worship, the planning meeting, the coaching meeting, and the cell group itself.

We allow for flexibility in our planning meetings, and each one is a little different. We have found, however, that most of the planning meetings follow a similar order, like the following sample order:

- *Prayer.* The leader will open in prayer, ask for prayer requests, and have everyone pray for one another.
- *Scripture.* We start with God's Word, and the leader might share something that God is laying on his or her heart in their personal devotion time.
- *Vision.* The leader reminds the group of the overall vision of making disciples through cell group ministry.
- *Results.* Follow up from the last planning meeting. Accountability is critical. The leader will ask whether people were visited and evangelized and whether the particular tasks were completed.
- *Planning.* Planning for the Saturday cell group. This is the main part of the planning meeting and takes the most time. The leader plans for the next meeting by doing the following:
  - *Visitation.* The leader will ask willing team members to visit those who have not been attending the cell.
  - *Sunday.* Prepare details about making sure each person has transportation to the Sunday celebration service. We want people in the cell group to also attend the Sunday celebration, and often transportation is a problem in San Salvador.
  - *Prayer.* We take personal prayer requests for those present at the planning meeting and pray about them.
  - *Announcements.* Finish with announcements about what's going on in the church in general.

> *Without a doubt, our cell ministry has
> been the most important multiplication
> factor at Elim Christian Mission.*

All this happens in one hour. We try not to go beyond the time limit, because we know people are busy. We have to constantly remind each core group about the importance of the planning meeting and why we are taking the time to meet together each week to plan for the Saturday night cell group.

We believe that the planning and coaching meetings are a key reason why our groups continue to reach out and multiply throughout the city. Our goal at Elim is to penetrate our city of San Salvador with multiplying cell groups. To make that happen, we need our people to be proactively involved in the process.

Mario's hero maker tip: Be patient and persistent in giving your leaders a chance to grow. I remember one of our pastors in an Elim branch church abroad took control of all the activities that were carried on in his congregation. He was in charge of the worship, then continued with the preaching, then collected the offering, then dismissed the people, and even provided counseling to those in need. When I asked him why he did this, he answered that he had to, because there was no one else in the church who could do these things as well as he could. He felt that in order to ensure that things were flowing properly, it was better for him to assume the responsibilities.

It was true that there were few people in his church who could do things as well as he could, but this was primarily because he had not created the environment for people to learn and grow. In his desire for control and perfection, he didn't provide the opportunities for people to effectively develop the skills to do the ministry. So the people settled in and became passive.

The same thing can happen at the cell group level when the leader does not allow the members to develop and grow as disciples through active participation. Things will not be done perfectly in the beginning, but we should only remember that this is the path we have all traveled at some point. If people who helped me had not given me the opportunity to try, fail, and try again, I never would have learned. It is essential to provide opportunities for people so that we can generate new disciples who in turn will generate new cell groups.[38]

The Apostle Paul Had the Same Message

I wonder if out of reverence for Jesus being divine, we sometimes dismiss his hero-making practices and think, *Well, that's because it's Jesus; he's God. Of course he's the best people developer in the universe.* So we admire how he mentored others who went out and changed the world, but we dismiss it as only possible for someone who is God incarnate. I've done that.

The apostle Paul didn't make that mistake. He heard Jesus' vision of God's kingdom, how we can bring that to be, and he recruited a young apprentice named Timothy (Acts 16:1–3). I love that Paul picked Timothy, because Timothy was a guy who didn't have a perfect life, and that makes him very relatable. Timothy's dad was not around; either he was an absentee father or he had abandoned Timothy and his mom altogether. Scripture describes Timothy as timid (1 Cor. 16:10–11). He was very apprehensive about whether his life could make an impact.

But Paul grabs him and even writes to him how they're going to change the world together: "The things you have heard me say in the presence of many witnesses entrust to reliable people who will also be qualified to teach others" (2 Tim. 2:2).

How many generations of apprenticeship do you see in that verse? Paul is saying, in effect, "Timothy, don't be content with being a Christ follower; think about others, the rest of the world. I know you have a hard time thinking about impact, but I want you to think *exponential* impact! Let's live our lives so as to impact at least four generations."

- First-generation apprenticeship: Jesus to Paul
- Second-generation apprenticeship: Paul to Timothy
- Third-generation apprenticeship: Timothy to "reliable people"
- Fourth-generation apprenticeship: "reliable people" to "others"

This verse calls us to mentor disciple multipliers to the fourth generation. That's exponential impact!

Paul was explaining to Timothy (and to us) that if we want to see disciples made in all nations—a movement of kingdom multiplication—it will happen through apprenticeship. Apprenticeship is the core competency of any movement of God.

What Paul discovered is the difference between impact and exponential impact. If we are Spirit led and committed to the mission, our lives can have an impact. But when we add the reproducing piece and even multiplying through apprenticeship, that is when exponential impact is possible. That's when we begin to see a movement of hero makers.

Simple Tool for Disciple Multiplication

FIVE STEPS OF APPRENTICESHIP

If Paul's goal of developing four generations of apprentices seems unreachable for you and your church, then I have good news for you. It is not. This goal is very doable if you and your church follow five simple steps.

I don't think I'm overstating my proposal: the simple tool I am about to give you is worth ten times the price of this book. This tool for disciple multiplication has the potential to exponentially increase the impact of your leadership. But you will get the value out of this tool only if you use it! Before you use this tool, pull out your dream napkin (the tool I gave you in chapter 5). Now ask, "Who are the specific people and leaders I want to develop now so that my dream napkin can become true someday?" Your next step is to take some of them through the five steps of apprenticeship.

Eric Metcalf is a disciple multiplier, and he has used the five steps of apprenticeship with other leaders as often as anyone I know. Eric doesn't shy away from a good challenge. The latest small group he led regularly drew sixteen people, and it was a challenge. Some were solid Christ followers; most were not. Some were single, some living together, and some married. Some partied really hard! And some were new believers, including one person with a Muslim background, another with a Jewish background (and a Catholic girlfriend), and another with practically no religious background at all.

You might imagine the lively discussions and lifestyle issues represented in those gatherings and conclude, "I think a pastor needs to lead a group like that!" Eric *is* the pastor for one of Community Christian Church's locations on the north side of Chicago. He and his wife, Erin, especially enjoy that group, but Eric knew he had a bigger calling than leading this diverse group alone. From day one, he was praying about which member (or members) he could train as an apprentice to take over this group or lead a new group.

"Hey, I have this idea, and I want to run it past you," Eric told the group. Then he continued, "For our group to reach more people, I'm going to ask some of you to consider moving into an apprentice leadership role and meeting with me on a weekly basis. We can meet for coffee or whatever, but during that time I will help you get to the place where you are confident and capable of leading a group." Grace, one of the Christ followers, said to Eric, "I really see a need to take some of the women in the group deeper into accountability with each other. I think I can help them do that, if you would let me lead them." Eric loved the idea, and she became his first apprentice.

Eric used the same simple five-step apprenticeship tool with Grace that he had used with dozens of other leaders over the years to help them grow in their leadership. Over the next eight months, Eric and Grace used these five steps as a guide to develop her to the place where she was leading her own group. Here's how it might have unfolded:

1. *I do. You watch. We talk.* As the experienced leader, Eric leads the group and tells Grace, "You just observe everything that happens in our small group, and then we will find a time to meet and discuss what you observed." Before the next small group meeting, Eric and Grace debrief, and this includes asking the following questions: "What worked?" "What didn't work?" and "How can we improve?" This time of debriefing needs to continue throughout the five steps.

2. *I do. You help. We talk.* In this step of development, Eric gives his apprentice, Grace, an opportunity to help lead part of the small group meeting. In this case, Eric asked Grace, "Could you lead the icebreaker time at the beginning if I lead the rest?" Grace agreed. Again, the small group meeting should be followed up with a one-on-one debrief between leader and apprentice.

3. *You do. I help. We talk.* Now Grace transitions from helping Eric to taking on most of the leadership responsibilities for the small group. Since Eric has had an exceptionally busy week, he takes the opportunity to ask Grace, "Could you lead most of the meeting this week? If you do, I will handle the icebreaker at the beginning and the prayer time at the end, plus I will be there with you the whole time." Grace agrees, and since she has seen him lead the group enough times, she feels very comfortable and does great. Eric is gradually releasing responsibilities to his new, developing leader.

4. *You do. I watch. We talk.* The apprentice process for Grace is almost complete as she grows increasingly more confident in her role as a leader. Eric has her lead the entire meeting each week while he watches her, and he gives her the responsibility of finding a service project for the group. At their debrief time, Eric says, "I think you are ready for leadership; do you think you are ready?" With a smile, Grace says, "I think I'm ready." With both leader and apprentice feeling ready for the

next step, they begin to plan whether Grace will take over the group or lead a new group, and what Eric will lead next.

5. *You do. Someone else watches.* This is where the process of multiplication comes full circle. Eric says, "Grace, you have done great! Have you started to think about who you can mentor and repeat this process with?" Grace says, "I already have two people who have expressed interest, and I'm meeting with one this week." Grace, the former apprentice, is now leading, and she begins developing new apprentices. Since Eric has developed and released several apprentices, he continues to work with Grace and other leaders in a coaching capacity.

The five steps to apprenticeship are really that simple! If you will constantly use these five steps, you can develop other leaders who will in turn already know how to develop other leaders. This is the second of five simple tools I offer (one per chapter), and they're all just as practical and accessible. My goal was to make each so easy that you'll conclude, "I could do that right now." And I hope you will.

A World of Disciple Multipliers in One Generation?

Let's wrap up the challenge to be a disciple multiplier with the stirring words of Admiral William McRaven, who, in a commencement speech, provoked graduates from the University of Texas with this exhortation: "If every one of you changed the lives of just ten people, and each one of those folks changed the lives of another ten people—just ten—then in six generations this class will have changed the lives of the entire population of the world, eight billion people."[39]

The admiral's words are a great challenge, not only for college graduates but for me, you, and the church! Since the church is far bigger than that graduating class, we've already got a running start. We've also got the Holy Spirit in us, and the God of the universe wanting it to happen. We can do it!

To change the world, we need to not only change people but also mobilize those people as change agents. If your efforts to mobilize people have ever felt like slot filling or just trying to get a task done, turn the page. By the end of the next chapter, you will discover a better way, through the hero-making practice of gift activating. I promise the fourth practice will be a blessing to you and to the people you are leading.

Hero Maker Discussion Questions

OPEN

- Who was a big spiritual influence in your life?
- In what ways did this person's influence involve ideas or practices of multiplication?
- What idea in this chapter is something you're doing well at?
- What was the biggest "Aha!" or "I need to work on that" for you from this chapter?

DIG

- Read 2 Timothy 2:2. If Paul gave you those instructions, how would you feel? Motivated? Overwhelmed? Why?
- Read John 3:22. In your ministry, how important is the idea of *diatribo*?
- Which statement is more true for you: "I do it if I have time" or "It's how I do ministry"? Explain.

REFLECT

- Who are some people you could mentor using the five steps of apprenticeship, starting today?
- Can you name some people your apprentice might be able to mentor?
- What's the most important action you'll take starting today, triggered by reading this chapter?

CHAPTER 8

Gift Activating

Big Idea: The practice of gift activating is a shift from asking God to *bless* the use of my own gifts to asking God to bless leaders whom I am sending out. Gift activating requires that we not fill slots but instead develop people's gifts and use simple tools like commissioning leaders to be sent out for ministry.

Blessing Dreams

"I dream of a different Chicago!" Duane Porter and his wife, Sauda, were being commissioned on a Sunday at a Community Christian location to plant a new church near where Duane grew up and around the corner from where Sauda worked as an elementary school principal. Duane said those words with the same conviction that Dr. Martin Luther King Jr. had voiced on the steps of the Lincoln Memorial. A recent *Chicago Tribune* headline had reported more than one hundred shootings and fifteen killed over a deadly holiday weekend. So when Duane shared his vision with such heartfelt passion, the auditorium erupted with applause.

When Duane and Sauda finished, they handed the microphone to Kingsley, another leadership resident at Community Christian, who was being commissioned to plant a multiplying church in his home country of Ghana. He started with a slow build. "I have seen churches planted, but only by adding one at a time." His enthusiasm grew. "But I'm going back to Ghana to help plant a reproducing church!" Then, with a full-throated shout, he yelled, "And I want to see my denomination begin to plant churches that reproduce churches. And I want to see reproducing churches all across the continent of Africa!" Again the auditorium was filled with applause.

Patrick O'Connell, the global director of NewThing, stepped forward and gave them two checks as a gesture of support. Then he challenged the people listening. "Maybe you are supposed to do more than applaud; if God is sending Duane and Sauda to the South Side and Kingsley to Ghana, maybe some of you are supposed to go with them! I want you to pray about that." Then he laid his hand on the shoulders of Duane and Kingsley while asking the rest of the church to reach out their hands as a sign of blessing. With every hand fully extended toward these three young people stepping into new leadership roles, we asked God to give them wisdom and provision. When Patrick finished his prayer and said amen, their apprenticeship as leadership residents was complete and their leadership gifts were fully activated.

Hero Making and Gift Activation

There is a direct connection between hero making and Duane, Sauda, and Kingsley being sent out to plant a church. It started with Community Christian's God-size dream that forced us into *multiplication thinking* (the first practice). This new way of thinking caused us to see the people God had put around us differently; we began to see leaders everywhere and started *giving them permission* (the second practice) through ICNU conversations. Soon *disciples were being multiplied* (the third practice) through apprenticeships in every ministry and at every level. Some of these apprenticeships lasted two months, some lasted a year, like Duane, Sauda, and Kingsley's leadership residency. What I described for you at the beginning of this chapter is the moment a leadership *gift is fully activated* (the fourth practice). It happens, in this case, with the laying on of hands and the blessing of leadership. (Figure 8.1 shows how all five practices fit together.)

The gift activation and the commissioning of a new leader can be as formal as a Sunday morning worship service in front of hundreds or as informal as a small group leader at a kitchen table giving a prayer and blessing to an apprentice who agreed to move into small group leadership.

I believe that gift activation occurs at a commissioning. What we have nicknamed the Great Commission in Matthew 28:19–20 was Jesus very specifically offering his authority and blessing to make more

FIGURE 8.1

A HERO-MAKING JOURNEY: GIFT ACTIVATING

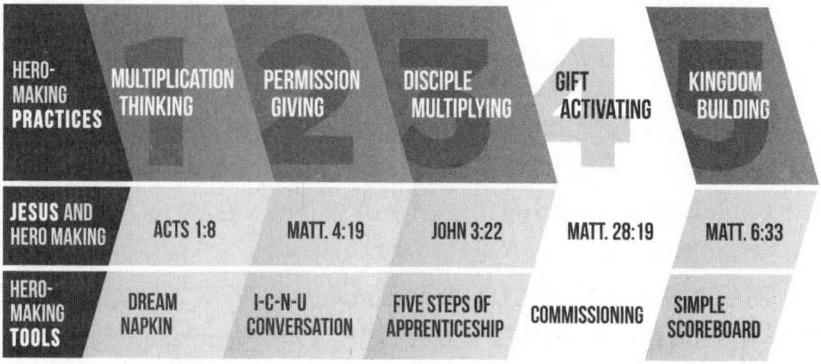

HERO-MAKING PRACTICES	MULTIPLICATION THINKING	PERMISSION GIVING	DISCIPLE MULTIPLYING	GIFT ACTIVATING	KINGDOM BUILDING
JESUS AND HERO MAKING	ACTS 1:8	MATT. 4:19	JOHN 3:22	MATT. 28:19	MATT. 6:33
HERO-MAKING TOOLS	DREAM NAPKIN	I-C-N-U CONVERSATION	FIVE STEPS OF APPRENTICESHIP	COMMISSIONING	SIMPLE SCOREBOARD

disciples, training them and baptizing them so they could join those who were already Christ followers.

In this case, Jesus commissioned eleven (his twelve apprentices minus Judas). I've seen gift activation occur with one person, two people, or thirty-one people at a time, as in my next story.

Never Seen That Before!

It was my first time at Nairobi Chapel, and I witnessed something I had never seen before. Their senior pastor, Oscar Muriu, and I had become good friends over the previous few years. He first contacted me after reading *Exponential: How You and Your Friends Can Start a Missional Church Movement*, telling me that the contents of the book perfectly described what he was doing and wanted to do. When he got invited to speak at Willow Creek's leadership summit in Chicago, he asked if I could meet him for lunch. I eagerly agreed, we totally hit it off, and that was the birth of a friendship. In time, he became a very important part of NewThing, providing us with apostolic leadership in Africa. I had him speak at Community Christian Church, and now at his request, I was in Nairobi to speak at his home church.

Nairobi Chapel is a large church[40] that does so many things well, but at the top of the list is mentoring and developing leaders and gift activation. Just prior to my teaching on that Sunday, Oscar invited to the stage thirty-one men and women who had just gone through the third and final track of their Kinara Leadership Program. As these graduates made their way up there, Oscar described their experience of apprenticing with experienced church leaders and spending time in the classroom learning from him and others. He went on to explain that the church was commissioning all thirty-one of these leaders to go and plant new churches in Kibera, the largest slum in Africa, located in Nairobi. He looked at the graduates, affirming his belief in their gifts and ability; then he looked at the congregation and asked them to join him in praying for them. As he prayed, he reached out his hand toward the new leaders to visibly express his blessing and great pleasure in what was happening. When the prayer concluded, the whole church sang out their approval and joy as thirty-one more church planters were commissioned for the Jesus mission.

Amazing! I have never seen that many church planters commissioned by one church on one Sunday! Pastor Oscar is a hero maker, and Nairobi Chapel is a hero-making champion continually activating and deploying the gifts of young leaders.

Gift Activation Gone Wrong

Back when spiritual gift inventories were all the rage, my coauthor, Warren Bird, did some research about where the process went south.

The sequence was fairly consistent. It typically started with the small groups or teaching team leading a church-wide emphasis on one of the New Testament passages that teaches that every believer has one or more spiritual gifts. Then everyone would be asked to complete a spiritual gift assessment, typically a survey that asks people how God has used them in the past, with a self-tally function that shows people which gift they're evidencing most often. Self-assessments are always interesting, and they left everyone with a sense of their gifts and eagerness for an assignment. So far so good, but the problems began with one of the following scenarios.

Scenario 1: "The Pile." In this church, the surveys were all collected and taken to the church office. The surveys were stacked in a pile on a desk and sat there and sat there and sat there . . . and are still sitting there. Many gifts were starting to be discovered, but none were activated.

Scenario 2: "Overwhelmed." In another church, the pastor didn't want the office to be the bottleneck, so after he preached a series on spiritual gifts, he asked everyone to take home a gift inventory and identify their gifts before the next Sunday. The following Sunday, the pastor asked for a show of hands and said, "Judging by what you learned, how many of you are *not* serving in your area of giftedness?" To his surprise, about 90% of the hands went up. He was instantly overwhelmed and couldn't imagine how to administrate that much change at once. So he didn't even try.

Scenario 3: "It Just Got Weird." In still another church, because of the emphasis on spiritual gifts, people began experimenting with their gifts, and some abuses occurred, such as disruptive worship and a preoccupation with gifts rather than a focus on the Giver—just as happened in some New Testament churches. The pastors and elders responded by shutting down the conversation on gift activation, saying, "We didn't realize that by inviting the Holy Spirit to show up, we were inviting chaos and weirdness too!"

Scenario 4: "Filling Slots." In yet another church, the staff eagerly grabbed all the surveys and held a draft. One after another, they took turns picking the name of the person who had filled out an assessment, not to help them activate their gifts but so they could contact them to ask them to fill a slot in their program. If you asked them why, they would tell you, "Without more volunteers, we can't continue our children's ministry (or first impressions team or fill-in-the-blank)." When they talked to volunteers, they would say, "It takes only a couple hours a week, and we really need your help." And if they got really desperate to fill a slot, they would add, "If you really love Jesus, you'll take your turn at volunteering for such-and-such ministry." It was all focused on running a successful program; that was the goal.

How Gifts Are Activated

What if we shift to an emphasis on people development? What if somehow running the existing program becomes secondary to helping people discover and activate their unique, God-given gifts? While assessments are good and helpful, they are not how spiritual gifts are activated. Hero makers understand that people are propelled into ministry, and gifts are activated, with a four-phase approach.

Assessments are good and helpful, but they are not how spiritual gifts are activated.

Phase 1: Dreaming big envisions gift activation. When we let God's Spirit inspire our imagination about doing greater things through others, we begin to envision the gifts of 100x more people being mobilized for mission.

Phase 2: ICNU initiates gift activation. It is in the moment of permission giving, when a leader says to someone, "I see in you . . ." and describes a preferable future, that the switch is flipped on for gift-based serving.

Phase 3: The five steps develop gift activation. It is in apprenticeship that gifts are tried and tested. Sometimes successfully, other times not so successfully, but this is a time of personal growth and discovery.

Phase 4: Commissioning fully activates gifts. When an apprentice thinks he or she is ready and the leader also thinks the person is ready, the new leader is ready to be released and have his or her leadership gifts fully activated. A commissioning, not unlike an ordination, happens when the leader lays on hands, prays, and asks God to bless the new leader's future ministry.

I will offer a few examples, and then at the end of this chapter, I'll give you a church-wide example of a commissioning service to help you become a stronger gift activator.

Start Them Young: Mentored and Commissioned

As a seventeen-year-old senior in high school, Obe Arellano found his way back to God and began taking his faith seriously. "I was so thirsty and hungry for more," he says. "As I focused on following God, I had big dreams. I knew that God wanted to do something big."

Obe (pronounced *Oh*-bee) recalls, "All I heard was no. I always felt like I was limited. I had no role model, no affirmation, and I got the strong message I was not experienced enough and not old enough. My pastor didn't mean to, but he kept shutting me down; I felt like I had no real gifts to be used."

A mentor from outside his church, Jose Cheng, would constantly say, "Obe, you have potential for more." He not only mentored Obe but also took him along on ministry events. On the way home one time, he told

Obe, "You have the leadership gifts and capacity to be a great pastor, and even to be a church planter." (Did you notice that both of these statements are examples of ICNU affirmations, which I introduced in chapter 6?)

Obe almost cried. "That rocked my world," he says. "I was only eighteen years old. I had felt like I didn't have permission to dream that big, being so young." Those words about his gifting were God's confirmation to Obe that he should pursue vocational ministry.

Obe continued to grow, he met and married a lovely woman, and together they dreamed of planting a church. When they thought the time was right, Obe left his job and they moved to the city of Aurora, Illinois, where they sensed God's calling. "We didn't know anyone there, and we didn't have any family there, but we sensed God wanted us there," he says. So he began meeting people, wanting to come alongside whatever God was already doing in that city.

At a pastors' prayer gathering, he met Kirsten Strand from Community Christian Church. She says, "I had a sense that Obe was the answer to our years of praying for the right person with the right gifts to help us launch a new location in Aurora."

Kirsten saw that Obe and his wife, Jack, were incredibly relational and connected equally well with first-generation undocumented immigrants and those who were more affluent. "Obe was sharp, articulate, passionate, and confident in a good way," she says. "Obe and Jack were incredible faith-filled risk takers and entrepreneurs." Using the ICNU approach that's second nature for many of our people at Community Christian Church, Kirsten gave permission for Obe and Jack to activate their gifting.

Obe and Jack began to explore a relationship with Community Christian Church, going through some of the training opportunities and ministry options that NewThing offered. When Obe came to understand the multisite church, he and Jack concluded, "That's what we've been dreaming about." Obe says that through a leadership residency, "a lot of people spoke confidence into my dreams, affirming my gifts and what God had shown me when I was eighteen!" Recalling the moment I approached him with the simple invitation to consider planting a location with Community, Obe says, "That blew my mind again."

Obe began to build a launch team and otherwise prepare. A few weeks before the opening day of the new campus, Obe, Jack, and the launch team were commissioned at one of our all-church leadership community meetings that brought together all our volunteer leaders and staff. "I was prayed for as an individual to lead the team to the best of my ability—and beyond, all with God's power and guidance—and ultimately to reproduce the mission in others," Obe says.

Obe planted a location in Aurora seven years ago, and along the way has poured himself into making heroes of other church-planting residents. One was a former worship pastor who was wrestling with God's call. "He had a restlessness, knowing he was supposed to do something but not knowing what." Obe encouraged him to do a leadership residency at Community Christian, through which he identified San Antonio as the place he should plant a church.

"I poured everything into him that I had received. It was a blessing for me to invest in someone, seeing their gifts come alive, as had mine. What joy that I, barely in my thirties, could already affirm the next generation of leadership," says Obe. Young Obe is becoming a hero maker.

Gift Activation through Tampa Underground

If Obe's story left you thinking that gift activation means finding a way into a church staff position, then let me offer the powerful marketplace example from Brian Sanders. He serves as the prime mover of the Underground, a family of church ministries based in Tampa, Florida, mostly led by bivocational people with a heart for Jesus and a love for what the church could become.

If Brian and his team of leaders are obsessed with anything, it is helping people find the calling and assignment God has given them, and then helping them follow through. They are gift activators.

They call these lay-led ministries microchurches. "The microchurch concept is entirely predicated on the idea of calling," explains Brian, who wrote a book called *The Underground Church*.[41] "For us, microchurches are not franchises like discipleship groups, cell groups, house churches, or even scaled parachurch ministries; they are customized and contextualized expressions of the church as unique as the people who start them."

Do you hear the idea of gift activation in that statement? That perspective has led them to activate the gifts of an amazing array of leaders, many starting microchurches focused on serving the poor. The target of these ministries ranges from at-risk youth to victims of the sex industry to the formerly incarcerated to refugees.

Brian and his team are making a difference, all of them heavily influenced by their focus on gifts and their willingness to dream boldly. They challenge people to ask the question, "What would you do if you were not afraid?" A microchurch starts with answering that question and obeying your calling. Then you build a community around that mission, with a focus on reaching people who are not encountering the gospel.

Brian explains what makes the Underground unique: "We are built to serve the needs not of the individual but of the *community* on mission. There is no way for an *individual* to join the Underground. Each microchurch is an expression of personal commitment and ecclesial innovation. This is not a strategy where we quickly reproduce the same thing. Each microchurch is a unique expression of the church that is as different as the people who start them."

Those who lead or support microchurches are known as missionaries, and about sixty Underground missionaries regularly office together in a rented workspace where about one thousand events are held each year. In total, some 175 microchurches are a part of the Underground, a number that has grown about 10% each year since their 2007 founding.

And yes, there is a commissioning moment. They wait one year so they know that the microchurch will last and the leader is committed. Then they formally commission them with laying on of hands and the community's blessing. This seems consistent with Paul's instruction, "Do not be hasty in the laying on of hands" (1 Tim. 5:22).

One outstanding example of a leadership gift activated and a microchurch coming to life was through Kathryn, a recent college graduate. Tampa Underground hired her for an administrative position, and when she met Brian, he asked her, "What is your deepest dream, your clearest sense of calling for your life?"

"I would love to one day run a free medical clinic," she quickly replied. Kathryn had a heart for the poor and for the healing a clinic could bring. Brian offered to help her pursue that dream, encouraging her as she went back to school for a master's degree in public health, raised money, and networked with medical professionals. As Brian saw her progress, he offered her two years of coaching to get the dream off the ground, and even allocated a portion of their existing facility to the new clinic. Brian spent two weeks of his vacation time to help her build it out.

Brian cheered with Kathryn at every milestone: when the clinic received its first big donation, passed county inspection, got their first doctor, and drew fifty patients on opening day. Brian now serves only in an advisory role but looks back on what Kathryn has done with pride, saying, "I love how this clinic has become a personal, dignified, inexpensive, evangelistic, and very real expression of the church."

Brian became a gift activator, in part, because others activated the gifts in him. Right out of college, Brian had, in his own words, "some really rough edges, but two courageous leaders at InterVarsity saw past my flaws and gave me a chance." They put him in a setting where they thought he would thrive most—an area with no InterVarsity ministry on a campus. "I loved the challenge to plant and pioneer," Brian says.

Looking back, he acknowledges that the leaders who mentored him found the just-right balance. "Even though I know I was often difficult and pushed against the system, they would both gently correct me and let me color outside the lines, try new and innovative things." That trust paid off, as it gave birth to the Underground. And now the Underground is making heroes of dozens and dozens of nonprofit leaders all over Tampa!

Simple Tool for Gift Activation

COMMISSIONING

God may never use you to send out thirty-one church planters in one day to represent Jesus in the slums. (But he might!) And you may never come alongside dozens of spiritual entrepreneurs and help them start nonprofits. (But it would be cool if you did!) But if you decide to be a hero maker, as Jesus promised his first followers, God will use you and those you influence to do "even greater things" (John 14:12). God will give you the opportunity to bless the people you are mentoring and activate their gifts through commissioning.

Commissioning is the simple process of blessing a person or team and affirming the use of the gifts God has given them. It will most likely involve two components:

1. Laying your hands on them as a sign of affirmation.
2. Praying for God to bless them as you send them out.

I have commissioned new small group leaders in a home. I have commissioned people who are leaving to start a new ministry or church at staff meetings in restaurants.

Commissioning can be done for a leader (or leadership team) starting a new group or team. It can be done for an individual (or a team) starting a new church. The commissioning is an important relational and personal blessing that hero makers give to those they are developing.

The first time we did a public commissioning at Community Christian, we were overwhelmed at the response. We concluded a message with the invitation, "If you believe God has called you to a specific ministry and would like to be anointed and prayed for, please come forward." We didn't have to wait long. Not just a few, not even a section, but the majority of the people got out of their seats and came forward. That happened not just at one service but at all of them that day. Wow!

It's now become an annual event at Community Christian Church. Once a year, we have a day on which we anoint and pray for everyone who wants to be commissioned for what we call the Jesus mission.

Once a year, we have a day on which we anoint and pray for everyone who wants to be commissioned for what we call the Jesus mission.

This Sunday celebration includes a commissioning for each of our small groups. We prime the group members by saying, "You need to be able to answer the question, 'Where and to whom are we commissioning you to go and bless the world?'" We make available a simple document that quotes Acts 13:2–4, where Barnabas and Paul are commissioned, and answers five questions:

- What is commissioning?
- Why should every group participate?
- Why commissioning?
- How can I create a culture within my small group where we live out the Jesus mission?

Then we ask anyone who wants to be commissioned to come to the front of the room where we are meeting, and we anoint them and pray for them. We consider it their ordination. In every way, we try to communicate, "We are for you, we are behind you as a church, and you have our blessing. Go out and accomplish that mission!"

We've done this for many years, and I am always blown away by the response. In particular, I'm stunned at how seriously they take this idea of being commissioned for a specific mission. Every year, I hear people say things like,

- "I don't want to merely coach my Little League team. I'm looking for opportunities to help many of those families find their way back to God."
- "We're going to adopt a child, joining many other Christian families who together dream of zeroing out our state's foster child waiting list."
- "I'm going to start a small group at work."
- "After going on three mission trips to Haiti, God's call is clear: we're going to move there, to make a difference."

Through the laying on of hands and praying a blessing on people, we convey a powerful message: if you are a Christ follower, we want to help you activate the unique gifts and calling that God has given you.

Hero Maker Profile: Joe Wilson

One of the most humble people I know is Joe Wilson. He was once a managing technician for an office supply company. But that is what he used to do! Since he became a Christ follower, a lot has changed. This friendly guy with a heavy Southern accent is now multiplying church-planting networks globally and is asking God to use his hero-making strategy to do it in every country on the planet!

I first met Joe at a gathering sponsored in Europe by Leadership Network, designed to help plant more than one thousand new churches over a five-year period. I was speaking on my book *Exponential*, which he had just read, and we hit it off. Joe had three big, burly Eastern European church planters with him, whom he introduced as "Dema, Dema, and Dema." After I laughed, one of them said, "And Joe's name in our language is also Dema."

Joe is partnered with NewThing and has a passion to plant churches and develop future leaders of Christianity in extremely underevangelized countries. It started in 2002, when Joe planted a single church in Minsk, Belarus, after starting an English as a Second Language school for Belarusians that offered practical help by teaching conversational English.

The government there shut down this church in 2005, forcing Joe to partner with a local church led by a like-minded Belarusian pastor. From this church, Joe helped catalyze a Belarusian team to plant churches. These efforts have grown from Belarus into other countries, like Russia, Albania, and nine others, where there have been 238 new churches started and twenty-three new networks.

Joe's secret weapon is gift activation. He always looks for Christ followers with apostolic impulses, leaders whom other organizations have ignored. He helps them fully activate their leadership gifts to convene other leaders, who then do incredible faith-stretching things together that none of them could have done alone. How does that work? Here is Joe's story in his own words.

Joe Wilson

NEWTHING
EASTERN EUROPE AND BEYOND

*From one church has birthed a vision
to catalyze a movement of reproducing
churches in the former Soviet Union*

As a young adult, I became a drug addict. If I had any money, I'd spend it shooting up cocaine and amphetamines. When I hit bottom, I asked God to help me. I knew that he was responsible for getting me off the drugs.

Three years later, at age thirty-one, I received Christ into my life. From that moment, I knew God had some kind of purpose for my life, but didn't know what. I felt God had called me to ministry, but there was no one to mentor me in my gifts. My church was happy for me to fill various volunteer slots they offered, but it didn't help me figure out how I was uniquely wired. No one provided a path for me to move forward.

After being a Christian for three years, I went through Henry Blackaby's *Experiencing God* book and was challenged by it to find out where God is at work and join it. Miami had been devastated by a hurricane, so I moved there with a group to plant a church. I learned the Blackaby book as I was practicing it. I began to identify the unique gifts that God had given me, and I saw that God could use someone like me to do things far beyond what I could ask or imagine, as Ephesians 3:20, one of my favorite verses, says.

A few years later, I was at a Bible study, and the passage was "The earth will be filled with the knowledge of the glory of the Lord as the waters cover the sea," (Hab. 2:14). That was the day the Lord put his finger on me, saying, "I want you on mission globally." That Sunday my pastor, not knowing anything about the Bible study I had attended, preached on the same verse with the same message. This was confirmation!

The book *Perspectives on the World Christian Movement* helped me find out more of what I was wired for, which was really apostolic ministry. God led me to go to Belarus to share Christ through an English as a Second Language ministry. It didn't really make sense, but I went and soon became involved with a local church there. By this point, I knew that I was good at Ephesians 3:20, getting people to practice big faith, and affirming, "You can do it!" When I see potential in someone, I affirm it. I would say things like, "God wants to do something great through you."

I try to do for others what I wish I had experienced. I look for hidden leaders, people no one else has spotted or believes in. My eyes are always peeled for people who haven't yet reached their potential, humble people with white-hot faith, who are contagious in a way that attracts others.

When I got the copy of Dave and Jon Ferguson's book *Exponential*, I read it in five hours. I was consumed with the message of the subtitle: *How You and Your Friends Can Start a Missional Movement*. I loved the simplicity. I resonated with the way Dave says, "You can do it." I still remembered my days of dreaming about God doing great things but everyone telling me that God couldn't do it through me—at least, that's the message I heard.

One of the people whose gifts I've helped to activate is Altin Kita. He was what I call an apostolic shepherd in hiding: someone with white-hot faith, a passion to do something great for God, and a contagious spirit that has drawn others around him. I helped him launch his second church, and I coached him to build an entire network of reproducing churches.

Within three years, Altin's teams had planted more than thirty churches across four countries. Altin hopes to reach the whole Balkan peninsula through this effort, and I believe his gifts are activated and in motion to do so!

Now I'm working in twelve countries. I find guys so much more talented than me, and I walk in their shadow. We operate together on mutual respect; I don't try to control them. I just try to help them figure out how to launch, structure, and develop a network. God tends to connect me at the point where they've gathered some people. I help them form the "together" part of it, and we begin helping each other extend God's kingdom—including the idea to cross borders into other countries. It's amazing the spiritual harvest that comes from the seeds that God has sown into so many people.

Joe's hero maker tip: People who want to move toward multiplication might want to read Steve Addison's book *Movements That Change the World*. It will help them know if they really want to go on this journey. It requires developing a white-hot faith that believes God for something they couldn't do themselves.

Also, they need to examine whatever ministry they lead to make sure they're focused on the right engine: reaching people far from God, bringing them to Christ, bringing them into the church, and developing them as leaders—who then develop other leaders. If you don't do those things well, you'll remain stuck where you are.

Exponential Commissioning

The last session of every Exponential conference for the past ten years has ended exactly the same—with a commissioning moment. I remember that the first year we did this, we had about six hundred attenders, and Gene Appel was the last speaker at the closing session. As Gene brought it to an end and music started to play, he said, "Some of you have felt God prompting you to plant a church. If that is you, we want to ask you in faith to come forward, and some of us who lead this conference want to lay our hand on you, anoint you as a sign of blessing, and pray for you. We are with you and for you!" And in some form every year, every closing speaker has issued the same challenge. The only difference is, now there are more than ten thousand attenders annually at our conferences, and we have more people come forward to be commissioned into church planting than were at our first conference. Could it be that some of that swell in numbers is because the churches that have been planted over the years have in turn raised up and activated other church planters?

I remember the first time I met Ryan Kwon, now the lead pastor at a California church named Resonate. I recall him telling me that it was at an Exponential conference that he came forward to be commissioned and made a commitment to plant a church. He was sitting in the middle balcony and decided to go forward, and it was then that his apostolic leadership gift was activated. Joby Martin, lead pastor at Church of Eleven22 in Florida (profiled in chapter 6), can point to the very place he was standing when he made a commitment to church planting at Exponential. He came forward, and Matt Chandler laid hands on him and prayed for him, and has since become a hero maker to him. Derwin Gray, lead pastor of Transformation Church in South Carolina (whose story is told in chapter 6), has told me the same story of making a commitment and being commissioned into church planting at Exponential.

I remember one year looking down from the stage, and my good friends Troy and Janet McMahon had come forward to be commissioned. I knew the talk of church planting had come to an end, and it was time for his leadership gift to be fully activated. I got to pray for them and bless them. What a great moment!

We have changed a lot of what we do at the Exponential conference, but the one experience that we have never changed is the commissioning moment to activate leadership gifts for planting new churches. Why? Because that is what hero makers do!

What's next? We've now covered four of the five essential practices of hero making: multiplication thinking, permission giving, disciple multiplying, and, in this chapter, gift activating. The next chapter, "Kingdom Building," is the one that will help your church or ministry have the greatest impact in robbing hell and populating heaven. Don't miss it.

Hero Maker Discussion Questions

OPEN

- Who has encouraged you to use your gifts? Is there some-one in your life who believed in you and your unique gifts more than you believed in yourself? If so, who and how?
- Which of the people in the stories about gift activation in this chapter do you most identify with or look up to? Why?

DIG

- Read Matthew 28:19–20 and then, without pausing, Acts 1:1–8. Where do you see gift activation and the sending out of leaders?
- Have you seen gift activation or commissioning practiced? If yes, how? If no, why not?

REFLECT

- Suppose you performed a commissioning, akin to what's suggested in this chapter, for your group, class, team, ministry, or entire congregation. What would it look like? When would you do it? What message would it convey?

CHAPTER 9

Kingdom Building

Big Idea: The practice of kingdom building is a shift from *counting* the people who show up at my thing to counting the leaders who go out and do God's thing. Kingdom building requires that we reject old ways of measuring success and use simple tools like a scoreboard that measures the number of current apprentices and total apprentices.

Unless you're really into high school basketball, you probably didn't hear the sad sports story that came out of Yukon, Oklahoma.[42] Two high school teams were playing in the first round of the state basketball championship playoffs. Hugo High was leading Millwood High 37–36 with less than four seconds remaining in the game. Hugo had the ball, and all they had to do was hold it and let four seconds tick off the clock. Then they'd advance in the tournament.

Hugo's star forward caught a pass, but instead of holding it, he took a shot—and made it. He raised his hands in victory and started running around the court, looking for teammates to celebrate.

Just one problem: he had just shot at the wrong basket and scored two points for the other team. He looked at the scoreboard and realized his team had just lost. The opponent, Millwood, had won 38–37.

I'm someone who played high school and college basketball, and also a parent who has coached his sons in basketball, so my stomach sank and my heart broke for that star forward. It was painful to watch the replay of him shooting at the wrong basket—and losing the game.

The application? Scoreboards never lie, even if the players get confused. Whether it's high school, college, or professional sports, when the time is up, the scoreboard tells you the truth. The scoreboard tells you the game's outcome.

That star forward probably didn't like what was on the scoreboard. It may not tell the whole story, but at least for basketball, it does tell you who won the game.

Churches Have Scoreboards

Hero makers and the churches they serve have scoreboards too, even if they're not as obvious as the one at a ball game. Most pastors and volunteer leaders I meet work very hard. But too often we're like that star forward. I sense confusion and disorientation in our efforts to win as we try to accomplish the mission of Jesus. Too many of us lack confidence and understanding of how we can put points on the scoreboard and know for sure that our church is winning and advancing the cause of Christ.

Let's narrow the focus for a moment to pastors. For too many, keeping score is a mystery. I hear more and more pastors questioning, "Is keeping track of attendance and the offering enough? How do we measure discipleship? What about community transformation? What about issues of justice? What about sending out missionaries? Should church planting count?"

This observation about pastors and church leaders was substantiated when I interviewed Warren Bird the researcher, long before we decided to work on this book. Leadership Network had just sent him out to interview 104 lead pastors, most of them leading what Leadership Network had determined to be the most innovative churches on our continent.[43]

When the study was done, I asked Warren what he took from those conversations. He told me, "Dave, the most significant takeaway is this: the leaders in those churches are looking for a new kind of scoreboard, a way to figure out what it means to win, especially in making disciple makers."

Did you hear that? Pastors and churches do want to win—and hero makers are no exception—but they're not satisfied with their current system of metrics. They want to advance the cause of Christ, but they aren't sure how to do it well, in terms of the most important scores to track.

That's what this chapter is about. As the graphics across this chapter

FIGURE 9.1

A HERO-MAKING JOURNEY: KINGDOM BUILDING

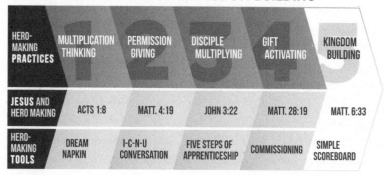

HERO-MAKING PRACTICES	MULTIPLICATION THINKING	PERMISSION GIVING	DISCIPLE MULTIPLYING	GIFT ACTIVATING	KINGDOM BUILDING
JESUS AND HERO MAKING	ACTS 1:8	MATT. 4:19	JOHN 3:22	MATT. 28:19	MATT. 6:33
HERO-MAKING TOOLS	DREAM NAPKIN	I-C-N-U CONVERSATION	FIVE STEPS OF APPRENTICESHIP	COMMISSIONING	SIMPLE SCOREBOARD

show, after looking at the role of kingdom building in Jesus' ministry, I want to help you create a new scoreboard grounded in solid theology and ministry practice, one that can tell your church whether God's kingdom is winning and whether the mission of Jesus is being advanced. It's about how to keep score of kingdom work. Clue: it's more than just counting people, but neither is it acting like people don't count!

Kingdom Winning

Jesus was all about the kingdom of God. Not only did he speak of it constantly, but he told his followers to make it a priority. Our Lord and hero maker said, "Seek first the kingdom of God" (Matt. 6:33 ESV). So how do we win at doing so?

Part of the reason people like winning is because winning equals success. This is where it gets tricky, because kingdom winning is not necessarily the same as this world's view of success. Jesus said that in his kingdom, the first will be last and the last will be first (Matt. 20:16). He also taught that whoever wants to be great has to be a servant (Matt. 20:26). The apostle Paul said that God chooses the foolish things of the world to shame the wise, and the weak things of the world to shame the strong (1 Cor. 1:27). You can probably think of additional verses that illustrate ways that Jesus' kingdom "is not of this world" (John 18:36).

There's also a strong theme in Scripture of faithfulness to God as a pathway of winning. Hebrews 11 is nicknamed "the spiritual hall of fame."

It uses the word faith thirty-three times, showing that by faith people conquered kingdoms, administered justice, shut the mouths of lions, quenched the fury of flames, escaped the edge of the sword, and more. Wow, almost anyone today would call that success. But the same chapter says that by faith people faced jeers and flogging, people were chained and put in prison, and people were stoned, sawn in two, or put to death by the sword. That's not how most people picture winning, but to God it was. "These were all commended for their faith," the chapter concludes (Heb. 11:39). To God, winning is faithfulness. Winning is a life that ends up with God saying, "Well done, good and faithful servant!" (Matt. 25:21)—words found in one of the parables telling us what the kingdom of God will be like.

In short, the more you read the Bible and the better you get to know Jesus, the more you understand that kingdom winning is not synonymous with the achievement and accomplishment prioritized in the Western world. So take a deep breath and breathe in God's grace. You don't have to be successful, only faithful.

If faithfulness is the sole measure of winning, that leaves the question, what must we be faithful in being and doing? Seeking first the kingdom of God, which I mentioned at the beginning of this section. If we are faithful in doing that, everything else falls into place. Our seeking starts on a very personal level, as this passage specifically deals with God's cure for our anxieties about daily provision. It reminds us that material provision is not unimportant, but our first motivation must be the will of God, which is to advance his kingdom. But the principle of this verse applies far beyond as we view all of life and ministry as seeing God's kingdom—his rule and reign (Luke 17:20–21)—take captive every spiritual stronghold as people respond to the gospel.

It is clear that Jesus' scoreboard is solely focused on advancing the kingdom of God. Notice the priority of God's kingdom in these verses:

- "Your kingdom come . . . on earth as it is in heaven" (Matt. 6:10).
- "As you go, proclaim this message: 'The kingdom of heaven has come near'" (Matt. 10:7).
- "I must proclaim the good news of the kingdom of God to the other towns also, because that is why I was sent" (Luke 4:43).

- "What shall we say the kingdom of God is like, or what parable shall we use to describe it? It is like a mustard seed, which is the smallest of all seeds on earth. Yet when planted, it grows and becomes the largest of all garden plants, with such big branches that the birds can perch in its shade" (Mark 4:30–32).

As I read the Gospels and compare them with leadership conversations today, I hear more about personal mission statements and churches' visions and goals, while Jesus seems to talk more about faithfulness to building the kingdom.

Counting Derrieres and Dollars

In many churches today, we limit ourselves to just a couple of measures: attendance and offering (also known as nickels and noses, butts and bucks, crowds and cash, or derrieres and dollars).

Beyond that it gets fuzzy. In fact, at a recent dinner I had with Todd Wilson and Warren Bird, Todd said to Warren, "Someone recently tweeted that you've done more large-church site visits than anyone alive, so here's my question: If all churches count finances and attendance, what's the third most popular metric?"

It was fun to watch Warren stutter! He eventually affirmed that there's no widespread agreement. We ultimately agreed, pooling all our experience, that the third most common scoreboard measure has something to do with measuring leadership development, often indirectly by how many people are involved in a church's small group communities, which go by lots of different names.

Jesus could never be accused of counting only crowd size and cash on hand. Instead his scoreboard—the measurement he spoke about most often—involved the gospel, the good news of the kingdom. This seems to be his way of measuring his mission "to seek and to save the lost" (Luke 19:10).

Jesus could never be accused of counting only crowd size and cash on hand.

Jesus had a full and powerful ministry. He healed the sick, showed compassion on those in need, proclaimed freedom to the oppressed, and otherwise modeled a perfect life of love for God and for people. But I believe that winning for him, according to Scripture, was measured most in multiplying God's kingdom.

In Need of a New Scoreboard

I remember going to a little rural church with my grandparents in Farber, Missouri. It had a wooden plaque on the wall that was updated every week. It was titled something like "Register of Offering and Attendance," and it gave the stats from the previous week and one year ago, enabling people to compare. No doubt, people felt that as long as the current numbers were increasing, then the church was winning. Many of us do the same thing today with spreadsheets.

But there are potential problems if the two categories of cash and crowds alone are our primary scoreboard.

It is entirely possible for a church's attendance to be growing, while the kingdom of God is shrinking. Today there are more people attending church on any given weekend in the United States than ever before. We could conclude that U.S. church attendance is growing, and therefore we must be winning, right? Wrong! While more people are attending church than ever before, it's a smaller percentage of the total population, a population that continues to grow with people who need Jesus. If we become content with that scoreboard measure, we'll never accomplish the mission of Jesus.

Also, it's entirely possible for a church's attendance to be growing, but the impact of the church is shrinking. I believe God is interested in a neighborhood's crime rate, the percentage of people living below the poverty level, the high school graduation rate, and more. Won't people who love God and love their neighbors—people whom Jesus calls the light of the world and the salt of the earth (Matt. 5:13–16)—make their community a better place?

It is entirely possible for a church's attendance to be growing, while the kingdom of God is shrinking.

In addition, church attendance says nothing qualitative about personal spiritual transformation. A church's growing attendance does not promise that people are growing spiritually. Attendance graphs that are up and to the right don't guarantee that people are faithful in following Jesus.

I'm not saying we should stop counting. Jesus and the New Testament writers counted people. I believe numbers simply represent people without showing their faces. Even references like those in Acts that say the church grew imply someone was counting, because otherwise eyewitness-dependent Dr. Luke, who penned Acts, couldn't make such statements.

My friend Reggie McNeal wrote the Leadership Network Series book *Missional Renaissance: Changing the Scorecard for the Church*.[44] I love the three shifts he suggests churches need to make.

1. Shift from an internal focus to an external focus. This means the church does not exist for itself. We exist primarily to do ministry beyond ourselves.

One of our sites at Community Christian Church is on the north side of Chicago, in a very diverse neighborhood. This new location understands what it means to be externally focused. For more than a year before ever having a celebration service, the campus pastor and his team volunteered every week in the local elementary school and at the alderman's office. When we had the first celebration service at a local elementary school, the place was packed not only with people who were part of Community but also with people who were part of several other nonprofits that we honored. During that prior year, we had built relationships with the school, the alderman's office, a garden project group, an environmental group, and others. Each of those partnerships was part of our grand opening, with booths set up in the hospitality area for volunteer recruitment. This new site of Community was both in and for the neighborhood from the very beginning.

2. Shift from program development to people development. Reggie rightly observes that over time, the North American church has largely become a collection of programs run by staff or lay leaders. The downside is that this emphasis has led to a scoreboard assessment of how well the programs are doing, not how well the people are doing. As Reggie says, "If instead you start with people, the programs then serve the people, not the other way around."

It's my conviction that the best kind of people development happens through apprenticeship, because that's a life-on-life relationship in which one person invests in another. That's why I devoted an entire chapter

(chapter 7) to the kind of disciple multiplication that resulted in the five-step tool for apprentice multiplication.

At Community Christian Church, we track and report every month how many apprenticeships are taking place and what percentage of our leaders have apprentices. That speaks to our commitment to people development and leadership development.

3. Shift from church-based leadership to kingdom-based leadership. Leading a movement is very different from leading an organization. Christianity was largely a street movement in its early days, when it turned the world on its head. Once we institutionalized it and put it largely into the hands of the clergy, we lost the virility of that movement.

At Community Christian Church, we try to measure kingdom-based leaders by what we call the family tree. Annually, each campus is asked to account for the attendance of not just their campus but all the campuses and churches they have helped plant and reproduce.

A great example comes from our Montgomery campus. It has a 1960s church building that was given to us and seats almost 200 people. Every weekend, they have two Sunday services and average about 350 in attendance. But if you look at their family tree, that metric reveals that they average a weekly outreach of more than 1,400 because of two campuses they have launched locally, as well as a church they planted in Boston.

Confusing the Scorecard with the Scoreboard

I remember the first Major League Baseball game I ever saw in person. My dad took me to Wrigley Field in Chicago, where the hometown Cubs played the St. Louis Cardinals. He bought me a scorecard and a pencil and showed me how to score the game. You could track dozens of stats on that scorecard: AB (at bats), 1B (single), 2B (double), 3B (triple), BB (base on balls), HR (home run), RBI (runs batted in), and lots more.

My love for baseball and stats might be why the movie *Moneyball* instantly became one of my favorites. In it Brad Pitt plays the part of Billy Beane, the general manager of the Oakland A's baseball team. The Oakland A's were a team in a small market with few resources, competing against big-market, big-budget teams like the New York Yankees and the Boston Red Sox.

It seemed that Beane and his team of underpaid overachievers could never become winners, but Beane knew there had to be a way. Beane meets young, Yale-educated brainiac Peter Brand, whom he hires to help him run his baseball team. Through statistical analysis, Brand offers Beane a brand-new strategy to win. "Your goal shouldn't be to buy players but to buy wins," Brand explains, "and in order to buy wins, you need to buy runs."

As obvious as it may sound, this was not how scouting had been done. Scouts largely recruited and drafted players by their general, overall feel about a player. But Brand wanted his scouts to forget how good players looked, how big they were, or even how fast they ran. The only stat and measurement that mattered was whether a player could cross home plate or help other teammates do so.

Billy Beane and Peter Brand changed the game of baseball forever, as the Oakland A's went on to have the longest winning streak in American League baseball history.

Church leaders are somewhat like those old-time baseball scouts. We have lots of impressions and stats about all kinds of things, mostly good things. I interviewed dozens of church leaders, and here are just some of what churches count.

- The number of people who attend a worship service
- The number of people who are in a small group
- The number of people who are serving both within the church and outside the church
- The number of people who are going through an apprenticeship
- The number of leadership residents, or people being trained to plant new churches or campuses
- The number of people who are in a small group that have a written mission statement and are commissioned
- The number of new churches or campuses started
- The number of people in new churches and campuses that the church started
- The number of first-time givers to the church
- The amount of money given to the church
- The amount of money given to organizations outside the church

- The number of other churches or nonprofits with whom you partner
- The number of missional communities
- The number of applications received for microgrants to fund community service projects
- The number of baptisms in a year
- The number of people who became a part of the church through personal invitation or connection
- The number of people who are customers of your café
- The number of people you send out from your church to other parts of the world as kingdom leaders
- The amount of resources you give away to invest in global engagement
- The number of relationships your congregation has with people who are unchurched
- The frequency with which your people connect with others in "third places" in their communities
- The number of volunteer hours you invest in the community
- The number of people who have completed a life plan and are pursuing it
- The number of invitations to events and outings received from non-Christians
- The number of new relationships formed in which people know each other's names
- The number of community-based initiatives your people are supporting with their time and money
- The number of leaders you are developing
- The number of Bibles purchased and given away
- The number of people who share their spiritual story
- The number of groups that are reproducing
- The number of people who are in small groups
- The percentage of people in a small group or missional community
- The percentage of people who are serving in a ministry or in the community

- The percentage of leaders who have an apprentice
- The number of people in intentional discipleship relationships
- A decrease in crime in a community
- A decrease in the number of children living under the poverty level
- The percentage increase in home ownership in a community
- The percentage increase of students graduating from high school
- The decrease in the percentage of marriages ending in divorce
- The number of people who have led or engaged in cross-cultural trips
- The number of significant legislative or policy changes influenced
- The number of people in recovery
- The number of children adopted by members of the church
- A decrease in the number of children waiting to be adopted in your city
- The number of children sponsored
- Dollars spent per person being discipled
- Dollars spent per person baptized
- The number of life-change stories that can be shared with the church
- The percentage of the budget given to causes outside the church
- The percentage of people with a self-identified mission
- The number of conversions
- The number of new and consistent givers
- The number of people who read through the Bible in a year
- The number of people who completed a Bible reading plan

In all our counting, I believe we have missed what matters most: Is the kingdom of God advancing? Kingdom building is the church's equivalent of baseball's runs.

My friend Dave Travis, a thought leader regarding the future of the church, made a very helpful observation about the church and keeping score: "Churches have to be careful not to confuse the scorecard with the scoreboard," he said. "The scorecard offers you lots of important and interesting stats that you can track, but the scoreboard tells you whether you are winning or losing the game."

So what should we count? And how do we keep track of kingdom building? Great question! Keep reading; I'm going to give you a simple scoreboard for hero-making churches and a simple tool for hero makers.

Simple Scoreboard for Hero-Making Churches

At Community Christian Church, we agree that you need to count the number of people who are attending, and we also keep track of dollars and cents. But we don't quit there. We prioritize two other measurements that lead to kingdom building: disciple making and movement making.

Let me explain these two ways of fueling and measuring growth in the kingdom of God.

1. MEASURE DISCIPLE MAKING

Are we making disciples? Isn't that what the Great Commission is all about? For the church, this is how we score runs. If we do this, we win. If we don't, we lose—even if our other metrics are great.

That question, "Are we making disciples?" isn't as easy as it appears, because it means I must first offer a definition: what is a disciple of Jesus? Besides all the good teaching in Scripture, volumes have been written on it.

The biggest mistake you can make as a leader is to ignore that definition. If you can't answer the question, "What is a disciple of Jesus?" you'll never know if your church is winning.

If you can't answer the question, "What is a disciple of Jesus?" you'll never know if your church is winning.

After answering the question, the next step is to boil down the definition to a few key measurements. You won't be able to measure every nuance of what it means to be a disciple, so don't try. Instead select a few of the key attributes and make those what you measure.

It was several years ago at Community Christian Church that we set out to create our very first scoreboard. After prayer, thoughtful study, and conversation, we concluded that a disciple is someone who is apprenticing with Jesus. We like the term apprentice because it implies a relational way of learning that includes both knowing and doing. Too often churches have made the mistake of equating discipleship with taking a series of classes or only gaining cognitive knowledge.

With that understanding of discipleship, we began to get more precise about a simple and measurable definition of an apprentice of Jesus. We determined that the simplest way of describing a disciple was to consider three primary, growing relationships. We call them the three 3Cs, and we find them throughout Scripture. One passage that embodies all three is the first description of the early church's activities, in Acts 2:42–47: "They devoted themselves to the apostles' teaching and to fellowship, to the breaking of bread and to prayer.... They broke bread in their homes and ate together with glad and sincere hearts, praising God and enjoying the favor of all the people."

We see those early apprentices of Jesus experiencing three primary relationships: celebrating, connecting, and contributing. (See Figure 9.2.)

FIGURE 9.2

 CELEBRATE: The focus here is our relationship with God, referenced above with words like "devoted themselves to the apostles' teaching" and "the breaking of bread." We measure this by weekly participation in celebration (worship) services.

 CONNECT: The focus here is growing our relationship with others in the church, referenced above with words like "fellowship." We measure this by participation in and doing life with a small group.

 CONTRIBUTE: The focus here is growing our relationship with those in our community and world who need to find their way back to God, referenced above with words like "enjoying the favor of all the people." We measure this by participation through serving in ways that advance the mission of Jesus.

When a Christ follower is celebrating, connecting, and contributing, we call them 3C. On a monthly basis, I get an update on our dashboard of how many 3C Christ followers we have and how that number has grown from the month and year before. I will be the first to admit that the 3Cs do not cover every aspect of what it means to apprentice with Jesus, but it is our simple and measurable response to the question, "What is a disciple?"

2. MEASURE MOVEMENT MAKING

When we first sat down as a group of friends from college and dreamed about what Community Christian Church could become, we scratched out the following three-phase dream on the back of a restaurant napkin.

Phase 1: Impact church
Phase 2: Reproducing church
Phase 3: Movement of reproducing churches

The most recent addition to Community's scoreboard is a metric to help us determine whether we are winning in our efforts toward phase 3 of our dream, to catalyze a movement of reproducing churches.

To measure movement making, again, you must first define it. As challenging as it is to define a disciple, defining a movement is even tougher. One of the best definitions I've seen comes from the research of Ed Stetzer and Warren Bird. In *Viral Church*, they define a church-planting movement as "a rapid multiplication of churches where a movement grows through multiplication by 50% in the number of churches in a given year to the third generation. For example, if they are 100 one year, they are at least 150 the next, and that growth is accounted for mostly by new converts, not transfers. Finally, this kind of growth continues to the third generation." While that is a very helpful definition to a network or denomination, I think a local church needs a simpler metric. We keep track of our movement-making efforts using the following three simple measurements.

1. *Apprentice leaders.* Apprentice leaders are people in training to lead small groups and ministry teams. These are entry-level leaders who oversee groups and teams of approximately four to twenty people. It is leaders who ensure that disciple making is happening,

and these apprentice leaders ensure that there are more and more people who will take the lead in making sure the movement is moving. At the core of every kind of movement is apprenticeship.

2. *Leadership residents.* Leadership residents are church planters in training. A residency lasts from six to twelve months. This high-level apprenticeship is the key mechanism for movement making. In an effort to catalyze a movement of reproducing churches, we challenge each of our campus pastors to have one leadership resident per year. An important movement-making measurement is our number of apprentice church planters, or leadership residents.

3. *Family tree.* The family tree is your church's weekly attendance plus the weekly attendance of all the churches you have planted. This metric was inspired by my mentor and friend Bob Buford. I've heard him say a hundred times, "My fruit grows on other people's trees." That is the hero maker's mindset, and that is what it takes if you want to see a movement. To plant new trees, which in this case is starting new churches, requires sending leaders, people, and resources. We wanted our scoreboard to reward and not penalize our campuses for sending money and people to start new campuses and new churches, so we came up with the metric called family tree. We are discovering that an important movement-making measurement is to determine how many people are part of each family tree.

Does counting apprentice leaders, leadership residents, and the church attendance of our family tree ensure we will catalyze a movement of reproducing churches? I have a strong conviction that it will, but only time will tell. However, I do know this for sure: now that we are keeping score of these three movement-making metrics,

My fruit grows on other people's trees.

—BOB BUFORD

we have a greater opportunity to see it happen than we did when we were not! So go ahead and ask the question, "What does it take to catalyze a movement?" Answer the question in a way that is simple and measurable, and add it to your scoreboard. If we want to see the mission of Jesus accomplished, it will come through a movement of multiplying churches.

I'm Playing to Win

My conviction about playing to win when it comes to the kingdom of God continues to grow. For the past several years, I've had the opportunity to provide leadership for Exponential as the president of the conference and chairman of the board. As I mentioned in the introduction to this book, I work alongside Todd Wilson, full-time director and CEO of Exponential, the mastermind who has taken this once-small church-planting conference and grown it to become the largest church-planting conference in the world (that we know of). The growth has been a tremendous grace from God and simply amazing.

It was after the Exponential East conference sold out for the first time that the question came to me: "How do we know whether the Exponential conference is really winning?" My first reaction was, "We just sold out and had tens of thousands of people joining us via webcast!" I continued to think, "It is the largest church-planting conference anywhere!" Then I told myself, "We are able to offer registrations to church planters at a very low price and still break even!" I concluded, "If we have more people attending than ever, and we have a model that is financially self-sustaining, we *must* be winning!"

That's when it hit me: "Dave, you are only measuring nickels and noses. How do you know whether Exponential is mentoring and deploying new church planters? How do you know whether Exponential is accomplishing its mission? How do you know that this conference is being used to accelerate movements?" I immediately sought out Todd. I said, "Todd, remember that conversation we had on the airplane when you challenged me to start measuring the things that I say really matter?"

He said, "Sure, I remember."

I had him right where I wanted him. "Todd, this time I want to challenge you. We say that what really matters to Exponential is mentoring church planters and advancing the mission of Jesus by accelerating movements, but right now we are only measuring butts and bucks. We need a new way of keeping score. How do we really know we are winning?"

Todd smiled and nodded his head in total agreement.

It was this conversation that led Todd and me to our four-to-ten mission. We refused to settle for a derrieres-and-dollars metric. Realizing that only 4% of all churches in the United States ever reproduce, we determined to put all our efforts and energy into moving the needle to 6%, then 8%, and ultimately 10%. That is our big dream. And the scoreboard of the Exponential conference is primarily measuring not how many people show up or how many people pay admission but how many churches are Level 4 and 5 churches! Why? Because a scoreboard will tell us whether we are winning; the scoreboard never lies.

Kingdom Builder Profile from India

I've told you what I do at Community Christian Church and at Exponential, but let me give you examples from other contexts. For instance, if any country of the world gives Christians a good excuse to hunker down, circle the wagons, and look out for their own, it's India. Mob violence and other persecution readily tempt Christ followers there to live in fear and to focus on watching your own back. At present, Christianity in all its forms is officially less than 3% of the population and, sadly, is an unpopular minority. Various government documents describe Christians as *enemies of the nation*, "and the phrase is common in the public discourse in social media," summarizes Vijayesh Lal, executive director of Evangelical Fellowship of India, in his annual report on hatred and targeted violence against Christians in that country.[45]

On my most recent trip to India, I spoke with Vijayesh. I expressed my concern, asking what we can do. He responded, "Don't pray that the persecution stops, because it is advancing the mission of Jesus! Instead pray that we will have the courage to withstand it."

That was one of the most courageous statements I have ever heard.

Vijayesh is not alone. One of the brightest lights in India, illuminating that country with the good news about Jesus, is his friend and mine Dr. Ajai Lall, pastor and missions pioneer, currently serving as director of Central India Christian Mission. In a coincidence of history, the home in which he was raised is the same house which earlier had been the home of global missions leader Donald McGavran, author of *Bridges of God*. As you hear Ajai's story, notice how his focus remains on being a kingdom builder.

Ajai Lall

CENTRAL INDIA CHRISTIAN MISSION
MADHYA PRADESH, INDIA

His "extremist" faith has seen twenty-five
hundred churches planted—with five hundred
thousand believers—in one generation.

My country of India is full of extremists: Hindu, Islamic, Maoist, and more. I have friends who were beaten or raped simply because they claim the name of Christ. Some of our church planters have been persecuted or even tortured in horrifying ways. I've been in a big city going to an appointment when a terrorist explosion was so close that the police made me turn around. My family has been attacked by several gunmen. Even Christian acts of kindness are being rejected, such as ending the decades-long child sponsorship programs by Compassion across India, closing 589 centers that were serving 145,000 children, funded by $45 million in annual donations.[46]

I believe that Jesus wants each of his followers to be Christian extremists, but of a different type. Not one who uses explosions or violence, but someone who shows an extreme love and compassion to enemies and prays for those who persecute us. If I don't have a heart of forgiveness, I am lost.

When my wife and I started our ministry thirty-five years ago, we wanted to be among people who have never heard about Jesus Christ. I had prayed to be in a situation that's challenging, where there's not enough vision of evangelizing and where baptisms happen only rarely. So we started in a difficult area of central India, one where less than 1% of the inhabitants are Christians. We wanted to preach and demonstrate Jesus' love and forgiveness.

Through those years, more than twenty-five hundred churches have been planted through the ministry of CICM, which now oversees a full-time staff of more than eleven hundred people serving more than five hundred thousand believers who are worshiping the Lord Jesus Christ all over India and the surrounding countries.

We have also started three regional centers in strategic areas, each offering full-time training to workers reaching out to the most unreached people groups. These church planters regularly risk their lives among terrorists and other violent extremists, where evangelists have been killed but people have not yet heard of Jesus.

In recent years, we've become a partner with NewThing. It's a great encouragement to us because sometimes you feel lonely, like you are Timothy without Paul. Working together is like a filling station. It also gives us a feeling that we are helping each other on global goals of planting churches. It reminds us of the bigger picture—that we make sure that before we die, every person knows about Jesus. We want to make an eternal impact as we say, "Follow me as I follow the model of Jesus."

India has the world's fastest-growing number of people. We add one "Australia" to our population every year. With such a great task, and so many open doors even through the persecution, how could we not develop the kind of churches that multiply?

Ajai's hero maker tip: To help people move toward multiplication, I encourage them to see things in light of eternity, to keep moving forward, and to never ever give up. I might have to sacrifice my life, and you might lose yours as well.

Your vision must go beyond what you can do to what God wants to do. We never looked into our resources; we never checked our pocketbook. God makes his presence known as you move forward. We must say, "It's not my life but your life; it's not about me but about you."

One of our preachers was tied up, and his attackers made him watch as they raped his wife. Some while later, this pastor told me about their most recent baptisms, which included the people who had brutalized them. This pastor and his wife had visited their attackers, prayed for them, and forgiven them. Only the love of Christ could motivate their actions.

Likewise, if I want to see the multiplication of hero makers, I must preach not just from my lips but from my life. As I live out what I preach, I must be "extreme" in pouring my life into others.

If I can do it with the help of God, you can too, wherever you serve. We stand together. We serve a great God.

Whew! See why I wanted Ajai to be the profile in this chapter? He is a great example of a multiplication thinker (the first practice of a hero maker). He always thinks about how to multiply and has always pursued big dreams. You can imagine his dream napkin saying something like, "Tell everyone in India about Jesus while showing them extreme love and forgiveness."

He also is a permission giver (the second practice). You can just hear him affirming those church planters with ICNU statements like, "If God is with you, then you can go anywhere and boldly proclaim Jesus without fear!"

Further, he models being a disciple multiplier (the third practice) with his emphasis on making disciples who make disciples. The level of commitment exhibited by the leaders he has multiplied is unlike anything I've seen in the West. They're actually building the five steps of apprenticeship into their training curriculum.

He's also a gift activator (the fourth practice) as he commissions most graduates of their centers to plant a church. And he excels as a kingdom builder (the fifth practice), putting all his efforts into developing leaders and church planters and advancing the kingdom. Can't you feel his burden and passion for people who have never heard the gospel or seen it lived out? His scoreboard emphasizes how many people have become disciples of Jesus.

Simple Tool for Kingdom Building

SIMPLE SCOREBOARD

Now it's your turn. Like Ajai's scoreboard, yours will help you focus on being a hero maker and not the hero.

You must also make sure you don't confuse the many stats on a scorecard with the most important statistic of "runs scored" on a scoreboard that tell you whether you are winning. And a winning scoreboard for a hero maker must show that you are faithfully building the kingdom. It will focus not on who is coming to your thing but rather on who is doing God's thing. For pastors and church leaders, it will shift priorities from counting how many you are *seating* in your church to counting how many you are *sending* out on mission.

I don't want you to shoot at the wrong basket, so let me suggest that as a hero maker, you keep track of only two measurements: first, how many apprentices you have; second, how many total apprentices you and your apprentices have developed. This is a simple scoreboard that you can easily keep on your phone, your laptop, or even a scrap of paper. Let me explain these two kingdom-building stats.

FIGURE 9.3

NOW		FUTURE	
TODAY	Number of Apprentices	Next yr	5 yrs
	Current Total		
	Cumulative Total		

1. Measure Current Apprentices

Ask yourself these questions: "How many people am I investing in?" "How many people am I mentoring to be commissioned to do great things?" "How many people am I taking through the hero-making process?" Apprenticing relationships are not hard to count. Usually leaders have only a handful of apprentices at a time. Jesus had twelve. I doubt I've ever had that many at any one time.

If you are a small group leader and you are developing an apprentice, that is one. If you are a ministry leader and you have a team of four whom you are growing and meeting with regularly to expand their ministry, that would be four. If you are a lead pastor and you have an apprentice in your small group, a leadership resident who is going on to plant a church, and your executive staff team of five whom you hope grow beyond you, that would be a total of seven.

This is intentionally simple but ultimately important. The first measurement on a hero maker's scoreboard is how many people you are mentoring.

2. Measure Cumulative Apprentices

The second measurement on a hero maker's scoreboard is the total number of apprentices that you and your apprentices have ever developed and released. The most proficient of hero makers have a hard time keeping track of this second measurement. That should be your goal—you develop so many leaders who develop so many leaders who develop so many leaders that you have lost count after the fourth generation.

However, until you get past the fourth generation, I would encourage you to keep track. When we started Community Christian Church, each of us started a small group and used the simple graphic in Figure 9.4 to challenge ourselves with the vision of reproducing beyond the fourth generation.

It showed us how, through the hero-making process, we could build God's kingdom to impact 320 people (ten per group)

FIGURE 9.4

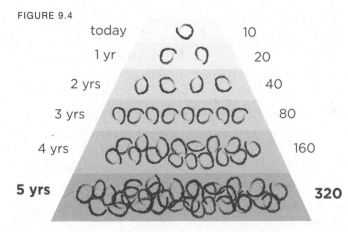

today   10

1 yr   20

2 yrs   40

3 yrs   80

4 yrs   160

5 yrs   **320**

each circle is a group of about ten

by mentoring a total of thirty-two leaders over a five-year period. For many of you who are type A and need to keep score of this kind of thing to know whether you are winning, this is exactly what I would encourage you to do.

Tracking Multiplication versus Addition

As you determine your scoreboard measures, be careful to pick values that lead to multiplication, not just addition. As Todd Wilson wisely observes in his Exponential ebook *Dream Big, Plant Smart*, "Possibly the single-largest obstacle to multiplication occurs when we position addition activities (new programs and ministries, new facilities, small groups, outreach events, church-wide campaigns) as our primary strategy for growth, rather than seeing these activities as a supporting element to healthy biblical multiplication."[47]

The reason why I recommend apprentice counting as your primary kingdom-building scoreboard measure is that it so readily leads to multiplication, as Figure 9.3 shows. Suppose you accept my definition that apprentices do not graduate until they have their own apprentice. If so, then when that graduation happens, you've already moved from Level 3 growth (you working harder and longer) to Level 4 reproduction (you reproducing yourself in someone else).

But wait, there's more! As soon as your former apprentice graduates his or her own apprentice, you have moved into Level 5 multiplication. Then, when all of you repeat the process (if next season or next year everyone takes on another apprentice) and a fourth generation emerges, you are solidly advancing God's kingdom through Level 5 multiplication. You are birthing a hero-making family, and so are each of the heroes you make!

What's Next?

You've now finished learning about the five practices of a hero maker, and for each one, you have a simple tool that you can put to work today. As you implement these practices, you will maximize your life and ministry, and God's kingdom will advance. But understand, it won't be easy. It will be hard. If it were easy and not hard, more leaders would have done it. The next chapters will help you anticipate what's ahead and show you how to lead through it. They'll also give some examples to motivate you, reminding you that the transition is worth it and that your new life as a hero maker is both manageable and enjoyable—and incredibly fruitful.

Take a breath, and then jump into your future by turning the page.

Hero Maker Discussion Questions

OPEN

- What was the first job you ever had?
- How did you know whether you were successful?
- Who do you know who has a kingdom-building score-board?

DIG

- Use a Bible app or Google to search for Bible verses using the word *kingdom*. Which verse with *kingdom* in it is the most meaningful to you and why?
- Read Matthew 6:33. How does Jesus' admonition to "seek first the kingdom of God" (ESV) affect your under-standing of success as a leader?
- What does it mean to you when you pray this line from the Lord's Prayer: "Your kingdom come, your will be done, on earth as it is in heaven" (Matt. 6:10)?

REFLECT

- Which do you celebrate more: people coming to your thing or people doing God's thing?
- Tell about a time when you saw God's kingdom win, but not your personal kingdom.
- What does your hero maker's scoreboard look like today? How many apprentices do you currently have, and how many total apprentices do you have?
- What would you like on your scoreboard in one year and in five years?

PART 3

HERO⚡

MAKERS

GET RESULTS

CHAPTER 10

The Influence of Hero Making

Big Idea: Hero makers have the opportunity to be used by God to move the needle on the church-multiplication gauge from 4% to 10%, creating a tipping point in the impact and influence of the Jesus mission.

You never wake up thinking, *Today something big will happen that changes everything*. But this day would be different.

It was a warm fall morning, and I was working out of a Panera Bread restaurant, finishing writing the first talk I would ever give on the multisite church. Leadership Network had convened a group of leaders of innovative multisite churches at Community Christian Church who were to start meeting after lunch. It was September 11, 2001. Yeah, *that* day. I finished up my notes and got in the car to drive to our meeting site. By the time I got there, the entire world had changed.

Do you remember that day? It was an inflection point in history, a turning point, an event that would forever change how we think and act.

"Inflection point" is a term made popular by a couple of business guys named Andy Grove, of Intel, and Clayton Christensen, of Harvard. In business terms, an inflection point is when a new opportunity presents itself or a new market opens up or a disruptive innovation appears, like the internet, the personal computer, or the smartphone. It's a turning point because customers from that point on will never think and behave the same.

> An inflection point is a turning point, an event that forever changes how we think and act.

The business world borrowed the term inflection point from the

FIGURE 10.1

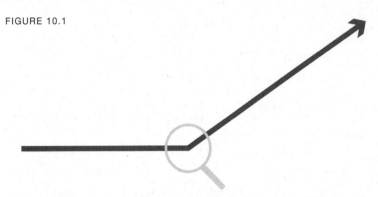

math world because when you put an inflection point on a graph, it looks like Figure 10.1.

I believe that the church in North America could be at a very important inflection point. I want to unpack this inflection point by explaining "what is" and then "what could be."

What Is . . .

Let me start by reminding you what is currently happening with the church in North America. Back in chapter 2, we told you how every church can be placed into five different levels of church multiplication capacity.

Level 1: Subtracting—churches that are declining in attendance
Level 2: Plateauing—churches that are holding steady
Level 3: Adding—churches that are growing
Level 4: Reproducing—churches that have reproduced one or more new sites or churches
Level 5: Multiplying—churches that multiply generations of sites or churches, showing movement behaviors

About 80% of all churches fall into the Level 1 (subtracting) and Level 2 (plateauing) categories. Our research at Exponential tells us that about 16% of all churches fall into the Level 3 (growing by addition) category. That leaves only the Level 4 (reproducing) and Level 5 (multiplying) categories. About 4% of all churches fall into Level 4, while there are only a couple examples of Level 5 churches in all of North America—like Ralph Moore and the more than twenty-three hundred churches planted through Hope Chapel (see chapter 5). Our hunch is that of the 4% of churches (roughly fifteen thousand) in Level 4, only about half reproduced with joyful intention. Many of those new churches were actually church spats or splits! Ugh. I hate that "what is" reality.

What Could Be . . .

Now let's take a look at what could be.

In our first ten years of the Exponential conference, we've been laser focused on multiplication, church planting, and movement making. During that decade, we have seen the annual number of conference participants grow from a few hundred to more than ten thousand, with another thirty thousand participants joining us online annually. Most people don't make it every year, and typically at least half are present for the first time. When I think of Exponential, I don't think of a conference as much as I think of a community with a cause that represents more than one hundred thousand leaders across every network and denomination. My point is this: there is a growing critical mass of church leaders who are committed to becoming hero makers!

> There is a growing critical mass of church leaders who are committed to becoming hero makers!

During that same decade, we've seen church multiplication slowly start to gain momentum. The number of new churches planted in the United States is increasing. Just over ten years ago, we were closing more churches than we were starting. The most recent statistics on this show that every year, we're seeing a net gain of more than five hundred new churches! Not enough yet, but we are gaining momentum. The church in the U.S. is starting to multiply, at least in a few places!

We're also gaining momentum over the past ten to twenty years with the innovation of the multisite church. On that fateful day of September 11, 2001, we convened with a dozen other multisite churches for the first time. At that time, there were fewer than one hundred multisite churches in the country. Today there are more than eight thousand multisite churches, and they make up the largest segment of growing churches in the United States. The faster you're growing or the larger your total attendance, the more likely you are to go multisite. Churches are starting to reproduce rapidly, at least among many high-visibility pacesetters!

Not only that, but I sense a subtle shift in what success looks like in the local church.

"Grow big." During the last couple decades of the twentieth century, many churches aspired to grow bigger. They defined their success by the size of their budget, attendance, and buildings. The church growth era ushered in a time when the church leaders who wrote the bestselling books spoke at conferences; leaders looked up to leaders who had grown very large ministries.

"Grow big and reproduce." At about the turn of the millennium, a new measure of success arrived with the multisite movement. The unstated measure of success had slightly shifted; now it was not just to grow something large but also to reproduce it at multiple sites. Again, the leaders who could achieve this drew the admiration and attention of other church leaders, who wanted to know how they could do the same.

"Grow and multiply." Now I sense that young leaders are rejecting the idea that success equals growing something big on their own. They are also not content with just growing their own ministry and then reproducing it in other places. There is an emerging strain of young leaders who understand that the mission of Jesus is accomplished through movement. They are also grasping parts of the secret that God's mission expands when you have aspirations for the kingdom and not just for your church. One research note that affirmed this last observation: Warren Bird ran a major survey through Leadership Network and found that 83% of pastors under age forty "have a future vision to plant/launch new sites or churches."[48] They may not yet know or understand the hero maker language I'm introducing in this book. But these young leaders are aspiring hero makers. I'm greatly encouraged by what I see in the next generation of church leadership.

I say all this to draw your attention to what could be. We have a growing critical mass of church leaders who have bought into the Jesus mission, the vision of multiplication, and the desire to be hero makers. We also have a growing momentum in which leaders see their role as hero makers and more and more church leaders want to lead Level 4 and 5 churches.

If all this is true—and I'm strongly suggesting it is—then we're looking at what could be an inflection point in the church and mission of Jesus Christ in the United States!

4% to 10%

These numbers weigh heavy on my heart, and I want to share something with you that is very personal but needs to be public. Figure 10.2 is a graphic based on a page out of my journal where I write out my prayers and reflect on how God is leading me. Almost every day in my journal in the lower right section, I write down "4% to 10%."

FIGURE 10.2

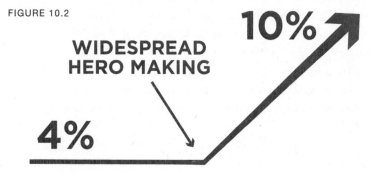

As I've said (you must have memorized this stat by now), only 4% of all U.S. Protestant churches are reproducing or multiplying. I strongly suspect these churches have hero-making leaders!

After I write 4% in my daily prayer journal, I write 10%. Why? I believe that in the coming decade, it will be possible to move the needle from 4% to 10% and see more churches become hero-making churches. If we get to 10%, I believe, we'll reach a tipping point for changing the church and reaching millions of lost and hurting people in the United States. For every 1% increase in reproducing churches, thousands of eternities will be changed. We have everything we need to see the percentage of Level 4 and 5 churches go from 4% to 6% to 8% to 10%!

So every day, I write this little equation in the lower right-hand corner of my journal as a prayer: "God, let us see the number of churches that are 4's and 5's (reproducing and multiplying churches) in the U.S. move from 4% to 10%."

A Hero-Making Challenge

So how do we leverage this opportunity?

I've spent a great deal of time thinking about what I'm going to say next. It makes sense to me that if only 4% of all churches are hero-making churches, it's probably also true that only 4% of all Christ followers are hero makers. Let me explain. I've had the privilege of working with thousands of churches and tens of thousands of church leaders over the past twenty-five years. One consistent observation I've made is that churches that reproduce and multiply macro (new sites and new churches) also reproduce and multiply micro (new disciples and new leaders). So the converse of that also makes sense to me: if a church doesn't reproduce and multiply macro, it is most likely made up of people and leaders who are not reproducing and multiplying micro.

So now for the challenge.

You now understand what it takes to be a hero maker.

You also have simple tools you can use today in your hero-making efforts.

But will you do it? I implore you: don't let this be another book that is interesting to read or gives you content to share on social media, but you never apply it or live it out! Integrate the five hero-making practices into your leadership. Use the simple tools routinely. I can't urge you strongly enough. Please, please, please, become a hero maker! The kingdom of God and the mission of Jesus are depending on you and me. The eternities of thousands of people rely on your commitment and daily resolve to become a hero maker who multiplies disciples.

> Please, please, please, become a hero maker! The kingdom of God and the mission of Jesus are depending on you and me.

If you will accept this hero-making challenge, God will use us together to move the needle from 4% to 10% to create a tipping point in the impact and influence of the Jesus mission in the United States.

In his bestselling book *The Tipping Point*, author and businessman Malcolm Gladwell says something that will help us take on this hero-making challenge: "To create one contagious movement, you often have to create many small movements first."[49] The following are three hero-making challenges. If you accept them, you'll be starting a small movement that can be part of creating one contagious global movement. Read each of these carefully. Then take them to heart. I do, and I'm committing myself to each of them. Will you?

Hero-making challenge 1: motives. "My only motive is advancing God's kingdom, not my kingdom."

The first challenge we all have to deal with is our motives. We have to ask ourselves the deep and probing question, "Is my motivation about God's kingdom or my kingdom?" Pause for a second and reread that question. Before you answer, let it sink into your mind—and your heart.

Every one of us wants to be successful. But hero makers give up their own success for the success of others and the advancement of God's kingdom. That might mean your group never grows very large. It could result in your ministry never getting the affirmation you think it deserves. Others may get the attention while you do all the work. Hero makers must strive to have the same motives as Jesus, "who, being in very nature God, did not consider equality with God something to be used to his own advantage; rather, he made himself nothing by taking the very nature of a servant, being made in human likeness. And being found in appearance as a man, he humbled himself by becoming obedient to death—even death on a cross!" (Phil. 2:6–8).

One of the best examples of hero making I know is my brother Jon Ferguson. We started Community Christian Church together. We also launched NewThing as a team. We have also coauthored several books. He has been an equal partner in everything we have accomplished by God's grace. However, sometimes people will refer to him as "the pastor's brother" or give me credit for the stuff he has accomplished. Still, his motives are always the same—advancing God's kingdom, not Jon's kingdom.

Jon and other hero makers know that their influence is multiplied and the mission is advanced by seeking the kingdom of God first and letting go of the need to be the hero. Their single, primary motivation is God's kingdom!

Hero-making challenge 2: methodology. "My missional method is multiplication, not addition."

Hero makers are always thinking about multiplying their efforts.

They are never satisfied with just doing. Nor are they content with just adding to their group, ministry, or church. Hero makers are obsessed with making everything they do reproducible and scalable. They have one eye on making a difference and the other eye on whom they can mentor to multiply what they are doing.

One of the most remarkable hero makers I've ever been around was also someone you'd least expect. First, he wasn't an adult; he was a student. Second, he didn't have a charismatic and charming personality; he was kind of nerdy. Finally, he didn't grow up in the church; he was new to faith. But he

A hero maker's methodology is not about creating a crowd but about multiplying a movement.

loved people! And when he started a small group, he did two things well: he loved the people in that group, and he made sure he had an apprentice who would learn to do the same. Over a handful of years, I saw him multiply and develop ten new leaders and reach more than one hundred people. Why? He was a hero maker! And a hero maker's methodology is not about creating a crowd but about multiplying a movement.

Hero-making challenge 3: measurement. "My measure of success is to send people, not create a crowd."

As I write this, Community Christian Church is in the process of launching another location. We have a goal to send more than three hundred people to help start this new location. We have seven months till we start, and already almost two hundred people have volunteered to go and serve, including twenty-two small group leaders.

How is that happening? It works only because we have campus pastors and staff from other locations who value sending more than creating a bigger crowd at the site they lead. These three-hundred-plus people will come from four of our locations that have leaders whose measure of success is to send people, not merely create a crowd.

Jesus brought together a ragtag bunch of followers and invested three years in mentoring them in the ways of hero making. The purpose of those three years together was not just to grow deep in understanding, nor was it to gather a mass of people. The purpose of the apprenticeship was to prepare Jesus' followers to be sent out in pairs to catalyze a movement of multiplication that would reach the lost, the least, and the lonely. If Jesus' measure of success was to create a loyal crowd, he failed miserably. Let's learn a lesson from our Savior and maximize our impact by making our primary measurement not crowd creation but people sending.

If each of us will accept these three hero-making challenges and make small movements ourselves, we can see missional multiplication movement in our lifetime! We will see the needle inch forward from 4% to 6% to 8% to 10% if we declare,

- "My only motive is advancing God's kingdom, not my kingdom."
- "My missional method is multiplication, not addition."
- "My measure of success is to send people, not create a crowd."

You may think, *But I'm only one person; what difference can I make?* The truth is, on your own it is hard to make much of a dent. But together our efforts are multiplied, and together we can make a world of difference! A shift from 4% of churches that reproduce or multiply to 10% means that millions more people will know the love and forgiveness of God through Jesus here on earth and then spend eternity with us in heaven. Worth it?

I'm not ending here, because there are some pitfalls that you need to know about. More specific, there are three tensions you need to manage along the way. That's what the next chapter is about.

Hero Maker Discussion Questions

OPEN

- Describe a time in your life (personal or ministry) that was an inflection point, where everything changed.
- Describe a time in your leadership when you tried to lead a team, group, or congregation through a change. What worked? What didn't?
- Did you feel anything from your past resurface as you read this chapter's challenge of helping move the needle from 4% to 10%?

DIG

- Read Acts 6:1–7. What challenges do you think the leaders of the early church felt in trying to lead a multiplying church while caring for the Greek widows?
- This chapter in Acts talks about the challenge of motives, methods, and measurements for a hero maker. How do each of those issues show up in Acts 6?

REFLECT

- Which of the three challenges is easiest for you to accept, and which is the hardest? Why?
- If you accept the challenge of this chapter, what's the greatest personal cost that you will likely pay?

CHAPTER 11

The Tensions of Hero Making

Big Idea: Hero makers courageously live in the tension of doing ministry both here and there, of growing and sending, and of funding facilities and also multiplying new churches.

The tensest moment in any relay race is the passing of the baton. Spectators at a track meet hold their breath until one runner reaches out and successfully hands off the baton to the next while still racing at full speed. It doesn't matter how fast you run if you don't cleanly execute the handoff. This lesson was learned and relearned at the Olympics by USA's women's 4x100 relay team.

In the 2000 Sydney Olympic games, the USA women's 4x100 team should have won. They had the fastest individual runners and the fastest team. But they were sloppy coming into the second exchange of the baton and ended up in third place behind the Bahamas and Jamaica.

In the 2004 games in Athens, Team USA once again had the four fastest individual runners and the fastest overall team. But as Marian Jones went to hand off to Lauryn Williams, she slowed down because of fatigue, and by the time she had passed the baton, they were outside the exchange zone. The women's 4x100 team was disqualified.

USA was favored again in 2008 at Beijing Olympics, but on the third exchange, Torri Edwards attempted the handoff to Lauryn Williams and dropped the baton.

For three consecutive Olympic races, Team USA should have won, but they lost even though their individual and team times were faster than all others. It was a trifecta of reminders that it's not about the speed of the individual runner if the baton is not successfully passed.

Then came the 2012 Olympic games in London. USA's women's 4x100 executed each of the baton exchanges flawlessly and in the process broke a twenty-year record!

Hero makers understand the lesson here. It's not about how great we are or how great our ministries become. It's about raising up more and more leaders, pouring into those who are coming alongside us and after us, and successfully passing the baton over and over again.

The Tensest Moments in Hero Making

To accept the challenge of passing the baton and being a hero maker is not the end; it's really just the beginning. If enough of us accept this challenge, then we will begin to band together as hero-making leaders and hero-making churches. That will be important, because we need each other's help. Leaders and churches who put God's kingdom first and prioritize multiplying and sending also have to be prepared to deal with a unique set of tensions. We don't necessarily work to resolve these tensions; instead we learn to live with them, acknowledging their presence and how they can stifle our commitment and efforts to multiply.

Let me explain three of the tensions common to every hero-making leader and church.

1. The Tension of Proximity: Do We Focus on Here or Do We Go There?

Hero-making churches focus on both here *and* there, not just ministry in their own immediate community.

If you're serious about hero making, you're also serious about leading and becoming a church that is all about reproducing and multiplying. Compelled by the vision of Acts 1:8 to go from Jerusalem to Judea to Samaria and to the ends of the earth, your church may start here, but it knows that it also needs to go there, there, and over there too! We create a proximity tension to focus on what we're doing here and have a vision for something over there.

When I speak at conferences or conduct workshops, I often pass out dream napkins (introduced in chapter 5). I tell people to write out on the back of the napkin the dream they have for their church, like I had you do.

I love it when I receive a tweet (@daveferguson) or get tagged on Instagram (fergusondave) or Facebook by a participant sharing with me his or her dream napkin. (Send me yours!) When I look at a dream napkin, I can tell within seconds if the creator is dreaming of a Level 3, 4, or 5 church. How?

- If the dream napkin has one symbol for one church in one city, I know the best it will ever be is a Level 3 church.
- If the dream napkin looks like something with a few spokes coming off the center, symbolizing a reproducing church, I recognize the potential of a Level 4 church.
- If the dream napkin resembles an atomic explosion multiplying both near and far, that tells me they are dreaming of a Level 5 church.

FIGURE 11.1

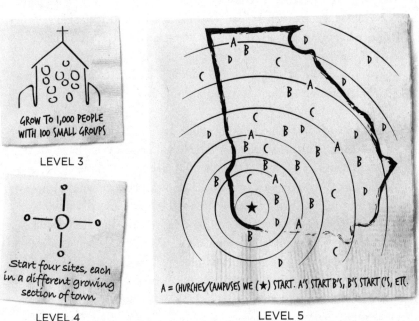

GROW TO 1,000 PEOPLE
WITH 100 SMALL GROUPS

LEVEL 3

Start four sites, each in a different growing section of town

LEVEL 4

A = CHURCHES/CAMPUSES WE (★) START. A'S START B'S, B'S START C'S, ETC.

LEVEL 5

One of the many things I love about Mission Church in Roselle, Illinois, is their desire to live in the tension of both here and there. Jon Peacock and Tommy Bowman started this church dreaming of what they call the Ten. The Ten refers to their dream to start ten new churches in the ten communities closest to Roselle.

I'd rather see one small church that is starting ten churches than a church of one thousand that's not starting any churches. Why? The latter has capped its impact at one thousand people, but the former has exponential potential because each of those ten churches is a reproducing and multiplying church!

I'd rather see one small church that is starting ten churches than a church of one thousand that is not starting any churches.

If you were to ask James Griffin of CrossPoint City Church and Jason Gerdes of Revolution Church about their dream napkins, they would tell you about the fifty new churches they're starting in and around the city of Atlanta. Both of these hero makers have decided to put God's kingdom ahead of their own kingdom by forming a NewThing network with nine other churches working together to plant new reproducing churches. That network is not for the benefit of their local church (here) but for the sole purpose of starting new churches (there).

If you're part of planting a new church, then start from the very first day with a dream of being a Level 5 multiplying church. Write it out on a napkin. Pray over it. Share the dream with others. *Never* give up on that dream.

If you're a part of an existing church, do what you can to facilitate a re-dreaming process. I've seen established churches begin to dream again. When Kevin Pike became the lead pastor at Ridge Point Church in Holland, Michigan, he took over a Level 3 church that had grown very large. Kevin knew that he wanted to use the resources and influence of Ridge Point to see it become a Level 4 or 5 church. He joined NewThing, in which every church fills out an annual MRP ("my reproducing plan"), and so Ridge Point made a commitment to not just being here but also planting new churches there. Kevin brought in new staff members, such as Bob Carlton, who had expertise in hero making and put into place a leadership residency program. After sensing the buy-in from the congregation, they have now set a goal to plant 235 new churches in twenty-five years! They are living in the tension of here and there.

All this dreaming is very motivating, but getting it done is hard work. I can guarantee you it will create a tension. You will have to lead, manage, and grow this church here while at the same time sending people and resources to the new churches you dreamed of over there. It's not easy, but it is so worth it!

2. The Tension of Priority: Do We Prioritize Growing or Sending?

Hero-making churches are both growing and sending; they prioritize sending capacity, not seating capacity.

This next tension is where you shift from having a dream on a napkin to deciding what is really important. This is the tension of priority; you'll be forced to ask and answer hard, telling questions.

- "Am I looking for volunteers and leaders to fill a slot in a program, or am I looking to commission Christ followers and leaders for the Jesus mission?"
- "Do I develop leaders for growing this church or for starting new churches?"
- "Is my priority growing my attendance or sending people out for kingdom work?"

Please make sure you hear this: There is nothing bad about growing! Let me be clear—healthy growth is good! Very good! But ask yourself, "*Why* do we want our church to grow? Are we growing to increase our *seating* capacity, or are we growing to increase our *sending* capacity?"

If you decide to be a hero-making church that both grows and sends, you will experience tension. I remember being asked by one of the largest churches in the country to do a consultation on how to reproduce. They wanted to start reproducing new sites and go from Level 3 to Level 4. This church was a beautiful example to other churches of how to do things right and with excellence. I gave them a complete presentation and explained the challenges and tensions I saw ahead for them.

As our time came to a close, a member of their executive team said,

"One of our core values is excellence; how can we focus on sending to start something new when we still haven't gotten this church right yet?" I couldn't help but think, *How much more right can you get?* But what that executive team member was feeling was the tension of priorities: growing or sending.

Someone who has managed this tension as well as any U.S. leader is J. D. Greear of Summit Church, in Raleigh-Durham, North Carolina. He believes God wants their church to plant one thousand churches by 2050. How could that happen? As he says, "If we plant fifteen churches a year, we won't get there. But if we plant churches that plant churches that plant churches, it just multiplies all over the place." Great plan, and J. D. and Summit Church consistently live in the tension of both wanting to grow *and* wanting to send.

He's changed their church's scoreboard from measuring *seating* capacity to measuring *sending* capacity. In fact, the joke at their church is, "If you've been on our staff a long time, it means you're not that good, because if you were, we would have sent you already!"

Can you feel the tension as he talks further about this dream? "We've grown to have the sort of culture where sending is the very air we breathe. Being a disciple means being sent, so sending should pervade *every* aspect of what a church does. First-time guests should know from the moment they set foot on our campuses that sending and kingdom are in our blood."[50]

The tension is real. The tension is challenging. But every time I lay hands on a new crop of church planters and bless their dream, or get to visit a church we planted, or hear a story of life change that happened there and not here, I know it is worth it. And you will too!

3. The Tension of Provision: Do We Fund Buildings or Church Planting?

Hero-making churches fund the planting of new churches, not just the construction of new buildings.

I remember our very first newcomers' reception at Community Christian. We were only four weeks old, and we were meeting on Sundays in the cafeteria of the local high school and had our newcomers' reception in the teachers' lounge. I finished my presentation with a group of about twenty new folks and asked if anyone had any questions. A short, bald, and very enthusiastic guy named George raised his hand to ask a question. (I remember him because he went on to become the mayor of our town for twenty years.) George said, "When are we going to have a church building?" I thought, *We can't afford a building. It's hard enough just trying to afford staying in this cafeteria!* But I told him, "We will build a building when it helps us better accomplish God's mission." And we have tried to stick to that ever since.

Just as you feel the tensions of proximity and priority, you will also feel the tension of provision. And one of the biggest outlays of cash will be for facilities and buildings. So let's have a candid conversation, because if you want your church to be a hero-making church, you will live in the tension of providing facilities but also funding new churches. And this is a very real tension.

On one hand, facilities can be a big help to the mission. I remember church growth and leadership consultant Lyle Schaller telling me, "The most overlooked aspect of new church development is the importance of space" and then reminding me how important spaces are to people. I also know that in many contexts, a permanent building brings credibility. When your church moves into a new space, a significant increase in attendance is often not far behind.

On the other hand, facilities are a huge expense. It costs lots of money and time spent raising the money. Once you get the building, it's very costly to keep it looking good. And usually we build bigger spaces, so we have to invest lots of hours to make sure we have enough people to fill the space. Those buildings also create culture and bring with them a lot of unintended consequences (some good, many not good over time). And this is always true: the building you will build today is not the building you would build in ten years.

I have a love-hate relationship with church buildings.

So if you want to manage this tension of provision, do what I and other aspiring hero makers do, and remember the following three provision principles.

Provision principle 1: Tithe to church planting. In the same way that you would tell a young believer to start tithing and trust God to provide, I tell young church planters to tithe to church planting and trust God to provide. At Community Christian, we have set aside at least 10% for many years for multiplication. The discipline of tithing has allowed us to have the funds to start new sites, plant new churches (both locally and globally), start a new church-planting network, and invest in innovative church-planting strategies. As we look at the next three years, we see Community helping to start twenty-eight new churches and sites. That wouldn't be possible if we were not setting aside a tithe to multiplying. If you really trust God, tithing to plant new churches is not an issue.

Provision principle 2: Plant before you build. Before we ever bought property or built a building, we had started a second and third site of Community Christian Church. We were sure that multiplying was the best way for us to accomplish the mission of Jesus. I believe that this decision moved us to becoming a Level 4 church, and now closer to a Level 5 church. Planting before we ever built was a clear signal to our people, leaders, and staff that we were not going to be about buildings; we were all about the mission of Jesus and advancing his kingdom!

Provision principle 3: Always ask, "What is the best way to accomplish the mission?" With every budget, spend some time prayerfully asking, "What is the best way to accomplish the mission of Jesus?" Once you've answered that prayer, you then know how to allocate the provisions with which God has resourced your church.

There will be occasions when you will need to invest dollars in facilities, but even then, look for creative ways to maximize facilities' use for the mission of multiplication. When we added a twelve-hundred-seat auditorium to our location, known as the Yellow Box, we also built our Leadership Training Center for training emerging leaders and church-planting leadership residents. So when I cast vision for this new space, I told our people, "This auditorium will help us reach thousands, but the Leadership Training Center will allow us to reach tens of thousands." And we are already seeing this happen.

We will never be able to build buildings big enough or fast enough to keep up with what God wants to do.

Remember, if the church is a multiplication movement, we will never be able to build buildings big enough or fast enough to keep up with what God wants to do. So always ask, "What is the best way to accomplish the mission?"

An Unexpected Team of Hero Makers

In the movies and comic books, there are times when the challenge is so daunting that one hero is not enough and you have to call for a whole team of superheroes. So you call on the Avengers or the Justice League or the Guardians of the Galaxy. The challenge before us is not something made up in the movies or in the pages of a comic book; it is real, it is eternal, and it requires more than a team of heroes. It requires a team of hero makers!

I recently met such a team. They didn't look like hero makers. And I certainly didn't expect hero making from a board of elders who were mostly in their seventies and who, together with their pastor, provided leadership for a declining church that was started fifty-four years ago.

This elderly group of men had asked me to meet with them, and I anticipated they would want to hear strategies for survival. I thought their goal was to be a Level 2 church, to just hold their own. I was wrong. Really wrong.

One of the elders, Ken, started the meeting by saying, "We believe God has a bigger vision for us than what we have been able to accomplish for the past few years. We believe God wants us to multiply." Inside I was shaking my head; this church had never reproduced anything that I recalled. He went on to explain the vision God had given him in prayer. Then another elder chimed in. "We believe it's possible to see an Acts 2 kind of church; we haven't given up on that dream." I was embarrassingly shocked and humbled. One other elder spoke up. "My home church has twenty people who show up every week in a huge auditorium. They should have sold their building thirty years ago. I don't want us to just survive; I want to be a part of something that thrives."

And what I heard next was stunning. "We think we can get two and a half million dollars for our building. We want to sell our building, close down this church, and invest all that money in the next generation of church planting." This group of older leaders understood that the goal of their leadership was not longevity but legacy. With great admiration, I spent the rest of that evening helping them figure out a strategy for multi-plying their impact, as I watched a group of unlikely hero makers change history! Clearly they understood the importance of passing the baton well.

But How Do I Make It Stick?

I don't want to leave you here. What comes next will help you see the greatest possible results from your hero-making efforts. It shows you very practical ways to instill hero making as part of the culture of your minis-try. The five practices are not a fad for this year, to be replaced next year by something different. Instead you want them to go deep and last, and the next chapter will walk you through what to do, step-by-step.

 Hero Maker Discussion Questions

OPEN

- Biology teaches us that physical tension is necessary for the body to grow and become strong. Tell about a time when you grew in your leadership as a result of tension.

DIG

- Read Mark 6:6–13, 30–46, which describes many ten-sions Jesus had to live with. Which one do you most identify with, and why?
- Read Acts 1:8. What's one tension that church leaders in the book of Acts had to manage?

REFLECT

- What leader or which church do you know that has been a good example of living in the tensions described in this chapter? Why?
- What did you learn from them that you will apply to your ministry or leadership?

CHAPTER 12

A Culture of Hero Making

Big Idea: Hero makers strive to create hero-making cultures so that the practices of hero making continue without them and after them.

Only one leadership move ensures a longer-lasting legacy than hero making does, and that is creating a hero-making *culture*. A hero-making culture empowers leaders to multiply their impact well beyond their sphere of influence and well beyond the life of any single leader. The very best hero makers do not just make heroes; they create a culture in which everyone around them implements the five essential practices of hero making. And these practices become so common that they are widely adopted over and over again without a second thought.

The first time I heard someone talk about culture and the power of culture, it was Erwin McManus, a Los Angeles pastor leading a church named Mosaic. I was at a conference he was hosting, and I was hanging on to his every word as he talked about creating a movement-making culture. Erwin defined culture this way: "Culture is spontaneous repeated patterns of behavior."

Ever since I heard Erwin's definition, I have worked to create leaders, teams, churches, and organizations that repeatedly produce hero makers. Culture is a leader's greatest asset. Culture is at work 24/7. Culture never rests

> Culture is spontaneous repeated patterns of behavior.
>
> —ERWIN MCMANUS

and is always influencing. Culture is reinforcing over and over again what is really important, through spontaneous repeated patterns of behavior.

FIGURE 12.1

7-STEP PROCESS FOR CREATING A HERO-MAKING CULTURE

DECLARE IT. | DO IT. | BRAND IT. | TEACH IT. | RECOGNIZE IT. | REPEAT IT. | INSTITUTIONALIZE IT.

Seven-Step Process for Creating a Hero-Making Culture

"I think this is the best part of your *Hero Maker* book."

I'm hoping that's what you'll say after you work through this section. It already has a good track record. I have taught and coached the following[51] seven-step process for creating a hero-making culture to hundreds of church leaders and consistently received good feedback, and I'm confident it can work across many different sizes and types of churches.

DECLARE IT. A hero-making culture starts with declaring it. There needs to be a pivotal moment. It can be public or private, but the important thing is the seriousness of the commitment and that you know this is the hill you are willing to die on and there is no turning back.

Jeff Pessina leads a NewThing church-planting effort in the Philippines through Frontline Christian Mission, which he started more than thirty years ago. After the first two decades, they had helped countless hurting people and seen millions make decisions at their crusades. But as Jeff began to evaluate their work, he felt they didn't have enough of a lasting impact to show for all their efforts. So he pulled his team together and declared that they were going to focus on multiplying churches and equipping Filipino leaders who would lead those churches. It was then that Frontline began to partner with NewThing. Jeff's declaration was a clear statement that a new day had come to Frontline. Since he made that declaration, they have planted thirty-four churches and are dreaming of more than a thousand new churches.

If you are ready to lead a hero-making group, ministry, or church, start with a solemn declaration. On your computer, in your journal, or on the back of a napkin, write out your declaration. I would encourage you to focus on the problem you are trying to solve and how a hero-making culture will solve it. Your declaration doesn't have to be eloquent or ready for publication; it just needs to be personal. Then keep it somewhere you will see it several times a week. Once you have done that, a new day will begin!

 After you declare it, the next step is to do it! Because many leaders in the church are also teachers, you will be tempted to teach it. Please resist. Before you teach it, you need to do it yourself. Culture is more caught than taught.

This second step in culture creation is recognizing that you are the primary culture creator. As a leader, you need to go first. You will reproduce what you do—not what you teach but what you do!

As I mentioned earlier, everyone on our original staff team had apprentice small group leaders before we started our church. This did more for creating the hero-making culture of Community Christian Church and NewThing than anything else. While I was the first person on our team to have an intern, all of us immediately started helping people move along the leadership path. When you do that, it creates culture. I may have supervised the first leadership resident, but it wasn't long before we were asking all our locations to have a leadership resident. As the leader, you need to go first.

 Once you declare it and do it, you may be thinking, *Okay, now can I teach it?* Please hold off just a little longer. The next step will help you with that. Your next step in creating a hero-making culture is to brand it.

The larger the scope of your leadership, the more important this third step will be. If you are leading a small group, this can easily be accomplished through conversation and a change in language and storytelling. If you are leading a ministry or church(es), it may require a memorable slogan and a communication strategy. "Hero Maker" is a memorable slogan. We created it as a brand for our Exponential conference, to help leaders understand what it means to be a kingdom-minded leader who multiplies generations of leaders. You should strongly consider using the phrase hero maker to help brand the new culture in your ministry or church! And use this book. Or think of something even better.

Some of the new language you will use to establish your brand will come from the pages of this book, terms like apprentice, intern, leadership resident, leadership path, ICNU, and more. And tell stories. Feel free to use the stories I've told you, but in short time you will need to tell your own stories. And the best stories are the ones you tell of other people who are being hero makers.

TEACH IT. Now you are ready to teach it. Did I mention that one of the biggest mistakes church leaders make is teaching too soon? We get excited about new ideas, and we regularly need content to deliver to listening people, so we end up teaching about hero making before we are doing it ourselves and have the language and our own stories to explain it. I applaud you for having the discipline to wait till you declare it, do it, *and* brand it before you teach it.

In teaching hero making, remember that the endgame is a new culture. With that in mind and with the branding work you have done, teach the concept of hero making to your leaders first, before you teach the rest of your group, ministry, or church. I have found that the best way to teach other leaders is to use a process referred to as "heart, head, and hands."

> *Heart.* Leaders often need to feel it in their hearts before they will ever live it out in their lives. This is why it is important that other leaders feel and see the passion in your life. You can help them feel it by telling stories or by having other leaders tell stories of people who were hero makers for them. This can be accomplished in person or by video.
>
> *Head.* Leaders also need to get it in their heads. They need to understand how hero making is grounded in biblical truth and know why this is so important. Change is always composed of both emotion (heart) and understanding (head), and that is how leaders are best taught.
>
> *Hands.* Leaders need to receive permission and encouragement to live it out for themselves. Part of equipping leaders has to be your

approval and confidence that they can be hero makers. Don't teach just for others to feel it in their hearts or get it in their heads; teach for them to live it with their hands. That is how you create culture.

Remember, leaders are culture creators, and once you get other leaders beginning to implement the practices of hero making, that dramatically influences everyone else. After you teach and equip your leaders and see they are doing it, you are ready to teach the rest of your group, ministry, or church. That is how culture is created.

The fifth step in creating a culture of hero makers is to recognize it.

In the words of Ken Blanchard, "Catch people doing it right." Most people live in environments and work in organizations in which they are constantly being told what they are doing wrong and how they need to get it right. There is a place for correction, but we need to be intentional about specific praise and letting people know that we see their efforts to be a hero maker. Remember, leader: what gets rewarded gets repeated. You can recognize hero-making efforts privately in hallway conversations or by sending a note, a text, an email, or a good old-fashioned letter that can be kept and reread. You can also recognize them publicly at staff meetings, at leadership gatherings, in teaching illustrations, through video, or via any of your social media platforms.

Another way to recognize hero-making efforts was covered in chapter 9: by encouraging every leader to use the simple scoreboard tool (see chapter 9). The reminder from the leader that efforts count is critical to culture creation. Whether you oversee a group, ministry, church, network, or denomination, a regularly updated dashboard that keeps kingdom stats is important to creating a hero-making culture. By the time you get to this fifth step in the process, making sure you recognize what you have declared, done, branded, and taught is vital.

This sixth step may be the hardest of them all, and that is to take a look at what you have done to create a hero-making culture and repeat it. I promise that you will get bored with some of this. You will not want to even say the phrase hero maker again, because you are so sick of it (for the moment). You may also decide that others who have heard it a hundred times are also bored and sick of it. Not true! It is just about the time when you are sick of it that it is starting to sink in and change the culture.

So don't stop repeating it over and over again. When it comes to creating culture, boredom is your enemy, and intentional repetition is your ally. Repeat it. Repeat it. Repeat it. (I think you get the idea.)

 **INSTITUTIONALIZE IT.** The last step of creating a hero-making culture is to institutionalize it. Knowing when a value has moved from being a good idea to being a part of the institution is hard to tell, but once it is written permanently on the wall, once it finds its way onto the annual calendar, once people rearrange their lives to experience it, you can be sure it is seeping into your DNA. The following are three examples of how to institutionalize hero making: leadership path, leadership community, and leadership residents.

Leadership Path

When you walk into our Leadership Training Center, what will immediately grab your attention is a few large graphics and other items permanently

FIGURE 12.2

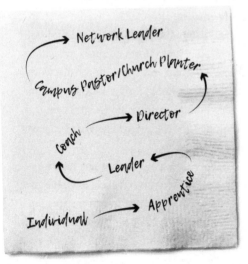

displayed on the wall, which include 2 Timothy 2:2, a replica of the original dream napkin with a napkin dispenser for leaders to write out their own dream, and our leadership path.

Often when I meet with an emerging leader who is excited about expanding his or her influence, I will find a scrap of paper and write out the leadership path in Figure 12.2. Then I will explain how someone can travel this path of expanding influence, using one of hundreds of examples, such as Patrick O'Connell.

When Patrick took his first step on this leadership path, by this world's standards he was a success: he was rising in the corporate world, happily married, and starting a family. But something was missing. His wife, Nancy, had gotten involved in a small group at Community Christian and found her way back to God. His first time attending Community was "just to be supportive" of his wife, who was being baptized. That began his journey of finding what was missing: Jesus. He started attending and joined a small group. It was there that he made a commitment to Christ and was baptized.

Seconds after Patrick was baptized, Scott, the leader of his small group, said, "Patrick, I see in you lots of leadership potential, and I want you to think about being my apprentice leader." Patrick said yes and took the next step on the leadership path.

Within a year, Patrick had gone through the five steps of apprenticeship (see chapter 7) and felt prepared to lead the group. Scott affirmed that step, and Patrick started leading a new group. Over the next couple years, Patrick did with others what Scott had done with him, and developed other leaders.

Having reproduced other leaders, Patrick took another step on the leadership path and began coaching them. But Patrick was just getting started.

Patrick explains, "I took a giant step forward in my leadership when Troy McMahon invited my family and me to move to Kansas City to plant a reproducing church. Troy had a big dream of starting a network of multiplying churches, and I wanted to be a part of it! I quit my job in wealth management, raised my own salary, and joined him. I have no regrets!" Troy, Patrick, and the team started Restore Church, which has grown to about one thousand in attendance at three locations while helping to start forty-one new churches so far.

Meanwhile, NewThing had grown from a few churches to a few hundred, and it needed someone who would be the day-to-day director while I helped provide the vision. With a hero maker's disposition, Troy told me that he knew Patrick could do the job and asked me to strongly consider his recommendation. After much prayer and conversation, Patrick took his most recent step on the leadership path and jumped from being a church planter to overseeing a whole network of churches. Patrick says, "I have this incredible opportunity to multiply disciple multipliers!"

Just a decade ago, Patrick O'Connell had yet to make Jesus Lord of his life. Today he is the global director of NewThing, giving direction to more than twelve hundred churches.

After sharing Patrick's (or another leader's) story, I will tell the emerging leader I am meeting with, "If you want to expand your influence in a similar way, I will be glad to help you." The leadership path helps create a hero-making culture in three ways.

- *The leadership path offers vision.* When I write out and share this leadership path with an aspiring leader, oftentimes their eyes light up and they say, "Yes, this is what I want to do, but I didn't know whether there was a way to do it." The leadership path is specific enough that it helps them see the future but generic enough that various leaders in different ministries can relate to it.
- *The leadership path gives clarity.* The leadership path also makes clear what the next step is in growing a person's leadership. Someone coaching that person can easily identify where they are, where they want to go, and what step they need to take next.
- *The leadership path is affirming.* Simply sharing the leadership path with a leader is an affirming exercise because you are explicitly saying, as Jesus did with his followers, "I see even greater things in you."

The leadership path started as an experience of a few leaders sincerely wanting to expand their influence to reach more people. We began to share their stories with other leaders. As we did, we found a simple way to illustrate their journey and share it with groups. In time, the leadership path became so important to our hero-making culture that we made a graphic and put it on the wall for all to see. That is the first of three ways to institutionalize hero making.

Leadership Community

As we were planting Community Christian Church, before we ever started a worship service, we first started small groups and a monthly event we called "leadership community." Leadership community has been a permanent part of our calendar, happening once a month (with July off) since *before* our beginning. Leadership community has become institutionalized.

A simple way to explain what we do at this monthly gathering of all our leaders (adult, student, children, and arts) is to think of it in terms of the global positioning system (GPS). Most of us use GPS every day to help us know where we are, where we are going, and how to get there. You can understand the components of our leadership community by thinking GPS, as follows.

- *G—Goal.* Leadership community is a once-a-month gathering that allows the senior leadership to share the vision and goals with all the leaders from every ministry. This can be a clear and compelling articulation of the next hill we are going to take, an explanation of the values we hold, or a platform opportunity for catching leaders doing it right. Vision fades, and leaders need an inspiring reminder of the mission and the goals before us.

- *P—Peers.* Leadership community is also a great time to break up into peer group huddles. Coaches meeting with leaders and apprentice leaders should facilitate the peer group huddle. During the huddle, the coach can simply use three questions: "Where are we winning?" "What are your challenges?" and "How can I pray for you?" These peer huddles are an important time of encouragement and support.

- *S—Skill.* A monthly leadership community is also a great time to offer skills training. At first you may offer various skills that all your leaders can use. As your leadership community grows, you may offer training that is ministry specific. For adult small group leaders, you might offer "How to facilitate a discussion," and for student ministry leaders, you might offer "Partnering with parents for spiritual growth in teens." Or you could take an elective approach and offer three or four skills that all leaders would benefit from, like "How to develop an apprentice leader" or "How to ask questions that develop leaders." Whatever skills you offer, from tips on developing a better prayer life to guidance on how to create community in your group, the emphasis is always biblical and extremely practical.[52]

Ask yourself, "Does my group, ministry, or church know the mission and goals that God has for us? Are we creating space for leaders to support and encourage one another? Do we offer the training that leaders need to grow their gift? How well do we perform each of these GPS functions for our leaders, both volunteer and paid staff?" Leaders need all three to move forward. And leadership community will help you institutionalize hero making.

Leadership Residents

I love our leadership path and leadership community, but if I had to pick only one way to institutionalize hero making, it would be through leadership residency. This is by far the best way for a church to accelerate the development of a hero-making culture! That may seem like a bold claim, but it also seems squarely to be the model of Jesus. He spent the majority of his ministry hours focused on what might be called a leadership residency for the Twelve. Those twelve took the culture they learned and experienced under Jesus—the multiplication thinking, the permission giving, the disciple multiplying, the gift activating, the kingdom building—and, as the book of Acts describes, they filled Jerusalem with their teaching about Jesus (Acts 5:28). As the number of believers continued to grow, churches multiplied to the point where the gospel reached you and me today.

If I had to pick only one way to institutionalize hero making, it would be through leadership residency.

Internships and residencies are not a class you teach in which the goal is to fill a notebook or get a diploma. Nor are they a strategy you use to hire a bunch of people to assist you in personally doing ministry. Rather they are a way to institutionalize a system of leadership multiplication. They're designed for people who are shifting from disciple to disciple maker, from caregiver to maker of other caregivers, and from minister to minister maker.

As we institutionalized a culture of apprenticeship across Community Christian Church, it was a natural extension to create opportunities for people who wanted an even more intensely focused approach to growing in these practices. Churches use all kinds of language for these programs, such as apprenticeships, mentorships, fellowships, or internships. We quickly gravitated to the term residency, as in church-planting residency.

It was similar to the medical world, in which doctors in training hone their craft under the tutelage of seasoned physicians.

We used residencies both for those in training to plant locations of Community Christian and for those planting a church beyond Community Christian: a nine- to twelve-month residency is now an expectation for any emerging leader who wants to start a church in NewThing. It's standard operating procedure for all new church planters. NewThing's slogan today is "One resident per site per year." As we institutionalize that value, the multiplication potential will reach exponential proportions!

What distinguishes a top residency program? My coauthor, Warren Bird, conducted Leadership Network research on more than three hundred churches that offer residencies (free download at *www.leadnet.org/ intern*). Then he interviewed more than fifty program leaders to discern the best practices among top residency programs. Here's his take on ten qualities that make a great residency program.

- *Committed to multiplication.* Residencies replicate the DNA of the sponsor church, and the best residencies are built around what the church does best. If the church champions multiplication, the residents will also.
- *Focused on full-time ministry.* Residents enter the program with clarity on specific ministry outcome (example: "God is calling me to plant a church overseas") versus a more general goal of becoming more effective in ministry.
- *Already seasoned.* Residents are generally older, with ministry experience, versus being college age or in their early twenties.
- *Top team oversight.* The senior pastor regularly interacts with residents, while another paid staff member owns the program's day-to-day management.
- *Trained trainers.* The sponsoring church also invests time and energy in developing and supporting the staff, volunteers, or outside resource people who will be training the residents.
- *Support raising.* Most residents raise some or all of their financial support. This cultivates their ability to do fundraising and makes sure they have skin in the game.

- *Hands-on emphasis.* A majority of the residency time involves hands-on ministry and consistent feedback. The classroom time does not exceed one-third of the program.
- *Leadership development.* Most churches indicate that leadership development is the top reason why they're offering the internship or residency program.
- *Multiple pathways.* The sponsor church offers multiple levels of internship (which goes by various names), with the highest level being residency (but not always using that name), and multiple tracks for each level.
- *Next-stop overlap.* The best residencies transfer seamlessly from the end of the residency to the next ministry for the resident; there has even been intentional overlap and preparation. So if a resident has a call to plant a church, the residency helps with all elements, down to selecting a location, developing a core group, and planning the initial launch day.

What would I do different in ministry if I could start again? I would have a leadership resident from day one, mentoring someone to start a new church. And I'd expand that into a leadership training center—a full leadership pathway institutionalized as part of how we do church.

At Community Christian Church, it took us nine years to start a second site, and nine more years to have our first full-time church-planting resident. That's unacceptable for being a multiplying, reproducing church.

If after reading through this book, you have concluded that Community Christian is a church that has it all together—a place teeming with Level 5 leaders, experiencing constant success in multiplication, having smoothly running systems in place at every level, and cultivating a waiting line of prospective residents—then I've mislead you. We are anything but the perfect model, and few days end without problems at some level. But if there's any structure we're betting the farm on, it's our investment in developing a healthy system of church-planting residents—and helping other churches do likewise.

One of the fifty people Warren interviewed was Gabe Kolstadt, pastor of a turnaround congregation named Westside Community Church, in Portland, Oregon. What got Gabe thinking about leadership residency was reading the book *Exponential* that my brother Jon and I wrote. As he told Warren, "We started building a culture of apprentices, and this demanded that we take it farther. We don't think we'll be faithful to Jesus if we don't develop leaders on a bigger scale."

As their culture of apprenticeship grew, people at Westside started saying, "I think I should be in ministry, but I haven't a clue where to begin or what to do." They didn't see themselves leaving their current life to be in seminary, but they could imagine spending part of their working hours with more involvement in their church.

The church was tight on funds, but that didn't stop them. As Gabe says, "We took the approach that we can engage bivocational people now. We're so glad we didn't wait. I tell everyone that you too can begin very small, and start now." When they launched, they followed a simple plan: "All the staff and lay leaders simply invested time. We let our interns and residents see behind the scenes, sit in meetings, and shadow us for the day, even on a Sunday." But church staff also gave out a number of assignments: create a podcast, run multiple groups, tackle the parking flow issue, and more. "They weren't to be just doers, but leaders who develop other leaders," he says. "That's how our residency program has become a culture-setting piece."

What does it look like when you have gone through those seven steps of culture creation? You will see people around you move from striving to be the hero to desiring to become hero makers. Sometimes those people do it consciously and sometimes they do it unconsciously. When you have a strong culture, you will develop and attract hero makers, as in the following stories of Doug and Matt.

The Seven Culture-Creating Steps
Develop Hero Makers

Doug was the guy who came to a Saturday night service and picked a seat closest to the outside aisle so he could easily escape after the closing prayer without talking to anyone. Doug had gone to church growing up but always felt like he was on the outside looking in. And he liked it that way. But Doug's anonymity came to an end at a neighborhood picnic when my wife, Sue, invited him and his wife, Mary, to a small group we were leading on parenting. Mary said yes for both of them. Wanting to stay happily married, Doug agreed and came along with Mary to our first group meeting. Doug so disliked the idea of going to a small group that he would always call it a "class." My hunch is that he was hoping that, as with a class, he would graduate and be done with us.

But over time, Doug found benefit in learning from other parents. All of us in the group started to become real friends. It was then that I announced to the group, "One of the necessary parts of us fulfilling the mission of this group is for me to have an apprentice leader. And Doug, I would like for you to be my apprentice." Silence. I could see him breaking out into a sweat.

Shaking his head in disbelief but still smiling, Doug said, "Okay." (Warning: I was pretty blunt. I don't recommend you put most people on the spot like this. I could have approached it as an ICNU moment, because I clearly saw that he had leadership potential, as did the whole group. I made my invitation public in this case because of Doug's personality and my healthy relationship with him and the rest of the group.)

Doug and I set a time to regularly meet, on Tuesdays at 5:00 p.m. at Starbucks. The first time we met, Doug said to me, "So if I'm going to be a leader, I guess I ought to be reading the Bible, right? How do you do that?" I explained how I did it on a regular basis, and his apprenticeship had begun.

Over the next several months, Doug and I continued to meet at Starbucks, and I took Doug through the five steps of apprenticeship (see chapter 7). Over time, he started reading the Bible, got comfortable praying in front of the group, and discovered he was a really good small group leader. It was about a year later that Doug thought he was ready to lead. I affirmed that he was, and I turned over the leadership of the small group to him and went on to lead another group.

Doug thought that was how this leadership thing worked everywhere—you lead and develop an apprentice while doing it.

A few weeks after Doug took over, I just happened to stop at Starbucks on Tuesday at 5:00 p.m., and I was so pleased with what I saw: sitting at the same table we had sat at for the previous year was Doug and his new apprentice, Brad. I don't remember telling

Doug he had to get an apprentice (although I'm sure it came up), but more important, Doug simply assumed that of course he would get an apprentice. Doug just thought that was how this leadership thing worked everywhere—you lead and develop an apprentice while doing it. For all Doug knew, that was how every small group leader in every church everywhere did it! His only experience was in a culture in which everyone thought that way. Doug was what you call "unconsciously competent" and because of the culture developed into a hero maker.

The Seven Culture-Creating Steps *Attract* Hero Makers

Matt Larson also experienced the power of a hero-making culture, but Matt did it consciously, with his eyes wide open. Matt was so attracted to our hero-making culture that he moved his whole family from Southern California to Chicago to do a leadership residency at Community Christian, taking in everything he could. Why? He explains, "Our dream was to plant reproducing churches in Southern California. We had been told by a number of people that we were ready to plant a church and didn't need to do a residency. But I knew that without a strong infusion of reproducing habits, practices, and some DNA transfer, we might be a 'successful' church plant but not a healthy, reproducing church that released people into the story that God had for them."

During Matt's leadership residency, he was a part of the launch of Community's Plainfield location. It was during this time that Matt learned firsthand about leading a reproducing church. Matt looks back and says, "I got to see a church live out 2 Timothy 2:2, reproducing to the fourth generation. I loved seeing how this applies in every area of ministry and not just in church planting. As a result of what I experienced, I was able to instill that same reproducing culture in the church I planted."

After Matt completed his residency, we commissioned him and his family, and they returned to Southern California consciously competent in planting a church that plants churches. And did they ever! In just ten years, Anthem Church planted first in Thousand Oaks, California, and then expanded the Anthem family of churches to locations in Camarillo, Ventura, and Denver, Colorado. In addition to Anthem locations, they have planted new churches throughout Southern California—San Diego,

Chula Vista, Chatsworth, Temecula, Downey, Santa Barbara, Orange County, another in Thousand Oaks—and they are currently dreaming of southeast Asia.

I love both Doug's and Matt's stories!

I love Doug's story because on a nearly daily basis, I still get to see Doug using his leadership gift. He is now on Community Christian Church's directional leadership team, and he is multiplying his gift through others and helping hundreds and thousands of people find their way back to God.

Recently, I had breakfast with Matt, and it was so rewarding to hear that our nine-month investment in his leadership residency has multiplied into a whole family of new sites and churches. Matt is just getting started!

The great thing is, Doug and Matt are not the only ones. There are so many others. Some of your church's hero makers might become church staff, but the majority will make heroes of others even as volunteer leaders themselves.

> Some of your church's hero makers might become church staff, but the majority will make heroes of others even as volunteer leaders themselves.

Just through the two organizations I know best—Community Christian Church and NewThing—there are now thousands and thousands of leaders who have been mentored and multiplied into implementing hero-making practices. Some of them are consciously competent, and some of them, fortunately, don't know any other way! Whether leaders are developed in the culture or attracted to it, hero makers are the result.

A Picture of a Hero-Making Culture

FIGURE 12.3

If you want to have your own stories of multiplying leaders like Doug and Matt who multiply other leaders, you first need to understand what a hero-making culture looks like. I want to give you a quick picture of one, using a simple diagram taught to me by Brian Zehr of Intentional Impact.[53] Any strong culture has three components: values, narrative, and behaviors.

1. VALUES

At the core of any hero-making culture is a strong set of values. These values are both the convictions of your mind and the passions of your heart. You are convinced that these values are grounded in the truth of Scripture. You can point to the life of Jesus and how he was a hero maker when he told his apprentices they would "do even greater things" (John 14:12). You can reference Jesus seeing in a ragtag bunch of fishermen and working-class guys more than they ever saw in themselves, when he said, "Come, follow me" (Matt. 4:19). They were shocked that he believed in them. Jesus spent time with them, and then he sent them out by twos, saying, "All authority in heaven and on earth has been given to me," and now I'm giving it to you, so "go!" (Matt. 28:18–19). And you see those hero-making values lived out by Paul, who passed them on to Timothy by insisting that his apprentice think in terms of four generations of reproduction (2 Tim. 2:2). These are strong values because they have theological integrity and are consistent with Scripture.

But they are also values because they are what makes your heart beat fast and what holds your attention late into the night as you talk about them and dream about them. Sometimes these values are made into a creed (see chapter 13), and you repeat them over and over to keep them prominent in your head and heart. Sometimes you print them out and post them on your wall to display your commitment, or download them and make them the wallpaper on your laptop or phone so you see them several times a day. Values are at the core of hero-making culture.

2. NARRATIVE

Narratives reinforce and bring values to life in a hero-making culture. Narratives are the language and stories of any strong culture. If you have ever worked in a place that had a strong culture or been a part of a team that had a winning culture, you know they have their own "speak."

If you have frequented Chick-fil-A, you know that if you say, "Thank you," they always respond with, "My pleasure." It's so predictable that I sometimes play a game by trying to see how many times I can get them to say, "My pleasure." My record is currently fourteen times in one trip! Chick-fil-A has a strong culture of customer service and a language that reinforces that culture.

There are certain words a culture may use that you don't hear in other places, and those words have special meaning in that culture. In a hero-making culture, those words might be apprentice or leadership path or ICNU.

Along with specific language are the stories that make up a hero-making culture. Doug and Matt are both great examples of hero makers. By telling stories like theirs in private, small circles or from the platform, I can give life and color to the concept of hero making, in ways that help create a hero-making culture. Such stories show you how to live out the values. Good stories make values sticky and become like folklore. You repeat these stories over and over because they remind you of the moments when you got it right, and so others remember them too.

Telling stories in private, small circles or from the platform is an important part of bringing the values to life in a hero-making culture.

I had told Doug's story to my coauthor, Warren, several years ago. As we were working on this chapter, he said, "I hope you'll tell your story about the guy you mentored at Starbucks." Not only had that story stuck with Warren all those years, but Warren had recently told it to someone he is mentoring at his church.

That's the power of a compelling story. But you're not limited to vintage stories, because hero-making cultures always birth new stories. The new stories are what you celebrate; they bring the emotion that tells the whole community that we will still trade our lives for our values!

3. BEHAVIORS

A strong hero-making culture needs more than the two components of revealing the values at its core and having an ongoing personal and public narrative to express those values. A third component is the most important: behaviors. Those are where you, as a leader, live out your message. Behaviors are you being a hero maker in real life.

Why do only 4% of all U.S. Protestant churches have a hero-making culture? I say that because at present only 4% of all churches ever reproduce a new site or church. Stay with me here: Why are there so few churches with a hero-making culture? It's not because lots of churches don't understand the values; they do! And it's not because they don't tell stories of disciple multiplying; they may have to get them from some other church or organization, but they do find stories to tell. I'm convinced that the most significant reason why so few churches have a hero-making culture is because their leaders do not live out the hero-making practices! Sorry if my words hurt! Your reading this book suggests that you want to be part of a church with a hero-making culture. But don't stop with just wanting it; you need to do it!

When we teach a set of values and tell stories to reinforce them but do not live them out personally, we are implicitly saying, "You just have to sit there and listen to me teach truth and tell good stories, but you don't have to really do it." Leader, you are the primary culture creator. Leader, you will get the culture you deserve. You will reproduce who you are!

When you put together values, narrative, and behaviors, you have a snapshot of a hero-making culture. You can't just have one or two of these elements; you need to make sure you have all three. When all three are working together with integrity, you will have the kind of culture that reinforces and encourages the adoption of hero-making practices 24/7/365!

Seven Steps—Might Look Simple, but They're Not Easy!

The seven steps in this chapter are a process for you to not only be a hero maker but create a culture that is continually encouraging hero making and developing hero makers. Just because I did the hard work of putting it into seven nicely outlined steps, don't think it is easy—or that any of us have arrived. Don't confuse easy to understand with easy to do. This may be the greatest leadership challenge of your life, but it will be worth it! I promise. If you create a hero-making culture, it will live far beyond you and far after you!

C'mon, commit yourself to being that and doing that. If you're ready for that kind of commitment, let's move to the final chapter, where I will show you how you can recommit yourself to that task every day.

Hero Maker Discussion Questions

OPEN

- Describe a time that caused you to really mature in your ministry abilities.
- Would you describe yourself as more "unconsciously competent" or "consciously competent"?
- If you've ever done a leadership internship, apprenticeship, or residency, what was the main benefit you gained?

DIG

- Read John 17, known as Jesus' high priestly prayer for his followers. What elements do you see of how Jesus created or prayed for a culture of hero makers?

REFLECT

- Of the many ideas in this chapter, which resonated most with you as something you'd like to explore?
- What one specific action from this chapter will you take this week?

CHAPTER 13

A Secret to Be Shared

Big Idea: Hero making requires that leaders make a commitment by signing the hero maker's creed and start each day by answering the hero maker's question.

Brian Bolt's journey from hero to hero maker almost cost him his life.

As a young man, he wanted to be somebody—the hero on the streets. He had been a drug user since age thirteen and later a military deserter who lived on the streets. One day he got into an argument and was shot point-blank in the head. "I watched blood come out of my head like a water fountain," Brian recalls. "I was glad, because I was so hopeless. I just wanted to die."

Yet God had another plan. When paramedics arrived, one of them said to Brian, "Son, you're going to die. Before you do, I need to ask you this question: Do you know Jesus as your Lord and Savior?" The EMT led Brian in prayer. "I asked Jesus into my life there in the back of an ambulance." But Brian didn't die.

Brian struggled with his new commitment to Christ, and he went back on the streets. But two men came up to him with ICNU words. "I thought they were going to jump me, but instead they began to speak life and potential into me," Brian says. "They were part of a church-planting church. They told me God has a plan for my life. They put me in a men's recovery home connected with the church."

Brian grew in his faith. "A passion came over me. I wanted to tell everyone about Jesus, that he could change anyone," Brian says. That journey led him over several years through an internship program in a Pennsylvania church, where he met a pastor from the suburbs of Pittsburgh. "I told Brian that I've been praying for someone to start something in the city," Jeff Leake says. "I believed in him and agreed to help him start a church." Brian moved to Pittsburgh and started a Hope Home outreach.

The partnership between Brian's inner-city center and Jeff's Allison Park Church was a win for both. "The church, when it's working right, is the greatest support system on the planet," says Brian.

Brian knew that hero making was a secret too good to keep to himself. Now his life goal is to equip others to be hero makers. Specifically, now Brian is holding ICNU conversations of his own, giving permission to all kinds of church planters in urban centers. "The Holy Spirit impressed on me that we wouldn't reach the whole city unless we plant more churches," Brian says.

City Reach Network, a church-planting organization Brian founded several years ago, has planted churches and Hope Homes throughout the northeastern United States. At one point, they launched twenty-seven churches in one day.

"We want to keep doing this all over the country," Brian says. "There's such a need in the city. God wants to raise up strong churches that can multiply and bring new life into cities. Church planting and multiplication changes the future for people."

Brian has come full circle. After finding his way back to God, he has come to embody multiplication thinking, permission giving, disciple multiplying, gift activating, and kingdom building. Brian is contagiously living out the secret of hero making.

How Will You Share the Secret?

Hero making was never meant to be a secret. My singular focus in writing this book has been to instruct, encourage, and inspire you to join me in becoming hero makers and to share this secret as often as you can!

We know by Jesus' example and instructions in God's Word that hero making is the model for how to lead in a kingdom movement.

We know by Jesus' example and instructions in God's Word that hero making is the model for how to lead in a kingdom movement. We also see it lived out by how Jesus trained and released the Twelve, and then how he empowered and sent out others, whether it was a group of 72 (Luke 10:1–2) or 120 (Acts 1:15;

2:1) or the continuation of Jesus' mission through the Holy Spirit as "more and more men and women believed in the Lord and were added to their number" (Acts 5:14; see also 4:4; 6:7).

I want to conclude by challenging you to make a life-changing commitment. I want to ask you to make a decision that will be a personal inflection point in your leadership. I want this to be a holy moment and marker event in which you turn away from any strivings to be a hero and instead aspire only to be a hero maker.

Will you do that? Will you join me?

If you are ready to make a commitment to being a hero maker, I want to ask you to respond in two ways: first, by signing the hero maker's creed (see next page); and second, by starting each day with answering the hero maker's question.

Wait! I'm serious about this being more than a moment when you nod your head in agreement. I want you to sign your name, put a date on it, and have two witnesses—people you serve with and see frequently—sign it as well. This is a real commitment! Then set a time when your witnesses can check in with you and confirm that you're sticking to your hero-making commitment, asking you how it's going and what you're learning.

Then let's carry it even farther. What if those witnesses also had a prayer of commissioning for you? Could they charge you, as in public "I do" moments you've seen in other church ceremonies like weddings, marriage renewals, or baptisms? Simply have them read the document aloud, with you responding, "I do" after each of the five statements, and then lay hands on them and conclude with prayer.

If you also want our church to pray for you, email your name to me personally at DaveFerguson@communitychristian.org (or tweet me @daveferguson). When we do our next church-wide commissioning of our own leaders, we'll pray for you as well.

The Hero Maker's Daily Question

Finally, to keep that commitment to the hero maker's creed alive on a daily basis, I want you to begin each day with the leadership question I gave you in chapter 2. Begin each day recommitting yourself by answering this question:

HERO MAKER'S CREED

Our Lord and Savior Jesus made this hero-making promise to *all* of his followers: *"Whoever believes in me will do the works I have been doing, and they will do even greater things than these" (John 14:12).* Therefore:

1. As a hero maker, I commit to *thinking* with a mindset of multiplying leaders and refusing to put limits on what God can do. My model is Jesus' vision of a movement from *"Jerusalem, and in all Judea and Samaria, and to the ends of the earth" (Acts 1:8).*

2. As a hero maker, I commit to *seeing* the leadership potential in others and not being afraid of those who may be better than me. My model is when Jesus said, *"Come, follow me...and I will send you out to fish for people" (Matt. 4:19).*

3. As a hero maker, I commit to *sharing* what I've learned by discipling leaders and not being satisfied until I've seen it multiplied to the fourth generation. My model is the *diatribo* way that *"Jesus and His disciples went out...where He spent some time with them" (John 3:22).*

4. As a hero maker, I commit to *blessing* leaders by sending them out and not holding on to them. My model is when Jesus said, *"All authority...have been given to me. Therefore, go and make disciples of all nations" (Matt 28:18-19).*

5. As a hero maker, I commit to *counting* only what advances God's kingdom and not just what increases my kingdom. My model is when Jesus said, *"Seek first his kingdom" (Matt. 6:33).*

Signed (your name, today's date)

Witness #1 (name and date)	*Witness #2 (name and date)*

AM I TRYING TO BE THE HERO, OR AM I TRYING
TO MAKE HEROES OUT OF OTHERS?

Include this "ask" during your daily prayer time with God, maybe personalizing it for each new day: "Lord, please show me which people to make into heroes *today*." In your journal, write out and then answer this question daily. You figure it out how and when, but you need to answer this question every day going forward. The simple practice of reflecting daily on this question will change the trajectory of your leadership. It will push you away from your kingdom toward God's kingdom. It will propel you toward movement making. More than anything, other than God himself, it will help you maximize your leadership. Recommit yourself daily by asking, "Am I trying to be the hero, or am I trying to make heroes out of others?"

Before you finish this book, there's one more thought: Remember my good friend Pastor Oscar Muriu, a true hero maker from Nairobi? Because of the inspiration he has provided me for hero making, I have asked him to close with a few inspiring words just for you (okay, for me too). Don't skip it.

Hero Maker Discussion Questions

OPEN

- Describe a time when you went public on something in a way that made a huge difference. Maybe it was your baptism as a youth or adult, maybe an honor pledge you signed at school, or maybe even the "I do" of a wedding ceremony or wedding proposal.

DIG

- Read Matthew 13:10–12, where Jesus talks about the secret of the kingdom of God. What is the secret he's referencing?
- How does it apply to the secret this book seeks to make public?

REFLECT

- Imagine your life one year from today, after sticking with the challenges you accepted in this chapter. What do you suspect the greatest spiritual fruit will be?

Afterword

A Call to Action by Oscar Muriu

If you want to go fast, go alone.
If you want to go far, go together.

Oscar Muriu is an inspiring example to me of hero making. Throughout the pages of this book, I have frequently mentioned Pastor Oscar because he is a world-class leader. I remember sitting around a conference table at our first NewThing global summit in Nairobi, Kenya. At the time, we had about three hundred churches that were part of NewThing, and we were talking and praying about what God wanted us to do next. That's when Oscar spoke up and said, "Ten thousand multiplying churches!" Everyone laughed—except Oscar. He continued, "We will plant two thousand in Sub-Saharan Africa; you can do three thousand in Asia; you can do one thousand in North America . . ." and around the globe he went on, assigning God-size goals for the nine different regions of the world. Oscar summarized his challenge by saying to us all, "Let's set a goal so big that it makes God sweat!"

That was the moment I knew I loved this guy, and it was also the moment that NewThing set its sights on seeing ten thousand multiplying churches globally.

Since that meeting, Oscar and I have been traveling the world, looking for leaders to start multiplying churches and networks. If that's you, we'd love to hear from you! And because Oscar has been such an inspiration and an encouragement to me, I wanted to give him the last shot at inspiring you to become a hero maker.

Not long after I became the pastor of Nairobi Chapel, it began to dawn on me that there was way more God wanted me to do than I could do myself. I could get only so far. I could do only what one person can do. I kept coming back to Jesus' statement, "The harvest is plentiful but the workers are few. Ask the Lord of the harvest, therefore, to send out workers into his harvest field" (Matt. 9:37–38). In his statement, Jesus gives us not only a problem but also a solution: he says the problem is that there are not enough workers, but the solution is to pray that God will raise up people around us. Jesus' strategy was to first find his leaders, invest in them, and then focus on the harvest. So I accepted that Jesus' words were absolutely true.

One of the young leaders that God raised up at Nairobi Chapel was Muriithi Wanjau. He was in college, studying to be a biochemist, when I began investing in him. It took two years of us journeying together for him to realize that God had called him to ministry. It was then I invited him to pastor one of the campuses of Nairobi Chapel. When I saw he was ready, I released Muriithi and that campus to become a new church, called Mavuno, where he is the lead pastor.

Today Muriithi not only leads that flourishing ministry of thousands but is also following a call to plant a culture-defining church in every capital city in Africa and in the gateway capitals of the world. As he has often said to me, "Pastor Oscar, you threw me into the deep end of ministry— and it forced me to swim."

What if Muriithi had instead continued his studies as a future biochemist, not seeing in himself that he would be a minister of God's Word? It took a couple years, but with Muriithi, I simply confirmed what God was already doing in his life. I discovered that the size of your harvest depends on how many leaders you have. The problem is not with the harvest. The harvest is plentiful. The problem is with the harvesters.

The size of your harvest depends on how many leaders you have.

There is an old African proverb that says, "If you want to go fast, go alone. If you want to go far, go together." Today there are still many people whom God is calling, but no one confirms or encourages. Too often if no one comes along and speaks into their lives, their doubts and anxieties drown out the call of God. Too many of us are going it alone.

When I note qualities of leadership in a younger person, I will often have a conversation over a cup of coffee. I affirm, "I see leadership in you," and then I ask, "Could it be that God is calling you?" So often I hear something like, "I thought that, but I wasn't sure. I didn't know what to do. I didn't know whom to turn to. Now that you say that you see something..."

I think one of the things we need to learn as leaders is the discipline of listening to the Spirit of God to discern what he's doing in raising up leaders around us. A few will be bold and ask, "Could you please mentor me?" Others just hang around you, eager and desirous to learn from you, but are not clear on what to do. Still others need you to reach out to them. How can we expect them to build something until someone has taught them how to do it?

Let me give you two challenges.

First, will you pray for leaders and then begin to work with those whom God is raising up around you? Too often today we don't take Jesus' promise to send workers as a personal point of engagement. We become so busy and caught up in the work of ministry that we have no time to invest in the next generation of workers and to raise up leaders. Instead we look to the graduating class of our theological institutions and seminaries—but that's not the solution the Lord gave. So pray and look around you to see whom God is raising up.

Second, will you get other leaders praying and looking for whom God wants to use? I regularly sit down with my own leaders and ask, "Who do we see around us whom we think God is calling? Let's pray about these people for two months, that if God is calling, it would resonate with them." We call that group our "hit list" because we approach hero making in a targeted fashion. We don't want to see the voice of God become drowned out in those lives!

If you are going to be a hero maker, it starts with prayer. It continues with pouring yourself into the people whom God has put around you. Then cultivate into them the practices of hero making: multiplication thinking, permission giving, disciple multiplying, gift activating, and kingdom building.

If you do that, and if I do that, and if we all do that, the mission of Jesus will be accomplished, and God's kingdom will come to earth!

Chapter Summaries

If, after you have read the book, you want to find something in it quickly, use this tool.

Introduction

- Definition of hero maker
- Overview of the book
- Comparison of "common practice" and "hero-making practice"
- Jesus as a hero maker

1. Jesus' Leadership Secret

- Basketball's Bill Simmons and Isiah Thomas
- Jesus' secret of "greater things"
- Paul's secret of the body of Christ as a team function
- Comparison of hero and hero maker
- Sam Stephens and 3.5 million believers in India
- Michelle Bird's apprenticeship team
- Hero making as a force multiplier

2. The Wrong Questions

- Asking Bill Hybels the wrong questions
- Five levels of churches defined
- Examples of Level 1, Level 2, and Level 3 questions
- Leaders who decide, "There has to be more."
- Hero maker question to ask yourself every day

3. The Right Questions

- The right questions from the business world
- Asking questions that lead to greater spiritual impact
- Comparing addition with exponential multiplication
- Examples of Level 4 and Level 5 questions

4. Leading as a Hero Maker

- Jesus' ministry emphasis was his twelve leadership residents.
- What "greater things" looks like for Community Christian Church
- Oscar Muriu from Kenya and the next generation
- MOPS as example of hero making
- Overview of the five hero-making practices
- Difference between hero and hero maker

5. Multiplication Thinking (Practice 1)

- For every hero, there is a hero maker.
- Twelve steps of a hero's journey
- Hero makers live and teach multiplication thinking.
- How Jesus taught a multiplication mindset
- How multiplication thinking changes the questions
- Example of women's small groups at Community Christian Church
- Examples from dream napkins
- Profile: Ralph Moore, Hope Chapel, Hawaii, as hero maker
- Simple tool: Dream napkin

6. Permission Giving (Practice 2)

- Derwin Gray, football, and Transformation Church
- Jesus sharing his authority
- Sean Sears being told, "No thanks, Dude, we're all set"
- Fears that keep us from giving permission
- Six levels of permission giving
- Simple tool: An I-C-N-U conversation
- Derrick Parks in Wilmington, Delaware
- Profile: Jerry Sweat and Joby Martin, Jacksonville, Florida, as hero makers

7. Disciple Multiplying (Practice 3)

- Jesus, John 3, and *diatribo*
- Apprenticeship and disciple multiplying
- Apprenticeship in the story of Community Christian Church
- Mary, Dr. Bill, and other disciple multipliers as volunteers

- Worship arts and apprentice multiplication
- Mentoring artists at Bayside Church
- Developing interns
- Profile: Mario Vega, Elim Christian Mission, El Salvador, as hero maker
- Apostle Paul's command to multiply disciples
- Simple tool: Five steps of apprenticeship

8. Gift Activating (Practice 4)

- Duane and Sauda Porter's dream of a different Chicago
- Jesus held a commissioning for his apprentices.
- Nairobi Chapel and the commissioning of thirty-one church planters
- How gift activation can go wrong
- How gifts are activated
- Obe Arellano's gift activation and commissioning
- Brian Sanders and Tampa Underground's microchurches
- Simple tool: Commissioning
- Profile: Joe Wilson, Eastern Europe, as hero maker
- Commissioning Ryan Kwon at Exponential

9. Kingdom Building (Practice 5)

- Basketball scoreboards don't lie.
- Jesus' standards for kingdom winning
- Kingdom scoreboard ideas from Scripture and from Reggie McNeal
- Moneyball and ideas for scorecards and scoreboards
- Community Christian's dual scoreboard
- Profile: Ajai Lall, Central India Christian Mission, as hero maker
- Simple tool: Simple scoreboard
- Ways to count and measure apprentices
- How to track multiplication versus addition

10. The Influence of Hero Making

- Looking for a spiritual inflection point
- Why only about 4% of all U.S. Protestant churches have ever reproduced

- Today's shift from "grow big" to "grow and multiply"
- Moving the needle from 4% to 10% to create a tipping point
- Motives, methodology, measurement

11. The Tensions of Hero Making

- Tension of proximity: here or there?
- Examples of Level 3, 4, and 5 dreams
- Tension of priority: growing or sending?
- Tension of funding: facilities or church planting?
- Example of a legacy church's investment in hero making

12. A Culture of Hero Making

- Seven-step process for creating a hero-making culture
- Institutionalize it by a leadership path.
- Institutionalize it by leadership community.
- Institutionalize it by leadership residents.
- Seven culture-creating steps *develop* hero makers
- Seven culture-creating steps *attract* hero makers
- Any strong culture has values, narrative, and behaviors.

13. A Secret to Be Shared

- Brian Bolt's journey to hero maker almost cost him his life.
- How Jesus shared the secret
- Hero Maker's creed
- Hero Maker's daily question

Afterword: A Call to Action by Oscar Muriu

- Oscar's story at Nairobi Chapel, including Muriithi Wanjau
- Pray for leaders and then begin to work with those whom God is raising up around you.
- Get other leaders praying and looking for whom God wants to use.

Tweet the Book

Hero Making in 280 Characters or Less

- Hero makers have discovered the secret that results multiply through others and not through themselves. @daveferguson in #heromaker

- I want to help you become a hero maker so you can help others be hero makers too. @daveferguson #heromaker

- A #heromaker discovers that dying to self & living for God's kingdom thru others is the secret of multiplied results and greater impact.

- Jesus told his followers that he was investing his life in them so they would do greater things than he would. #heromaker

- The "secret" is simple: think about the kingdom of God more than about yourself or even your church. @daveferguson in #heromaker

- When I begin to seek God's kingdom more than my kingdom, his power and purposes are revealed to us and through us, says @daveferguson

- It's not about your personal stat line. It's not just about growing your church. It's about the kingdom. @daveferguson in #heromaker

- Hero makers know that if we focus only on addition, we never get to multiplication. @daveferguson & @warrenbird in #heromaker

- I asked the wrong questions, not hero-making questions but rather questions about how I could be the hero. @daveferguson #heromaker

- Ask this one question every day: Am I trying to be the hero, or am I trying to make heroes out of others? @daveferguson says #heromaker

- Hero makers understand that if we focus on multiplication, we can see God-size results. @daveferguson & @warrenbird in #heromaker

- Hero makers shift from being the hero to making others the hero in God's unfolding story. @daveferguson & @warrenbird in #heromaker

- Jesus was explicit about his desire to equip his followers to do the heroic. #heromaker

- Jesus was a hero maker. @daveferguson @warrenbird in #heromaker

- Jesus' ministry emphasis, in terms of where he put the biggest amount of time, was with his twelve leadership residents! @daveferguson in #heromaker

- Too often even our best difference-making efforts are oriented around positioning ourselves as the hero. @daveferguson in #heromaker

- Hero making is something anyone can do, and when accompanied by a leadership gift, it becomes explosive. @daveferguson in #heromaker

- Hero makers create a platform and then invite other people to stand on it. @daveferguson & @warrenbird in #heromaker

- Multiplication thinking requires that we dream big and use simple tools. @daveferguson & @warrenbird in #heromaker

- Heroes are made and not born. For every hero, there is a hero maker. @daveferguson & @warrenbird in #heromaker

- Multiplication thinking is most often catalyzed by the vision of a greater cause, a more important battle, or a bigger dream. #heromaker

- Even more than we need heroes, we need hero MAKERS who think big! @daveferguson & @warrenbird in #heromaker

- There is far more that God wants me to do than I can do all by myself. @daveferguson & @warrenbird in #heromaker

- Beware of doing a little ministry and forgetting about the bigness of God. @daveferguson & @warrenbird in #heromaker

- God can use anyone who is surrendered to make a hero of others. @daveferguson & @warrenbird in #heromaker

- I knew that to do what God said, we had to multiply churches. I needed to become a hero maker. @rmhawaii quoted in #heromaker

- The practice of permission giving is a shift from what God can do thru my leadership to what God can do through other leaders. #heromaker

- Leaders look into the soul of a person and say, "I see what you could be; my role is to bring that out of you." @DerwinLGray in #heromaker

- Jesus says to his apprentices, "I've got all the authority. I'm giving you access to it. Go spread the good news everywhere!" #heromaker

- If you are going to be a permission giver, you need to develop a yes reflex. @daveferguson & @warrenbird in #heromaker

- The reflex of a hero maker is to be a permission giver and say yes. @daveferguson & @warrenbird in #heromaker

- @daveferguson says, We call I C N U the four most important letters of the alphabet. #heromaker

- Disciple multiplying requires we do life with other leaders with the goal of 4 generations of multiplication. @daveferguson #heromaker

- One test of whether we're a #heromaker is whether we're reproducing and multiplying other Christ followers, who in turn do likewise.

- Whatever ministry you lead, to become a hero maker, you need to first be a disciple multiplier. @daveferguson & @warrenbird in #heromaker
- Even the Son of God, God in the flesh, didn't try to change the world on his own. @daveferguson & @warrenbird in #heromaker
- Jesus was a hero maker to the few and in so doing changed the world. @daveferguson & @warrenbird in #heromaker
- When you're committed to being a disciple multiplier, the impact reaches beyond your church and your city. @daveferguson in #heromaker
- 2 Timothy 2:2 calls us to mentor disciple multipliers to the fourth generation. @daveferguson & @warrenbird in #heromaker
- Apprenticeship is the core competency of any movement of God. @daveferguson & @warrenbird in #heromaker
- Gift activating requires that we not fill slots but instead develop people's gifts. @daveferguson & @warrenbird in #heromaker
- Assessments are good and helpful, but they are not how spiritual gifts are activated. @daveferguson & @warrenbird in #heromaker
- Once a year, we have a day on which we anoint and pray for everyone who wants to be commissioned for the Jesus mission. @daveferguson
- Kingdom building requires that we reject old ways of measuring success. @daveferguson & @warrenbird in #heromaker
- To God, winning is faithfulness. You don't have to be successful, only faithful. @daveferguson & @warrenbird in #heromaker
- Jesus could never be accused of counting only crowd size and cash on hand. @daveferguson & @warrenbird in #heromaker
- It is entirely possible for a church's attendance to be growing, while the kingdom of God is shrinking. @daveferguson in #heromaker

- In all our counting, I believe we have missed what matters most: Is the kingdom of God advancing? @daveferguson & @warrenbird in #heromaker

- If you can't answer the question, "What is a disciple of Jesus?" you'll never know if your church is winning. @daveferguson in #heromaker

- "My fruit grows on other people's trees," says Bob Buford, quoted by @daveferguson & @warrenbird in #heromaker

- Hero makers have the opportunity to be used by God to move the needle on the church multiplication gauge from 4% to 10%. @daveferguson

- Only about 4% of all churches in the United States have ever reproduced a new site or church. @daveferguson & @warrenbird in #heromaker

- There is a growing critical mass of church leaders who are committed to becoming hero makers! @daveferguson & @warrenbird in #heromaker

- I'm strongly suggesting we are looking at what could be an inflection point in the mission of Jesus Christ in the U.S. @daveferguson

- I believe the church is reaching a tipping point for reaching millions of lost & hurting people in the U.S. @daveferguson #heromaker

- Hero makers must strive to have the same motives as Jesus. @daveferguson & @warrenbird in #heromaker

- A hero maker's methodology is not about creating a crowd but about multiplying a movement. @daveferguson & @warrenbird in #heromaker

- If Jesus' measure of success was to create a loyal crowd, he failed miserably. @daveferguson & @warrenbird in #heromaker

- I'd rather see one small church starting ten churches than a church of one thousand that is not starting any churches. @daveferguson

- Are we growing to increase our SEATING capacity, or are we growing to increase our SENDING capacity? @daveferguson in #heromaker

- If you really trust God, tithing to plant new churches is not an issue. @daveferguson & @warrenbird in #heromaker

- We will never be able to build buildings big enough or fast enough to keep up with what God wants to do. @daveferguson in #heromaker

- Hero makers strive to create hero-making cultures so that the practices of hero making continue without them and after them. @daveferguson

- Culture is spontaneous repeated patterns of behavior. @erwinmcmanus quoted in #heromaker by @daveferguson & @warrenbird

- You will reproduce what you do—not what you teach, but what you do. @daveferguson & @warrenbird in #heromaker

- What gets rewarded gets repeated. @daveferguson & @warrenbird in #heromaker

- If I had to pick only one way to institutionalize hero making, it would be through leadership residency. @daveferguson #heromaker

- Some of your church's hero makers might become church staff, but the majority will make heroes of others as volunteer leaders. #heromaker

- Values are both the convictions of your mind and the passions of your heart. @daveferguson & @warrenbird in #heromaker

- Telling stories in small circles or from the platform is part of bringing values to life in a hero-making culture. @daveferguson

- Leader, you will get the culture you deserve. You reproduce who you are. @daveferguson & @warrenbird in #heromaker

- We know by Jesus' example and instructions in God's Word that hero making is the model for leading in a kingdom movement. @daveferguson

- Hero Maker's Daily Question: Am I trying to be the hero, or am I trying to make heroes of others? @daveferguson & @warrenbird #heromaker

• • •

Here are various sayings by contemporary Christian leaders, all of which communicate the idea of what a hero maker is and does.

- "My fruit grows on other people's trees" (Bob Buford).

- "I want to be a cheerleader who gives permission, encouragement, and accountability to release the potential in others" (Bob Buford).

- "Push others into the spotlight" (Carey Nieuwhof).

- "The greatest contribution you make to the kingdom might not be something you do but someone you raise" (Andy Stanley).

- "I'm the bow and others are the arrow; my job is to help send the arrows" (unknown).

- "The hero maker plays the role of the wind beneath someone's wings" (Larry Osborne).

- "Multiplication lives and dies on leaders who are willing to pass the baton and empower others to lead" (Ralph Moore).

- "If you delegate tasks, you create followers; if you delegate authority, you create leaders" (Craig Groeschel).

- "Most leaders focus on finding the right strategy; the best leaders focus on empowering the right people" (Craig Groeschel).

- "Mature leaders know they are worth more to the team when they know they don't have to be the star of the team" (Christine Caine).

- "Our best leaders, regardless of position, must assume the role of mentor and guide, rather than seek the hero's spotlight" (Chris Fussell).

- "The measure of a leader is not what *you* do but what people do *because of you*" (Howard Hendricks).

- "The church is not an audience gathered around one anointed leader. It's a leadership factory" (J. D. Greear).

Multiplication Resources

But wait, there's more! Don't miss the many excellent resources described below.

1. Official Book Website

See *HeroMakerBook.com* for a free discussion guide and other resources to help you maximize what you gain from this book.

2. Resources from NewThing

- *Exponential: How You and Your Friends Can Start a Missional Church Movement.* I cowrote this with my brother Jon, who is cofounder of Community Christian Church. It lays out the idea of a multiplication strategy, giving practical how-to's for reproducing Christ followers, leaders, artists, groups, teams, venues, sites, churches, and networks of churches. We illustrate it with the story of God's amazing work through Community Christian Church. *Exponential* is the anchor book in the Exponential Series. Available from any bookseller.

- *On the Verge: A Journey into the Apostolic Future of the Church.* I coauthored this with my friend and missiologist Alan Hirsch. This book blends both the theological and the practical with great urgency to explain how a church can make a shift to be more missional in its approach. It offers a simple change management approach that will empower Christ followers to influence their friends and neighbors and the church to impact their neighborhood and city. *On the Verge* is a part of the Exponential Series and is available from any bookseller.

- *The Big Idea: Aligning the Ministries of Your Church through Creative Collaboration.* When our church embraced what we call the big idea, it changed everything. Three of us—me, my brother Jon, and Creative Arts Director Eric Bramlett—wrote this very practical tool for the Leadership Network Innovation series to show how to creatively present one laser-focused theme each week to be discussed in families and small groups. *The Big Idea* shows how to engage in a process of creative collaboration that brings people together and maximizes missional impact.

- *Developing an Apprentice Field Guide.* Within these pages are some of the most practical and insightful ideas you'll find to guide you on this journey of not only leading but leading others to lead to change the world. This guide is used by all areas of ministry at Community Christian Church to develop leaders and further the Jesus mission of helping people find their way back to God. (Also available in Spanish.) See *www.newthing.org/store/.*

- *Mentoring a Leadership Resident.* This guide is for pastors, mentors, and coaches who want to see a reproducing church movement in our lifetime. In seventy-six pages, you will get a step-by-step plan for identifying, recruiting, and developing what we call leadership residents (apprentice church planters), who will eventually be sent out to plant a new church. In six chapters, this guide will answer the most common questions on how to do this effectively.

- *Coaching Guide Book.* Coaches play a valuable role in equipping leaders for the movement of God in our churches and cities. Leaders flourish and thrive under the practical care that a coach can provide. If you want to see the leaders in your ministry (including small group leaders) grow stronger, more resilient, and better able to develop others, then you will need coaches who know the game plan! This guide will give you tips and tools to help you be an effective coach to the leaders in your care.

- *LARN.* This stands for Leading a Reproducing Network, NewThing's one-year coaching opportunity for leaders of influence interested in starting and leading a reproducing network of churches. The goal of the training is to help leaders start new, reproducing networks of churches. To do this, we want to help you grow in your understanding of movements while providing you with practical insights on how to lead one. NewThing provides content while working alongside each church to create a specific action plan for its context. For more information, see *www .newthing.org/leading-a-reproducing-network/.*

- The Catalyst Community consists of three separate, facilitated sessions conducted over the period of one year. During these sessions, networks will establish a process that enables church teams to work together to build vision, identify and remove barriers, and create collaborative opportunities to accelerate and sustain the growth of the network. Each community includes catalyst facilitator training for selected individuals, to allow for multiplication of the network using this approach.

3. Resources from Exponential

A. EBOOKS

There are more than ten free ebooks in our multiplication library. Authors include Jeff Christopherson, Ralph Moore, Larry Walkemeyer, Bobby Harrington, Tim Hawks, Greg Wiens, Will Mancini, Todd Wilson, and many more. These leaders of multiplying churches share their journey of creating a sending culture of multiplication.

These ebooks are in addition to the more than eighty existing free ebooks in Exponential's resource library. Check out *www.exponential.org/ ebooks* to download these books.

B. PODCASTS AND VIDEOS

More than one thousand hours of audio and video training from national and international leaders are available on our website, including entire workshops from Exponential conferences (see *www.exponential.org*).

C. EXPONENTIAL CONFERENCES

Don't miss the opportunity to gather with like-minded church multiplication leaders at Exponential's many annual events.

Our national event convenes thousands of church multiplication leaders and features 150+ speakers, 150+ workshops, and 10+ focused workshop tracks.

Our regional events bring the full punch of the national event theme in a more intimate gathering that helps leaders save travel expenses. Regionals take place across the continent.

For a complete schedule of upcoming conferences and locations, see *www.exponential.org/events*.

D. FREE ONLINE ASSESSMENT TOOLS

Discover your church's level and pattern of multiplication by using our free online tool at *www.becomingfive.org/heromaker*.

Discover your profile and pattern of disciple making by using our additional free online tool at *www.becomingfive.org*.

E. FREE ONLINE MULTIPLICATION COURSES

The Becoming Five Course is designed to delve deeper into the practical elements of church multiplication. Leaders wanting to multiply their church will find valuable, work-at-your-own-pace training in the form of audio, video, and written content supplied by dozens of multiplying practitioners. Visit *www.exponential.org/school* to register.

The Dream Big Course is designed to help you and your church identify, select, and move forward on your pathway toward multiplication. You will be able to diagnose where you are, discern where you believe God wants you to be in the future, and determine the necessary practical steps to move into multiplication. Visit *www.exponential.org/school* to register.

F. DIGITAL ACCESS PASSES (TRAINING VIDEOS)

Exponential offers downloadable content from all main sessions via our Digital Access Pass (a separate pass for each conference theme) at *www.exponential.org/dap/*.

2015: "Spark: Igniting a Culture of Multiplication"
2016: "Becoming Five"
2017: "Dream Big: Discover Your Pathway to Level 5 Multiplication"
2018: "Hero Maker"

Paying Interns and Residents: Legal Requirements

By David O. Middlebrook, The Church Law Group

Many churches offer an unpaid internship or residency program which provides ministry-related skills and experience as well as suitable skills for a secular workforce. Sometimes these are a requirement for a student's degree program; at other times, it is just a matter of someone desiring to gain practical ministry experience prior to entering full-time ministry.

What do employment law experts say about whether unpaid internship programs (whatever you call them, such as residency) violate state and/or federal wage and hour laws? Some states have increased their investigation of this issue, and other states may follow, given the prevalence of such programs. It is therefore imperative that your church or ministry understand the legal requirements and implications for unpaid internship programs so they may be structured appropriately.

Is the Person an Employee?

One of the primary legal issues that arises in this area (and the focus of this appendix) is worker classification: when may an intern be classified purely as an unpaid intern rather than as an employee entitled to compensation? Failing to properly classify an intern can result in fines and can lead to litigation which would likely far exceed the cost of simply paying the intern. Since it is incumbent upon the employer to properly classify its interns, how do we evaluate who qualifies as an unpaid intern and who must be classified and compensated as an employee? A 1947 Supreme Court Case and subsequent guidance provided by the Department of Labor goes a long way toward answering this question.

In the case of *Walling v. Portland Terminal Co.*, 330 U.S. 148 (1947), the Supreme Court evaluated the classification of several individuals who participated in a pre-employment training program that was a required precondition of employment. The Court held that during such training the individuals were *not* employees for purposes of the Fair Labor Standards Act (FLSA), and *not* entitled to compensation. In reaching that decision, the Court placed particular emphasis on several factual circumstances present, which the Department of Labor (DOL) later utilized in issuing a six-part test to determine whether an intern must be compensated.

When You Don't Have to Pay

According to the DOL, if all of these criteria apply, "an employment relationship does not exist under the FLSA" and therefore *the intern need not be paid if:*

1. the internship, even though it includes actual operation of the facilities of the employer, is similar to training given in an educational environment;
2. the internship experience is for the benefit of the intern;
3. the intern does not displace regular employees but works under close supervision of existing staff;
4. the employer that provides the training derives no immediate advantage from the activities of the intern, and occasionally its operations may be impeded;
5. the intern is not necessarily entitled to a job at the conclusion of the internship; and
6. the employer and the intern understand that the intern is not entitled to wages for the time spent in the internship.

While this six-part test was originally developed and applied to for-profit entities, it remains helpful guidance for the nonprofit sector. In the same document in which it sets forth the six-factor test, the DOL also states that there is a recognized exception "for individuals who volunteer their time, freely and without anticipation of compensation for religious, charitable, civic, or humanitarian purposes to nonprofit organizations," and that unpaid internships in such a circumstance are "generally permissible."

When to Pay

Besides the six factors set out above which describe situations when an unpaid internship is appropriate, the DOL has also set forth examples of when an intern should be considered an employee for payment purposes— that is, when an intern is not really an intern. The presence of *any* of these factors, otherwise known as the "Unpaid Intern Prohibited Factors," means that an intern *should be classified as an employee if*:

1. the employer uses the intern as a substitute for regular workers or as a supplement to its current workforce; or
2. but for the intern, the employer would have hired additional employees or asked its existing staff to work additional hours; or
3. the intern is engaged in the employer's routine operations and/or the employer depends upon the intern's work.

Under these factors, if your organization uses an intern for seasonal work, such as for summer camps or holiday services, they may be called an intern but *likely should be paid at least minimum wage* if they are being used to augment your current workforce or if they exist in lieu of hiring additional staff.

Must All Six Criteria Apply to My Situation?

While the DOL's guidelines are helpful and should be considered by your church or ministry in establishing any unpaid internship or residency program, it is important to understand that sometimes it may not be necessary for all six of the above-referenced factors to be satisfied for a worker to be classified as an unpaid intern. In fact, in at least one case the six-factor test was eschewed entirely in favor of what was termed the "primary beneficiary test" (*Glatt v. Fox Searchlight Pictures, Inc.*, 811 F.3d 528 [Second Circuit 2015]).

In that case, the Second Circuit opined that the six-factor test was "too rigid" and not applicable for analyzing internships at all workplaces.

Instead the Court stated that "the proper question is whether the intern or the employer is the primary beneficiary of the relationship." To make that determination, the Court set forth several nonexhaustive *considerations that should be weighed, with no one factor being dispositive.* Those considerations, some of which overlap the DOL's six-factor test and which are aimed at determining the "economic reality" of the situation, are:

1. whether the intern and the employer clearly understand there is no expectation of compensation;
2. whether the internship involves training similar to that which would be given in an educational environment;
3. whether the intern receives academic credit for the internship;
4. whether the internship is conducted in a time frame corresponding to the academic calendar to allow the intern to fulfill their academic commitments;
5. whether the internship's duration is limited to the time in which the internship provides the intern with beneficial learning;
6. whether the intern's work complements rather than displaces the work of paid employees; and
7. whether the intern and the employer understand there is no entitlement to a full-time position at the conclusion of the internship.

How to Decide

Unfortunately, *there is no bright-line legal rule on this issue that would provide a definitive answer to every situation.* For this reason and because of the number of factors the DOL and courts say should be considered, it is easy for churches and ministries to suffer from "paralysis by analysis." This need not be the case.

It is clear that, whether viewed through the lens of the DOL's six-factor test or viewed through the analysis of various courts, *the primary focus is on training and education: the internship must primarily be in furtherance of the education of the intern and for the intern's benefit rather than the employer's.* Internships that are part of a formal academic experience, such as where the intern receives course credit from their educational institution, are generally considered appropriate unpaid internships by the DOL. This can be very helpful for those churches and ministries with college and seminary students serving as residents or interns, and for students whose degree program *requires* internship experience. In contrast, the more directly related an intern's tasks are to those that might otherwise be performed by paid staff members, the more likely the intern will be considered an employee under the FLSA and entitled to compensation.

In addition, because of the fact-specific nature of the analysis required, we recommend that your church or ministry always seek legal counsel when developing an unpaid internship or residency program, who can assist your organization with appropriately structuring the program in furtherance of your organization's purposes. At the Church Law Group, we regularly assist clients around the country with these issues, and it would be our honor to assist your organization.

The Church Law Group, a practice division of
Anthony & Middlebrook, P.C.
4501 Merlot Avenue
Grapevine, TX 76051
Phone: 972-444-8777
Email: churchlawgroup@amlawteam.com
Website: *www.churchlawgroup.com*

Acknowledgments

After writing a book titled *Hero Maker* and creating the *HeroMakerBook* .com website, it makes sense for Warren and me to acknowledge the people who were hero makers to us, building the platform upon which we get to stand.

First, I want to acknowledge my parents, Earl and Pat Ferguson. My dad was the first church planter role model I had as a young kid. I remember helping him set up chairs in Blackhawk Elementary School before church started. He was a hero maker for me and continues to lead like that while in his seventies. My mom was the single greatest permission giver and gift activator in my life. She helped me believe I could be anything I dreamed I could be. Thanks, Mom and Dad.

And thank you to my wife, Sue, who was being a hero maker before I ever started talking about hero making. You are a hero maker at home, consistently sacrificing for our kids and me. You are a hero maker for your friends, doing the little things without notice that make a big difference. And I love how you have been a hero maker through Connections and small groups at Community Christian, developing and mentoring countless leaders. And thanks for your help on this book too! I love you a lot!

There are few better at hero making than my brother Jon Ferguson. He has partnered with me on so many new ventures, from D & J Lawn Care as kids to cofounding Community Christian Church and NewThing. Thank you, Jon, for caring more about the mission than about who gets the credit. You embody hero making.

Thank you to my friend and teammate in the four-to-ten mission, Todd Wilson. You have built more platforms for other leaders than anyone I know, and I have yet to see you step into the spotlight. Thanks for your willingness to make heroes out of so many of us. Your fruit is growing on the trees in many orchards! The Exponential team also deserves a special shout-out for creating conferences and resources to fuel a movement of multiplication.

Thanks especially to one of Todd's many gifted team members, Lindy Lowry, for dozens of thoughtful and helpful editorial suggestions as she helped this book's contents to fully align with the Exponential conference and publications.

And thank you to my longtime, amazing administrative assistant Pat Masek. The first question I most often get when I am teaching at a conference or meeting new people is, "Who is your assistant?" Then it's followed by, "She is amazing!" More than anyone else, you kept this book moving forward and on course. Thanks for being so amazing!

Thanks too to Corissa Durst for going the extra mile on the outstanding graphics that appear throughout the book.

A heartfelt thanks to the people of Community Christian Church. You get it! You understand that the best way to help people find their way back to God is through a multiplication movement of new sites and churches. And I've seen so many of you embrace the idea of multiplication: mentoring others who in turn mentor others. I love being on this mission with you!

Throughout the book, I have featured my friends through our international church-planting network, NewThing, as outstanding examples. I am grateful to be partnered with so many hero makers who are passionate about the Jesus mission.

Thank you to what I'm calling the Becoming Level 5 think tank, which gave clarity to many of the concepts developed in this book. Participants are: Bill Couchenour, Dave Browning, Wade Burnett, Jeff Christopherson, Bill Easum, Tim Hawks, Daniel Im, Chris Lagerlof, Mike McDaniel, Ralph Moore, Dave Rhodes, Brian Sanders, Larry Walkemeyer, and Greg Wiens.

Thanks also to the many people who took time to meet with us to talk about specific material in the book or to review an early manuscript. They include: Eric Bramlett, Dave Dummitt, Jon Ferguson, Kep James, Greg Ligon, Keri Ladouceur, Doug Leddon, Skipp Machmer, Mike McDaniel, Troy McMahan, Tammy Melchien, Eric Metcalf, Patrick O'Connell, Jon Peacock, Ian Simkins, Ed Stetzer, Geoff Surratt, Jessie Vacca, Larry Walkemeyer, and Eddie Yoon.

Leadership Network, with its vision to foster innovation movements that activate the church to greater impact for the glory of God's name, has had an incredible influence on both of us for many years. There are few ideas in this book that haven't been in some way influenced by its approach of helping church teams move from ideas to implementation to impact. I'm proud to be on its board of directors, and Warren on its staff as their research director.

The Zondervan team, especially Ryan Pazdur, Jesse Hillman, Brian Phipps, Robin Schmitt, and Kyle Rohane, has given us pivotal feedback at many junctures and has always shown grace when we asked to incorporate a new idea or other adjustment into the book.

Finally, my coauthor and good friend Warren Bird enthusiastically echoes my words above—especially since he helped write them (!), as this book was truly a collaborative authorship.

Warren adds his gratitude to his wife and best friend, Michelle, who, like Warren, has been on the journey this book describes of moving toward greater spiritual reproduction and even multiplication. In fact, we tell a story about Michelle as an apprentice multiplier in chapter 1.

Most of all, Warren and I thank God for letting us play a part in challenging ourselves, and you as our readers, to multiply our efforts in ways that can exponentially increase the population of heaven. That's the eternal difference we pray this book will make.

Notes

1. "Barry" is the compilation of two friends. All subsequent stories are about the individuals named and are told with their permission.
2. Actually, Todd quoted Dave Rhodes, who had said there needs to be "a shift in the hero story for the prime leader from being the hero to becoming the mentor who creates heroes that become mentors." See Todd Wilson with Will Mancini, *Dream Big, Plan Smart: Finding Your Pathway to Level Five Multiplication* (Exponential, 2016), 55. This ebook is a free download at *www.exponential.org*.
3. Thanks to our friend Will Mancini for pointing out this pattern to us. Will is author of *God Dreams* (coauthored by Warren Bird) and *Church Unique*.
4. Bill Simmons, *The Complete Book of Basketball* (New York: Ballantine, 2009).
5. Ibid., 39. The narrative that follows is adapted from pages 38–41.
6. Ibid., 38–39.
7. Ibid., 51.
8. Ibid., 54.
9. Exponential has compiled lists of specific characteristics for each multiplication culture. To learn more, download a free copy of *Becoming a Level 5 Multiplying Church* at exponential.org.
10. Michael Slaughter with Warren Bird, *Real Followers: Beyond Virtual Christianity* (Nashville: Abingdon, 1999), 28.
11. David Sturt and Todd Nordstrom, "Are You Asking the Right Question?" *Forbes* (October 18, 2013), *www.forbes.com/sites/davidsturt/2013/10/18/are-you-asking-the-right-question/#b73fdaa76c5d*.
12. Ibid.
13. Alan Hirsch and Dave Ferguson, *On the Verge: A Journey into the Apostolic Future of the Church*, Exponential Series (Grand Rapids: Zondervan, 2011).
14. Calculations and terminology come from *www.webmath.com* with help from Dianne James Russell.

15. Personal email from Eddie Yoon to Dave Ferguson, August 13, 2017.

16. Todd Wilson and Dave Ferguson, *Becoming a Level 5 Multiplying Church* (Exponential, 2015), 31–32, analyzing Protestant churches. Free download at *www.exponential.org*. See also Todd Wilson, *Multipliers: Leading beyond Addition* (Exponential, 2017), also free download at *www.exponential.org*.

17. Matthew Philips, "Minority Rules: Why 10 Percent Is All You Need," Freakonomics (July 28, 2011), *http://freakonomics.com/2011/07/28/minority-rules-why-10-percent-is-all-you-need/*.

18. Danny Iny, "Why Asking the Wrong Questions Could Be Disastrous," *Inc.* (March 16, 2016), *www.inc.com/replacemeplease1455908276.html*.

19. See appendix 4 for these and other helpful free resources.

20. Sturt and Nordstrom, "Are You Asking the Right Question?"

21. These thoughts are inspired by Dann Spader's writings, such as *Discipling as Jesus Discipled*, *Four Chair Discipling*, and *Growing a Healthy Church*.

22. Lyle Schaller and Warren Bird, *Wisdom from Lyle E. Schaller: The Elder Statesman of Church Leadership* (Nashville: Abingdon, 2012).

23. Both accolades are cited and sourced in Schaller and Bird, *Wisdom*, x.

24. Ralph Moore, *Defeating Anxiety: Overcoming Fear before It Overwhelms You* (Honolulu: Straight Street, 2013).

25. "Study Examines the State of Faith in Hawaii," *Hawaii Free Press* (November 13, 2011), *www.hawaiifreepress.com/ArticlesMain/tabid/56/ID/5437/Study-Examines-the-State-of-Faith-in-Hawaii.aspx*.

26. Quotes adapted from Derwin Gray, "Pro Football Was My God," *Christianity Today* (March 3, 2014), *www.christianitytoday.com/ct/2014/march/pro-football-was-my-god-derwin-gray.html*.

27. Derwin Gray, *The High Definition Leader: Building Multiethnic Churches in a Multiethnic World* (Nashville: Nelson, 2015). See also *www.derwinlgray.com/about/*.

28. Kara Powell, Jake Mulder, and Brad Griffin, *Growing Young: Six Essential Strategies to Help Young People Discover and Love Your Church* (Grand Rapids: Baker, 2016).

29. Larry Walkemeyer, *Flow: Unleashing a River of Multiplication in*

Your Church, City and World (Exponential, 2014). Free download at *www.exponential.org*.

30. Abigail Jones, "Murder Town USA (AKA Wilmington, Delaware)," *Newsweek* (December 19, 2014), *www.newsweek.com/2014/12/19/ wilmington-delaware-murder-crime-290232.html*.

31. Acts 18:3. See also 1 Thess. 2:9; 2 Thess. 3:7–8; Acts 20:31–35; 1 Cor. 4:12. See "What Is a Tentmaker?" at *www.worldwidetentmakers.com/ education/what-is-a-tentmaker*.

32. David R. Wheeler, "Higher Calling, Lower Wages: The Vanishing of the Middle-Class Clergy," *The Atlantic* (June 27, 2014), *www.theatlantic.com/business/archive/2014/07/higher-calling -lower-wages-the-collapse-of-the-middle-class-clergy/374786/*.

33. Dave Ferguson, Jon Ferguson, and Eric Bramlett, *The Big Idea: Aligning the Ministries of Your Church through Creative Collaboration* (Grand Rapids: Zondervan, 2007).

34. *www.thriveschool.info/worship-major*.

35. *www.highlandscollege.com*.

36. *www.arcchurches.com/about/history*.

37. The church website is *www.elim.org.sv*. For a list of other global megachurches, see *www.leadnet.org/world*.

38. This account, reviewed by Mario Vega, is drawn from a variety of sources: Pastor Mario's presentation at Exponential East 2015, a personal interview by Warren Bird, and personal interviews by Joel Comiskey, a worldwide expert in the cell movement, who received the church's blessing to research a book that describes the church's development, *Passion and Persistence: How the Elim Church's Cell Groups Penetrated an Entire City for Jesus*.

39. Adapted from *https://news.utexas.edu/2014/05/16/mcraven-urges -graduates-to-find-courage-to-change-the-world*.

40. If you're curious about the growth of Christianity beyond North America, Warren Bird maintains Leadership Network's list of global megachurches at www.leadnet.org/world. It's believed to be the only active, sortable compilation of almost one thousand very large churches in Africa, Asia, Australia, Europe, the Middle East, South America, and Central America.

41. For more on his remarkable story, see Brian Sanders, *The Underground Church: A Living Example of the Church in Its Most Potent Form*, Exponential Series (Grand Rapids: Zondervan, 2018). Many of the quotes in the following narrative are adapted from the book.

42. This story and many others in this chapter are adapted from Dave Ferguson, *Keeping Score: How to Know If Your Church Is Winning* (Exponential Resources, 2014).

43. For the full report, a free download, please see Warren Bird, "Heartbeat of Rising Influence Churches" (Leadership Network), *http://leadnet.org/wp-content/uploads/2015/04/RESEARCH-2011 -DEC-PastorsWhoAreShapingtheFuture-Bird-Taylor.pdf.*

44. Reggie McNeal, *Missional Renaissance: Changing the Scorecard for the Church*, Leadership Network Series (San Francisco: Jossey-Bass, 2009).

45. "Hate and Targeted Violence against Christians in India" (Evangelical Fellowship of India, Alliance Defending Freedom India), *http://files.ctctcdn.com/523942c3501/271ca9a9-f085-4006-a08b -051ed9cd51c8.pdf.*

46. Sarah Eekhoff Zylstra, "Compassion: Why We're Leaving India, but Still Have Hope," *Christianity Today* (March 1, 2017), *www.christianitytoday.com/news/2017/march/compassion -international-leaving-india-child-sponsorship.html.*

47. Wilson, *Dream Big*, 15. Free download at *www.exponential.org.*

48. For a free download of Leadership Network's reports on church planters and campus pastors, see *leadnet.org/portable.*

49. Malcolm Gladwell, *The Tipping Point: How Little Things Can Make a Big Difference* (Boston: Back Bay Books, 2002), 192.

50. Quoted in ibid., 84.

51. This "blank it, blank it, blank it" format was inspired by a podcast from Andy Stanley called "Creating a Culture of Continual Improvement."

52. The GPS model was adapted from the VHS model of leadership community. For more on VHS meetings, see Carl George, *Prepare Your Church for the Future*, ed. Warren Bird (Grand Rapids: Revell, 1991), especially 135–45. See also Carl George with Warren Bird,

Nine Keys to Effective Small-Group Leadership: How Lay Leaders Can Establish Healthy Cells, Classes, and Teams (Taylors, SC: CDLM, 1997).

53. Brian Zehr is cofounder of Intentional Impact *(www.intentionalimpact.com)*.

Scripture Index

Meet the Authors

Dave Ferguson is the lead pastor of Community Christian Church, a multisite missional community that is passionate about "helping people find their way back to God." Community has grown from a few college friends to thousands and has been recognized as one of America's most influential churches. Dave also provides visionary leadership for the international church-planting movement NewThing and is the president of the Exponential conference. He is an award-winning author of books that include *The Big Idea*, *Exponential*, *On the Verge*, *Finding Your Way Back to God*, and *Starting Over*. Dave and his amazing wife, Sue, have three great kids—Amy, Joshua, and Caleb—and live in Naperville, Illinois. Feel free to email him with questions, ideas, feedback, or introductions at daveferguson@communitychristian.org. Website: *www.daveferguson.org*. Twitter: @daveferguson. Instagram: @fergusondave.

Warren Bird, PhD, after pastoring many years, is research director for Leadership Network *(www.leadnet.org/warrenbird)*. He is widely recognized as among the nation's leading researchers of megachurches, multisite churches, large-church compensation, and high-visibility pastoral succession. He also oversees the world's only active, sortable list of global megachurches *(www.leadnet.org/world)*. Warren has authored or coauthored twenty-nine other books, including *How to Break Growth Barriers: Revise Your Role, Release Your People, and Capture Overlooked Opportunities for Your Church* and *Viral Churches: Helping Church Planters Become Movement Makers*. Warren and his wife, Michelle, live just outside New York City and have two grown children. Website: *www.warrenbird.com*. Twitter: @warrenbird.

HeroMakerBook.com is the official book website, with a free discussion guide and other helps.

About the Exponential Series

The interest in church planting has grown significantly in recent years. The need for new churches has never been greater. At the same time, the number of models and approaches is expanding. To address the unique opportunities of churches in this landscape, Exponential Network, in partnership with Leadership Network and Zondervan, launched the Exponential Series in 2010.

Books in this series:

- Tell the reproducing church story.
- Celebrate the diversity of models and approaches God is using to reproduce healthy congregations.
- Highlight the innovative and pioneering practices of healthy reproducing churches.
- Equip, inspire, and challenge kingdom-minded leaders with the tools they need in their journey of becoming reproducing church leaders.

Exponential exists to attract, inspire, and equip kingdom-minded leaders to engage in a movement of high-impact, reproducing churches. We provide a national voice for this movement through the Exponential Conference, the Exponential Initiative, Exponential Venture, and the Exponential Series.

Leadership Network exists to accelerate the impact of 100X leaders. Believing that meaningful conversations and strategic connections can change the world, we seek to help leaders navigate the future by exploring new ideas and finding application for each unique context.

For more information about the Exponential Series, go to *www.exponentialseries.com*.

DOWNLOAD ADDITIONAL RESOURCES

HeroMakerBook.org